"Mister Abbott"

"MISTER ABBOTT"

* * *

George Abbott

Random House New York

To my best friend

Overture

I would like to apologize for the title. It is Bennett Cerf's, not mine. When he first suggested it I thought for a moment that he had forgotten I was the one who was writing this book. I protested; I complained that it made me sound conceited but he didn't seem interested in my state of mind. "It's what everybody calls you," he said. "It's a natural."

In any argument about a play title I would have had a definite and perhaps stubborn opinion, but in the book world I had to admit that Random House was likely to be more knowledgeable than I. So I stopped objecting, but I plan to leave town on the day of publication and flee to some far-off state like Florida, where they don't read books.

Perhaps I am being too self-conscious. Perhaps the very idea of writing about myself is so conceited that the picture isn't greatly altered by the addition of an egotistical title. People who talk at length about themselves have always seemed to me to be bores—yet here I am presuming to write a whole book on that subject. It has taken me a long time to decide to attempt it for I did not think it worth while to turn out one of those autobiographies which are merely a recitation of important people one has met, and which ignore the thoughts, the motives, and even the sex of the author. On the other hand, to indulge in too much candor could be thought bad taste. I have decided to err on that side. I shall try to be honest about myself and if it proves embarrassing to my relatives, I am sorry.

"Mister Abbott"

*

Part One

THE ALLEGHENY RIVER runs through the center of the town of Salamanca, New York. I remember it as deep and treacherous and violent. Sometimes it was filled with floating ice which piled up against the abutments on the town bridge and then there was wonderful excitement—many opinions—danger. Later, in the spring, the logs would be floated down the river. The log jams were equally exciting, perhaps more spectacular because of those incredible river men leaping from log to log in the swirling stream to keep the pack moving. Across the river you could see the Allegheny Mountains; the big mound on top of one of them was said to be an Indian burial ground, where one could find arrowheads.

That's the way Salamanca looked to me. When I visited it many years later, as a member of the University of Rochester Glee Club, I found that it had lost its fierceness as well as its size and that the mountains were unimpressive foothills. But in my boyhood the mountains were high and the river was a fascinating menace. There was a flood nearly every spring and the men would gather in little knots, looking important, speculating on the extent of the danger and arguing about what should be done. The women gathered together too and worried, while the children rushed about gleefully shouting the news of each new calamity.

All of this was long ago, before the chestnut blight. Salamanca had a grove of chestnut trees, in fact, the surrounding hills were full of them. Not those mealy things one calls chestnuts these days, no, a hard nut, delicious, as you'll learn when the trees grow back again. Salamanca also had a tannery. We set our clocks by its whistles. Early in the morning strange men—foreigners, Polacks—went trooping up the street by the river carrying their lunch pails, and at night they returned. I don't know where they lived—the town didn't recognize them officially—I only remember that they were Catholics. Sometimes a group of adventurous boys would visit the tannery and we would walk across the narrow wooden planks which separated the great vats of boiling tanbark. I daresay that nowadays such recklessness is not permitted.

I had a brother named Burwell McLaury Abbott, known to us as "Mick, Mick, the wild Irishman," or simply Micky for short. He earned this elaborate title because he lost his temper occasionally. I also had a sister, Isabel, seven years younger, who was an angel. She was named after a great aunt, Isabel Sparks, with perhaps the hope that she might inherit some of her money. But a set of china was all that ever materialized, and eventually, while a student at Vassar, she became known as Polly, a name which stuck to her thereafter and which fits her admirably.

Occasionally we visited our grandparents, who lived in Forestville, New York, on a farm which was no longer worked. Grandmother McLaury was a trained nurse, and she would go to Buffalo to work for a while and then return to the farm. Apparently Grandfather McLaury had not been a very successful businessman. I know nothing about him except that he was very religious—a devout Methodist. If the hay was in the field and it rained on Sunday, he wouldn't take the hay in. He said, "If the Lord wets it, the Lord will dry it." The Lord, however, neglected his responsibilities in this respect and my grandfather died leaving his widow debts and a mortgaged farm.

Once I was in the kitchen watching my grandmother prepare dinner. There was some cayenne pepper on the shelf and when I asked if I could taste it, she said, "You won't like it." I took some anyhow. It burned and I cried. Grandma said, "I told you you wouldn't like it," and went right on working without giving me any sympathy. Even through my tears I admired the inflexible rightness. She was my kind of woman.

It is hard to believe that just a short time ago there were people—good, honest, sincere people—who thought that card playing and dancing were wicked, who thought that music had a suspicious taint of evil and that laughter on Sunday should not be permitted. But thus it was in the McLaury home, and apparently that is what my mother rebelled against. I don't know how much of this rebellion took place in Forestville, but I do know that when she got to Salamanca, she declared her emancipation by becoming an Episcopalian—or at least attending the Episcopal Church because she said it had nice people and good music.

We children were never brought up to feel affiliated with any one church. Being left to ourselves in that respect, we shopped around for the one that had the best Christmas parties and the best summer picnics. None of us was baptized; Mama said she wanted us to wait and make up our own minds. Later, out in Cheyenne, Wyoming, I thought seriously of going through the rites because I was greatly attracted to one of the girls who was going to be confirmed. But in the end, my self-conscious fear of the ritual I would have to endure became stronger than my passion for the maiden, and I reneged.

The most illustrious member of the McLaury family was my Aunt Anna, Preceptress of the Fredonia Normal School. She was a big, calm woman and very good to us children although we probably annoyed her. After she had died, my mother confided to me that Aunt Anna wore a wig. Once there was a great fire in the school and Aunt Anna was nearly burned up because, after reaching the fire escape, she realized that she was without her hair and went back to get it. She would rather have burned to death than be exposed to ridicule.

We saw much more of my Abbott grandparents. My grandfather was a country doctor who had lived all his life in Hamburg, New York. He had been a colonel in the Union Army, and his war stories were a constant delight. Theoretically, my grandfather was a teetotaler, but if he had a slight cold or other indisposition, he, as a medical man, prescribed for himself a whiskey sling. Some of my pleasantest childhood memories are of sitting on his knee, slightly dizzy from the alcoholic aura which he breathed out, listening to the marvelous tales of his doings during the Civil War. He had been in charge of the federal prison at Elmira, New York, and had trapped many a Johnny Reb attempting to escape by assuming a Southern accent and going down among them to spy upon their doings. He had come out covered with "graybacks," which in a later war carried on as cooties.

Grandpa loved parades. He would sit on his porch and review the troops on all occasions. Later on, in his senility, he was discovered one day on the front porch reviewing a funeral and waving his handkerchief to the passing troops. Grandma hustled him into the house.

Grandma Abbott inspired awe. She was a big, grim-lipped woman, and when she put on one of her sulks, let no dog bark. She openly henpecked Grandpa, and I remember how delighted we children were when he rebelled on one occasion and threw a hoe in her general direction. Of course, he had to pay for that with many weeks of contrition.

Grandpa had retired as a practicing physician but had a small farm in Hamburg, as well as much land around and about. There were horses and an orchard and beehives and other things that interested a boy. Grandpa was a demon with the bees. They would sting us children if we went anywhere near them, but Grandpa would walk in their midst and even take off the tops of the hives to remove honey without being stung. Once the bees went berserk and gave him twenty-two stings. It was an exciting night.

The Abbott attic was full of interesting relics from the Civil War: flags, sashes, sabers, muskets, horse pistols and uniforms. We were not only outfitted to play soldier; we could outfit half the town and sometimes did. Little did those old people know as they saw us heading for the back lot on one occasion with one of the muskets, that we had purchased powder and were about to try an experiment with a muzzle-loaded weapon. We rammed home the charge and tried to set it off with a match. This was a failure, and by the time someone had informed us that we needed a cap to explode the charge, our powder was wet and we had lost interest and embarked on some new adventure.

Living with my grandparents was an old-maid daughter, Aunt Eliza, probably one of the homeliest women ever invented and with very few redeeming chracteristics. Her spirit had been completely broken by her strong mother: she was over-sweet and weak. Instinctively we realized her inability to cope with us and were, I regret to say, unfeelingly cruel. We didn't obey her; nor did we return the love which she so longed to find. Aunt Eliza was always wanting to kiss us, and I still cringe in thinking of those unattractive wet lips and the way her eyes were magnified by her glasses when she closed in for the embrace.

People think that children like to kiss. In their wish to cuddle the cute little things, adults willfully forget the distress which the same advances caused them when they were young. Hugging yes; kissing no. I never kiss a child because I remember how I hated it. How vividly I remember the repugnance I felt for the tobacco smell and the whiskers of the men, or the musty odor of the women. Often you see a child struggling in the arms of some grownup. Both are laughing, the child in a rather strained fashion, but the adult patronizingly, confident that he is helping overcome the little one's shyness. Don't believe it—the kid hates it. Kiss babies, but when they get of an age to struggle against you, settle for hugs, even if you are stronger than they are.

Adult kissing might be tempered a bit too. I don't mean real kissing, I mean the empty formality, the lipstick smear on the cheek which is now part of our social convention. Benjamin Franklin, when he was in Paris, complained about the society kiss of that era, the custom being to kiss on the mouth practically any woman whom you met. Wise old Benjamin said it wasn't worth while because for every good kiss he received he had to take ten bad ones. Family kissing generally means nothing and some of it is unattractive. When Russian men kiss each other it looks a little on the gooey side. I much prefer the greeting customary between men who are good friends in Latin countries— *el abrazos*—a quick hug and a pat on the shoulder.

It would be interesting to know the kissing habits of the human race through the ages, and the reason for the different national attitudes on the subject. I know that many Oriental nations abhor the idea, and that in India they delete from our films all such revolting contacts. You don't read of much kissing among the Romans and Greeks, but the Elizabethans apparently regarded the recreation as we do. At least Shakespeare's description of a kiss assures us that the two gentlemen from Verona used the same technique as the two juniors from Harvard.

Whenever we visited Hamburg, we were given a heavy dose of the local Methodist Church. As might be expected, my aunt was quite a worker, committee woman and doer of good deeds. My grandparents also were important members of the congregation, and the minister often had dinner with us. He would be asked to say grace, which was a somber moment followed by great relief when it was over.

In 1894 there was widespread unemployment, and a man named Coxey organized a protest march of the jobless from Massillon, Ohio, to Washington, D.C., to prod the authorities into remedial action. In the minds of the middle-class respectable people, Coxey's army was a mob of riffraff. I don't recall what effect the march had upon the authorities in Washington, but I remember well the effect it had on me, a seven-year-old boy. On a hot July day there was great excitement in Hamburg—excitement bordering on consternation—for Coxey's army was to pass down Main Street en route to Washington. I listened to the talk, to the women who were locking up their valuables, to the men who wanted to keep folks off the streets until the army had passed, and to all the speculations about the conduct of the oncoming horde. I entered into the spirit with a daring suggestion that my brother and I dress up in some of Grandpa's Civil War uniforms and review the army from the carriage block in front of the house. Micky and I got dressed in the ornate regalia from the attic—gold epaulets, swords, horse pistols and so forth—and basked in the attention we had created. We took our places and waited. Some older boys came running down the street—the

army had passed the cemetery, it was on the way! The glory of
the enterprise was beginning to fade and a slight trepidation was
beginning to steal into my heart. Suddenly we saw them coming.
The whole width of the street was filled with rough men sham-
bling along silently. As they came toward us I quailed; I began to
fear that these toughs might not like to see two children in uniform. I fled into the house, followed by my brother; and we hastily disrobed and then returned to the porch disguised as normal,
good little boys watching the somber and menacing parade.
Afterward my cowardice preyed upon my mind and I wished I
could have relived the incident and been braver. I still do—but
life doesn't always give us a second chance.

But when I was about ten years old I did become a hero. In
those days in a small town there was no such thing as a regular
swimming pool. Boys learned to swim in the old swimming hole.
In Hamburg, there was a swimming hole in the Eighteen Mile
Creek just in back of the cemetery. After a long walk down a
dusty road, we would cut across the cemetery and down the hill,
take off our clothes and jump in. We stopped at a mausoleum,
which had been built by the village atheist, and shouted into it
to hear the echo. Our atheist did not want to have his body in
consecrated ground, so on a hill just outside the cemetery proper
he had constructed a tomb with this verse on the door:

> No orthodox fiend
> With cloven hoof
> Or barbed tail
> Shall ever be seen
> In this pleasant vale.

His will had stipulated that he was to be buried there. When,
however, he died prior to his wife, she double-crossed him, tore
up the will and had him buried with the orthodox fiends up
above.

At the bottom of the hill was the swimming hole; it was as orderly as a modern locker room. You found yourself a little space
in the grass and piled your clothes neatly. Then to protect yourself from getting a cramp you were supposed to urinate on your
leg. I guess it worked; I don't recall any drownings. At any rate,

on this occasion I was down swimming with the big boys, having recently been graduated to that honor, and with us was Arthur Ricart, Grandpa's hired man, whom I had persuaded to play hooky from his chores at the farm. There was a little raft by the bank, and the fellows would dive off that, swim around, climb up again and then repeat the operation. Suddenly there was a thrashing about in midstream—someone was in trouble. It was Arthur. He couldn't swim but had been watching us enviously. Finally he decided that all that was needed was the nerve to do as the others did, and he jumped in.

The crowd became frantic. They ran up and down the bank yelling, "Get a pole. Help! Help!" But nobody helped; everybody seemed paralyzed. I sat on the edge of that raft and thought to myself how am I ever going to face my grandparents with the fact that I had lured Arthur from his work and that he was now dead. I watched him go down once and then twice, knowing that it wasn't safe to approach him while he was still strong or he would drown us both. Finally when he went down for the third time, I swam out and pulled him to shore. The older boys grabbed him and dragged him across the raft, filling his belly with splinters. After a good deal of rolling around, he vomited up the water and was on his groggy feet. We all trooped back to Hamburg, and in the excitement over my great deed, Arthur was forgiven for playing hooky and I was a hero. There was even some talk of nominating me for a Carnegie medal.

I would like it better if I could write this ego recital backwards and talk first about myself as I am now. For at the age of seventy-five, I find myself pleased with life. I have enough money, enough work, and friends whom I love and who love me; and while one can never have enough health, still I am well off in that respect. Today I enjoy a sense of well-being, but as a boy I did not. My memory of myself is that I felt abused, unappreciated and insecure. I felt misunderstood. Many of the things I remember about myself in that stage give me a sense of shame, and I would prefer to sweep them under the bed and forget about them.

To start with, our family life was not a happy one. An air of tension prevailed in most things domestic; and it was only years and years later that I came to realize that a home could be a place where there was no nagging, no fault-finding, no grim silences.

My father was about six feet tall, very erect and handsome. He was one of Salamanca's prominent citizens and had been a mayor for two terms; and the town's fire department—the Abbott Hose Company—was named after him. I never felt important in Salamanca and I imagine the reason that I got so little satisfaction out of my father's position was that instinctively I realized that it was not the same at home. I can never remember my mother saying a word against him, and yet I was perfectly sure that she didn't respect him. He walked with a slight swagger, as though he thought he was very important—and, indeed, he wanted to feel very important. He had a smiling, debonair exterior. My grandparents had financed him to a wholesale tailoring business in Salamanca, and he made the uniforms for the B.R. & P. Railroad, which paid its debts, but most of the other customers did not. George B. Abbott was much too fine a fellow to ask anybody to pay up, especially if it was going to cause unpleasantness. This was all part of the need for public approval on which he had been fed in the Abbott home. Innately he was shy, and although I did not realize this until many years later, he had begun to drink to help overcome that shyness. It turned out that he had a great tolerance for alcohol, and although a heavy drinker, he was not a drunkard at that time.

What did my mother look like? She looked like a mother. I don't know; she looked good to me. However, I do remember that judged objectively she was slightly stoop-shouldered and that she cleared her throat too much, a habit which her oldest son picked up from her and in which he still indulges. She was very bright and ambitious, not for herself but for her family. She was a perfectionist, an idealist, who had hoped for great things and who was finding them hard to realize. She despised bunk and therefore she preached a philosophy opposite to that upon which her husband had been reared. The Abbotts were very anxious to be well thought of. If we went to a party, the first question our grandparents would ask when we came home was if anyone had said anything nice about us. Mother, on the other hand, refused to make any gesture to conform. She incited us to be individuals unswerved by the opinions of neighbors.

Mother was incredibly brave. She went through some great trials without losing hope or deviating from her duty as she saw it. Best of all, she had a wry sense of humor which made her see every crisis in a funny light. She may not have been an ideal wife, but she was an ideal mother. Her struggle for improvement was always going on. She tried to seek out what she called "nice friends." She was an ardent member of the Salamanca Salamagundi Society, a local literary organization dedicated to self-improvement, to the study of literature and to the reading of papers on these subjects.

My father disappointed her and she disappointed him. She had given up her teaching to marry G. B. Abbott, thinking that she was getting a debonair knight in shining armor. She found herself yoked to a man who became less and less attentive, less and less communicative, who stayed out with the boys drinking instead of coming home, who lent his money to strangers to prove he was a good fellow, but didn't pay the family bills. She was anchored to the house by her children, and she had lost her independence. My father, on the other hand, found that when he married the bright and witty May McLaury, he had also married his severest critic. He had exchanged that strong woman, his mother, for another woman equally strong; one who wished him to be the best and who never ceased telling him how to achieve it. And in the bargain, he probably had a cold wife. In those days sex was sin and something you didn't talk about. There were a great many frigid wives, and I suspect that she was one of them.

The problems of a young boy's life are difficult for an adult to understand. Even though I can remember clearly some of the tragedies of my own boyhood, I realize that I am completely unaware of the things that may be bothering my grandson.

When I started school, it was discovered that I had bad eyes, and this defect was further aggravated by the fact that I suffered from granulated lids. It was necessary for me to be taken to Buffalo to see an oculist, and my father was elected to accompany me on the trip. We sat in the train like two diffident acquaintances and tried to make conversation with each other. Actually, my father was something of a stranger. During the week my brother and sister and I saw very little of him. He arrived at about the time we were being put to bed, or he was not there at all because of some business or social obligation. When he was home on Sundays, he generally spent his afternoons sleeping on the living-room couch. This habit was always associated in my mind with a strange personal odor, an odor which I learned a great many years later was alcohol.

Arriving in Buffalo, my father took me under one arm and tried to jump off the train before it had come to a stop, thus provoking an altercation with the brakeman. There were some violent words, Papa shouting and swearing, which raised him in my estimation. The other thing I remember about the trip is going to one of the first nickelodeons which was showing motion pictures. This one showed Niagara Falls and the rapids below the Falls, and I saw it three times while Papa was busy.

Another great humiliation of my youth was that I was a bedwetter. They say that this traumatic experience is avoided in most cases by the modern psychological upbringing of children, that it is the attempt to housebreak them too early which causes the obsession. I was never really scolded for this, and yet of course I felt a great sense of sin. If my mother's calm face did not rebuke me, the sheets hanging on the back line did. During my life I have done many things for which other people might feel guilt, and yet I have felt none; but in my adolescence I felt degraded beyond words because of this weakness.

Sex also raised its ugly head about this time. I envy the children who are given a natural and normal introduction into this mystery of life. I was not. I have a bad memory and recall very few episodes in my childhood, but one particular day of revelation is still crystal clear. Three or four of us were standing down by the river under the bank when one of the older boys asked us if we knew that boys and girls were "different." This we disputed hotly, considering it a hoax on a par with the Santa Claus myth. But Harry Rogers' arguments were so convincing that a new world was opened up: not a beautiful or natural one, but a nasty one.

When I think back to Salamanca, I remember a strange assortment of things. I remember once canoeing down the river with some of the older boys, who were going for a swim. When they undressed, I was startled and repelled by the sight of that bunch of hair at their middle. I remember being out on our porch one day when three men came by chasing a fourth. The hired girl yanked us into the house. It turned out that they were policemen chasing a burglar. I worried about that fugitive for days, and for some reason I am still always on the side of the fugitive, criminal though he may be. I remember once we were fishing from a railroad trestle when suddenly there was the sound of an approaching train. There was not sufficient time for us to climb back to the safety of the shore so we stood on the ties outside of the bridge proper and hung on to some stanchions, paralyzed with fright, as the train came thundering by, giving the bridge a frightful shaking. Of course it didn't thunder by—it was an old freight train and it lumbered by—but that was how it felt to me.

In 1898 an important event took place: we moved to Cheyenne. My father had received a political appointment as Government Land Agent for the State of Wyoming. His business in Salamanca had failed, and he went into bankruptcy. Mother explained to us children that bankruptcy was not necessarily a disgrace, that Sir Walter Scott had gone into bankruptcy, that as a result he became a novelist in order to pay back his debts, and that my father would also pay his eventually.

Papa went West first, and a few months afterwards we followed. My Aunt Anna went along to help take care of the children during the three-day train ride. I loved the trip West. I was ten years old, big enough to get off at the stations and then get on a different car up front, thereby causing some highly satisfactory consternation among my relatives who were fearful that I had been left behind at the last station. I loved also to talk to the porters, who seemed to be interested in my tales of our family grandeur: our mansions in the East, our ranches in the West. I was a terrible liar during this period of my life, though I felt that my lies were a degrading weakness in my character. I didn't realize then that this tendency to fantasy was something which could be used to make money.

When we pulled into the station at Cheyenne, Wyoming, on a sunny, spring morning Papa was waiting for us and took us to the Interocean Hotel for breakfast. I looked out the window and saw a cowboy herding thirty horses up the main street; men were slouching along with their rattling spurs; there were Indians from the Reservation wearing new yellow shoes. It was a dream come true: cowboys and Indians. What more could a boy want? And later I discovered that every September there was Frontier Day, which is the best of all rodeo shows.

Cheyenne was a romantic place. It stood on the flat prairie as though it were in the middle of the world; you could look east to the horizon and west to the Rocky Mountains. The air was so clear that they seemed close, within walking distance, but they were really forty miles away.

Cheyenne is different now. It has paved streets and neon lights. I passed through there when we took a road company to the coast. While the Union Pacific took on water, I strolled through the town. It was a great disillusion. But back in those days, even though there were nine thousand people there, it seemed like a small town—a big Western village.

My father had rented a house for us on Capitol Avenue. It was not grand, but it was respectable. It had plumbing; it had oil lamps; and it had a picket fence and a barn. The altitude made us a little short of breath at first, and of course we were inept at the things that a Western boy could do. We were tenderfeet. To throw a rope, to ride a horse, to be able to shoot were essentials for every boy if he was to be accepted at all. I practiced roping the picket fence at first, and then I used my brother and sister as targets, until finally I put it to more practical purposes. There were lots of stray horses around Cheyenne, so anyone could easily get some experience in riding.

What kind of games do you suppose the boys in Cheyenne played? Oddly enough, cowboys and Indians. You'd think that with the streets full of them, the romance would be lost. But they were our heroes just as big-time athletes are the heroes of a boy in the East today. Of course we had our athletes too. Cheyenne had a baseball team made up of men working in the city. I particularly admired one player who worked in the railroad shops and who had a swaggery walk (which I later used in characterizing a part of *Zander the Great*). Papa would go down to the players' bench during games and whisper advice to the players but even as a child I realized that they did not listen very avidly.

There are five little lakes around Cheyenne. Lake Minne-haha is a natural lake; the others were reservoirs, but at the time I only knew they were places to swim, and to shoot and skate. I had become a pretty good swimmer. This was entirely cause and effect—because I had "rescued" a man, I was a swimmer; and the psychological result was that I blossomed out in this direction. I am not sure how big these lakes are—probably much smaller than I remember them, but certainly big enough and deep enough so that mothers would shudder if they knew that a little boy was swimming across them without any safeguard whatsoever. Our greatest fear was of the weeds which grew at the bottom. We had a superstition that these weeds would reach up and grab us and pull us under.

Every Western boy was supposed to be able to shoot. There were things to hunt the year round—sage hens, prairie dogs and so forth. But the excitement began in the fall when the migrating ducks put down on our lakes. Every morning before sunrise, these lakes would be surrounded by eager hunters, young and old, armed with everything from a twenty-two rifle to an eight-gauge shotgun. The sunrise was awesome and wonderful. At first a false sun came up as big as the Empire State Building, followed later by the real sunrise. We boys would stay there hour after hour; after the men had gone home, we would still be prowling around the lake trying to get a wounded bird that had been left behind, or trying to shoot a helldiver. A helldiver, really a mud hen, is an incredible animal. I have seen one sitting twenty-five or thirty yards off shore. The hunter aims and fires and the pattern of the shotgun forms a circle around where the head has been, but the bird has dived and later surfaces over on the other side of the lake. Once I killed a loon with a twenty-two rifle. They are not supposed to be good to eat, but Mother cooked it (under the impression that it was a goose), and we thought it delicious.

One of the most exciting experiences in this world was seeing the wild geese fly by. Before they came into view we heard the rumble in the sky, as though a freight train were approaching, and then the V appeared. The geese went over in their magnificent formation: one big V and perhaps two or three little ones, with the thunder of their wings and their continual honking. They were always well out of range; where they stopped, I don't know, but Cheyenne was not one of the places.

One of the great tragedies of my youth was concerned with hunting. I wanted a shotgun. I had been planning and scheming and saving to get one. Up to this time all my shooting had been done with other people's weapons. One boy would own a gun, and the rest of us would carry our own ammunition and take turns using it. So my whole existence centered around the thought of owning a shotgun of my own. Then I got the word from Mama: I was to get one for Christmas. I walked on air.

Christmas came. My father was not in close touch with us children, and in any case to him a gun was a gun. What I found on Christmas Day was not the shotgun about which I had dreamed, but a twenty-two rifle. I hated it; I could have spit on it. Not only had I very little use for this type of gun, but its very acquisition made the owning of a shotgun forever impossible. If they had only given me the money and let me buy my own gun; Christmas was a double-crossing hoax; there was no joy or justice in the whole damn world. I guess I've never forgiven Christmas for this disappointment; ever since then I have refused to enter into the proper spirit of that great holiday.

We came to Cheyenne in the spring of the year, so the school season was interrupted. I re-entered the fifth grade, and from that time until I went to college my schooling was a thing of utter confusion. I didn't know why I was studying anything. The rules of grammar and the rules of mathematics were things to learn by rote, without any sense whatsoever. I was a poor student. I was one of the many who "could be good if he would only apply himself." Luckily, English, history and geography were interesting. I was all right there, and I saved myself from being stupid by becoming a great reader.

I remember once hearing my Aunt Anna, who was visiting us for the summer, arguing with my mother that I should be forbidden to read dime novels. Some shady publications—*The Adventures of Dick Merriwell, The Life of Harry Tracy*—had been discovered among my possessions. Mother said no, it was good to read, to read anything, and that I would learn to like better books later. She was right; pretty soon I graduated to H. T. Henty, then to Scott, then to Dumas, later to Conrad. One of the great thrills of life is the discovery of a new author. There follows the impatient reading of everything he has written. This, I think, applies mostly to the storytellers, although I confess that in my mature life I read Emerson and Montaigne almost as avidly as I do novels. Shaw one reads only half-excitedly, propelled by the knowledge that it is the thing to do. Shakespeare one rediscovers. I think Lamb's *Tales from Shakespeare* or any other short cut to the plots is a very bad thing to put into the hands of the young. One gets the idea that if he knows the plot, he knows Shakespeare; and thus he denies himself the pleasure of reading the plays carefully later on. The sonnets, I confess, elude me completely and yet when Gielgud recites them, they seem as clear as crystal. Most of the acting of Shakespeare is pompous, pretentious and wrong. He was writing shows. He had not the slightest thought that anyone would ever read them, and he meant them to be acted so that they would seem real. Or, as he himself put it, he wanted to hold the mirror up to nature.

All my young life, reading was my solace. There in the world of make-believe I could forget the troubles which beset me in this cockeyed world where I was not appreciated and where there was no justice. Of course it made me a little difficult at times. It is a bitter thing to be wrenched from the romantic atmosphere of *The Three Musketeers* to the practical matter of drying dishes.

But on the whole I was a pretty good helper around the house. My mother was quite ill at times. I can never remember her being sick in bed, but on occasion she had terrible headaches which almost incapacitated her. And she had rheumatism in the shoulder, which made work difficult. I was paid for taking on certain household duties—in fact, we were all paid for what we did around the house. Mama thought it was much more sensible to earn our money than to give us a handout. We never had allowances; we always earned our spending money by doing chores.

I earned money in other ways too. Mama always tried to inspire us to be fearless, aggressive and to seek action in the world. America was the land of opportunity; anyone could succeed who had the energy and the intelligence; a penny saved was a penny earned. Edison became deaf and it made him a greater inventor; every liability could be turned into an asset. My mother used her influence over us not to smother us, not to keep us in the home, but to push us out, to make us self-confident and independent. For instance, she informed us that frogs' legs were a great delicacy in the more sophisticated sections of the world. My brother and I went out to the lakes, speared a number of frogs and sold them from door to door. There weren't a great number of sophisticated frog-eaters in Cheyenne, but we did make a small profit, and what was left over was eaten at home. I also raised chickens and pigeons in our barn. I would sell the squabs from door to door and make a little profit that way. One day I met an ingratiating boy from the other side of town who suggested that we go into partnership in the pigeon business. Mama warned me that he was a little bit too flattering and pleasant and that I ought to go slowly in taking in partners, but I would have none of her pessimism. He cheated me out of my pigeons, and in that way I learned to beware of smooth-talking strangers.

One development of the chicken business was the raising of fighting cocks. I didn't say game cocks, I said fighting cocks. Any rooster in the neighborhood was liable to be called into service by a boy whose family owned it. Once, at great expense, I sent out of town and bought by mail order a real game cock. He was a young one, hardly grown yet, but he was a beauty. The day after he arrived, while I was away from the house I put him under a basket to keep him from getting mixed up with the other roosters in the yard. A woman who had come to help with the washing was sorry for him and let him out. He got in a fight, was too young to defend himself, and when I came back I found my game cock had one blind eye. And that, believe me, was a tragedy.

One of my better jobs was delivering papers. I had to get up at five in the morning. The alarm clock was tied to the head of my bed and would yank me out of my dreams with a terrifying jangle. In fact, I grew to hate that sound so much that I automatically awoke just before it went off. To this day some automatic time piece within me lets me awake at the hour I have set for myself. Five o'clock in the morning in a heatless house, in a Wyoming winter, is a pretty dreary affair. The first job was to get down to the station, where the papers were dropped off. There we counted out our quota and went about delivering them. By this time it was light, and it wasn't such a bad job except for the hazard of vicious dogs. You would go along dreaming your dreams and occasionally meeting other early-rising acquaintances. Also, there was a small system of graft connected with the operation: when you counted out your papers you counted more than you needed, and you sold them as you went your rounds to make an extra profit for yourself. I did not invent this, but I soon fell into the general practice.

A more interesting job was the one I had on Christmas vacations. A neighbor of ours was the manager of the Western Union Telegraph office and he told my mother that he could use me during the vacation if she wished me to take the job, but that she must realize that part of the work would require that I answer calls down in the red-light district. Mama thought that I might as well learn about life, and so it was agreed. She warned me that I must be very careful there, that if I even so much as touched a wall with a sore finger, I might get a fearful disease.

The job was more fun than delivering papers but just as dishonest. I was immediately initiated into a double standard of conduct. More than half of our calls were from the red-light district, sometimes to take telegrams, but mostly to fetch beer. They would ring for a boy and hand him half a dollar and a pail. He would go to the saloon, get the beer and return with it. If we got such a call from a hotel, we would return with fifty cents' worth of beer, but if we got a call from one of the houses down on Eighteenth Street, we would get thirty-five cents' worth of beer and keep the fifteen cents for ourselves. If they ordered thirty-five cents' worth of beer, we would bring them twenty-five cents' worth, and so forth. There was a regular knock-down rate which every cooperative boy had to respect. Should he not be cooperative, he wouldn't last very long. I can understand from this experience how difficult it is for a policeman to be honest. How almost impossible it is to stand out against the established practices of graft which are firmly entrenched: five for you and five for the sergeant.

The red-light district in Cheyenne was on or adjacent to one street, and the houses ranged from the swell joint, "707," where the rich people went, to family institutions run by a mother and daughter, to the colored brothels largely patronized by the

soldiers who were stationed in Fort Russell just outside the city.
At "707" they never sank so low as to send for beer by a messenger boy. Once, however, I got a call from there. I approached
with trepidation and rang the doorbell at this great, silent house
where all the blinds were drawn. The door opened about three
inches on a chain, and a Negro maid peered out. I told her who
I was, and she took me to a room upstairs. There was a very
pleasant, well-dressed young man and a fancy lady, fluffy and
sweet-smelling and, to a boy's eyes, pretty but rather grim. The
young man was smiling and looked sinful. She opened a drawer to
get something and I saw a revolver in the drawer. Then she left
the room, and the man took her purse and said, "Here kid," and
gave me some of her money. She returned and gave me some
clothes to return to a department store. I suppose the man was a
pimp, but from a boy's point of view, he seemed charming. People who give you money are likely to be.

Often the whores would tell the messenger boy their troubles. Once I was called at about ten o'clock in the morning to one
of the moderate-priced places, and a woman in a negligee was
weeping and screaming about how she had been deserted by
the man to whom she was sending a telegram. She kept asking
me for sympathy. Another time I went to a mother-and-daughter
institution. The mother and daughter were having an argument,
and a cowboy sitting there waiting kept saying, "Come on, let's
go upstairs." The daughter, who was busy getting a letter ready
for me to deliver, nearly lost a customer. After they had finally
gone upstairs, the mother gave me a long lecture on the ingratitude of her offspring.

One woman, who operated a house all by herself, was called
Sweet Hannah. She was a buxom, matronly-looking woman,
whom I would cast for a boarding-house keeper but never for a
prostitute. She had a little cottage set between two of the larger
institutions, and she had a reputation for being very stingy. When
I was delivering papers, I gave them to her at a cut rate, which
of course was clear profit since I had stolen them. Then as a messenger boy, I was called one evening and she came out, shut the
door so that the men inside couldn't hear, and sent for ten cents'
worth of beer. The men had probably given her fifty cents for the
beer, and she was making a profit. When I got to the saloon, I

didn't know how to cut that amount. No one had ever ordered as little as ten cents' worth, but I asked for a nickel's worth. The bartender said, "Who asked for that, Hannah?" and I nodded. He splashed a little beer in the bottom and give it back to me. I delivered it to Hannah and fled. She complained to the Western Union office, but they gave her no heed.

The cheaper joints were more exciting and more terrifying, probably because there were more people there and it was noisier. Once when I entered in response to a call, there was a roomful of men, girls and smoke. The men were sitting around the room and the girls sitting astride their laps facing them. They were all laughing and whooping it up. When I entered one of the girls came at me, calling out, "Oh, let me kiss the handsome messenger boy." I thought I was surely going to get some horrible disease; I gave her a terrified push and the patrons roared with laughter.

One of the books that made the greatest impression upon me was one given to me by my Aunt Anna called *Tales of a Grandfather* by Walter Scott. On my mother's side, I had some Highland Scottish ancestry, and I quickly identified myself with these wild heroes. I thought of myself as a Scot. Robert the Bruce and the Black Douglas were much more my ideals than George Washington and Honest Abe, so when it was arranged that I spend a whole summer on the BA Ranch at Iron Mountain, Wyoming, owned by a Scot named Allen, I was overjoyed. Mr. and Mrs. Allen had lost their only son, a boy about my age, and it was thought that I might be a comfort to them and in a sense a substitute for their son. It was agreed that I was to work for my board and live in the ranch house with the Allens rather than in the bunkhouse with the men.

Mr. Allen turned out to be not exactly the Black Douglas type. He was a small, dark, uncommunicative, unsmiling man, and throughout the summer he regarded me, or so it seemed, with a jaundiced eye. If he thought about me at all in connection with his son, it was only that the memory of the lad shone more brightly in contrast with the eccentricities of this fresh stranger whom he had allowed in a weak moment to be pushed into his home. Mrs. Allen was also small and quiet, a broken spirit. She probably felt deeply and warmly, but she showed very little. Oh,

don't think there wasn't humor in the Allen home. There were
frequently some lusty jokes. Mr. Allen was a pretty good deadpan artist, and if he made a joke he never laughed at it himself,
but the cowboys did. One of the best jokes occurred when Mrs.
Allen's favorite pony broke its leg and had to be destroyed. They
cut the horse up and took it down to the house as a side of beef.
After Mrs. Allen had eaten heartily of her favorite pony, they
told her what she had just consumed. The good male merriment
shook the house.

Ranch humor was never very subtle. One of the favorite
jokes concerned a simple-minded cowboy who worked over at
the Bar-L outfit. He was sickeningly in love with the owner's
daughter. The cowboys told him that there was one sure way to
land her. If he could just get her to put her hand on his most private and personal member, she would not be able to resist him.
So when out for a ride one day, they got off their horses to look at
the view. While her eyes were averted, he opened his fly and
quickly placed her hand on his flesh. She screamed in horror and
fled, and of course he was chased out of her life and off the
ranch. But he certainly gave the boys a lot of laughs.

Though my tone in retrospect is cynical, my attitude at the
time was entirely different. I regarded the cowboys with romantic
admiration, and they were very good to me in their fashion. I had
to be the butt of some jokes, of course, but they taught me how
to tie knots, how to rope and ride, and how to shoot. If their
jokes were cruel, so was their life. Most of them were without
women for the balance of the year, and then they had only prostitutes when they went to Cheyenne for a brief vacation, getting a
dose of clap as a matter of course and spending the next year
curing it. By the time they were thirty-five or forty, they were
old men. They sang a lot of merry, sexy songs, all having to do
with the conquest of women—usually school teachers. I remember in particular one that ended, "I walked up to her and down
she did fall, for she longed to be a-playing with my long peganal."

The food on a ranch is vile, or at least it was in those days.
I remember well my inability to eat my first dinner, the noon
meal; it was composed of a boiled potato and salt pork. Sometimes there was sage hen, or rabbit, or antelope, but generally nobody bothered to go out and shoot.

My jobs were varied. One of my specific tasks was to bring the horses in from the pasture in the morning. Of course, most of the stock runs loose on the range, but the few horses that would be needed the next day are kept in a fenced enclosure, maybe a mile square, when they are turned out at night. In the morning I would saddle up and ride out to drive them back to the corral. When Mr. Allen first said, "Go bring in the stock," I was paralyzed by the uncertainty of how to perform my task. I tried hesitatingly to get instructions. One of the cowboys said, "Oh, just get on old Doc. He'll do it for you."

A trained cowpony is a marvelous thing to watch. They put me on old Doc and I went out across the prairie not believing that I could possibly accomplish this difficult task. Soon I found that all I had to do was to hang on; Doc would do the rest. He rounded up the herd. If one of the stragglers tried to get back, he'd cut him off, and he brought the six or seven ponies in the pasture back to the corral. He nearly lost me a couple of times when he did a quick turn, but I hung on and thus survived the first test. I felt that at last I had become part of the great wild West.

Later in the summer, when I had become a bit more skillful and perhaps more useful, I really was part of the wild West. At roundup time I was given the job of roping the calves, throwing them and holding their legs while the hot branding iron was placed against their flanks. At first my sympathies went out to the squealing calves, but as the day wore on and as I grew tireder and tireder, I began to hate them for kicking at me. The air was full of dust and the smell of burning flesh. It was a bloody affair too, for the calves were castrated. The testicles were thrown in a little pile in the corner of the corral and later the cowboys cooked them over the fire used to heat the branding irons. I was offered a change of diet, but I discovered that I wasn't hungry.

During the roundup, a stallion brought into the corral with a great number of amorous mares finds himself involved with an almost continuous love life which gets to be too much for him. Weakened by the end of day, he becomes disgusted with sex and kicks any mare in the face who shows the slightest sign of coquetry. The whole thing was very educational to a small boy.

Sometimes the Allens had attractive guests. One was a big

Scot, the type of man I had hoped Mr. Allen would be, with a twinkle in his eye, an easy manner and, best of all, a bagpipe. At night when the sun had gone down, he'd sit out on the porch and play this wild instrument; and it was a beautiful thing to hear it keening over the prairie. Another guest was a beautiful young lady about twenty-two years old. The cowboys, who were inarticulate with admiration, disguised this under a thin layer of rowdy bunkhouse jokes. In her honor, we had a snipe hunt one night. I was given a burlap bag and sent down the creek to hold it across the water while they flushed the snipe into the bag. I stayed there waiting for the snipe, while it got darker and darker. There were, in fact, quite a few low-flying night birds but none of them went into my sack. Finally I came home and learned that I had been the victim of an old joke.

I was assigned to be the young lady's protector, and I used to take her out riding. I discovered that when racing at a gallop her skirt would work up over her knees. This gave me a tremendous thrill. She was led into quite a lot of fast riding, and I got bawled out by Mr. Allen for getting the horses too hot.

Sometimes I was entrusted with riding fence. The ranches in that part of Wyoming are fenced with barbed wire and in the course of time the wires are liable to come loose from the post and need to be repaired. The fence rider does a complete circuit, looking for places that need repair and then driving a staple in to make the wire taut again. I wasn't very good at it, but I liked the feeling that I was a cowboy doing a cowboy's job.

Once I was on an errand with one of the cowboys when we found a nest in a cottonwood tree containing two baby hawks. We brought one of them back to the ranch. Later when this bird had a wing spread of four or five feet, a visitor at the ranch identified it as an eagle. I'm not sure what it was, but its name was Hawkie, and I raised it with loving care. Mr. Allen was dour about this unorthodox addition to the animal life at the place, but he said it would die in a couple of days anyhow, so he let me try to raise it. I served Hawkie prairie dogs I had shot and frogs which I got from the pond next to the ranch house. Shooting a prairie dog is no easy task. They are easy to hit, but usually they get down their hole before they die. However, when you have a young mouth to feed, you are moved to unusual heights of skill and ingenuity. I fed Hawkie, and I also taught him to fly long before a bird of his age should have known anything about it. I would take him up on top of the windmill and toss him off. He couldn't fly, but he could sail down clumsily. When it became apparent that he was going to survive, the fear grew that as he developed in size he would attack the chickens. To forestall this, I threw him down next to a rooster while he was still very young, and the rooster whammed him in the ribs with spurs and knocked his wind out. I thought this single lesson ought to inspire respect for chickens in Hawkie's mind; besides I was moved by sympathy from any further attempts to educate him.

Later Hawkie moved to the haystack beside the barn and whenever any strangers happened by the ranch I was instructed to show off our pet. I'd yell "Hawkie, Hawkie," in my high nasal voice, and this white head would peep over the top of the haystack and then Hawkie would come flapping down to see what was going on. Because he had thrived on them when he was young, he had acquired a taste for frogs, and he would fly round and round the pond with one leg hanging down waiting to surprise a dreamy tidbit.

Hawkie became an institution after a while, and I ceased to play with him. Then one day, I put my hands on him and he reached up with one talon and ripped my buckskin glove from one end to the other. From that time on, I didn't touch him. Later he got tired of the frog diet and carried off a chicken. Mr. Allen said that was enough and I had to get rid of him. Feeling like Judas Iscariot, I hid a big club behind my back, called Hawkie to me and beat out his brains. If he had only laid off the chickens for one more week, I could have taken him back to Cheyenne with me, where he would have been a sensation.

I had another pet that wasn't so successful; I roped a young coyote and started to train him. He bit me in the finger, and it must have been quite a good bite because I still have the scar. I was making very little progress in taming him when an edict came from Mr. Allen. "This ranch is getting to be a goddamn menagerie—get rid of that animal." I had to shoot him, but he was a stranger so it didn't matter so much.

I returned to Cheyenne with one great worry—I was old enough now to change to long pants, and I feared that I would be a figure of ridicule. Since all boys had to go through this transition I don't know why I was so self-conscious about it, but it caused me hours and hours of distress.

Distress came quite easily to me in those days. All adolescents, I am sure, feel unattractive. It is a miserable age. I felt that nobody liked me, really liked me, except maybe my mother and the librarian; that I was constantly being visited by injustice; that the world did not appreciate me (though someday I was going to show them); and finally that I was quite an objectionable person.

By this time, at the age of thirteen, I was tall and gangling. I walked with a stoop trying to make myself look shorter, and I shuffled along to show the world that I didn't give a damn what anybody thought about me anyway. I had blondish, dishwater-colored hair, white on top where the sun had bleached it; sometimes I was called Cottontop. Although the word was not then in vogue, I was close to being a juvenile delinquent.

I suppose the basic trouble for a boy of this age is sex. He begins to think about the female of the species—day and night, night and day, as Cole Porter says. And like the beat, beat, beat of the tom-tom, sex is hardly ever out of his consciousness. I had never touched a girl; I knew nothing about them; I merely thought about them all the time. They came to me in my fantasies as willing mermaids. The girls I met in real life I treated derisively to show that I didn't care.

Once another boy and I drew some dirty pictures and left them where the girl next door would find them. Being a good girl, she took them to her parents, her parents took them to my parents, and this guilty victim was tracked down and brought before the judge and jury of his mother and father.

Occasionally I got into fights. The one I remember particularly was with a boy named Conner. He accused me of snitching on him in school and challenged me. We were led off by a large crowd of the older boys to a back alley to settle the affair of honor, and there he gave me two black eyes. I bawled, and it took me a long time to forgive the Irish race.

Cheyenne was big enough to have its tough gangs. One day some of us were out swimming at the reservoir when a gang was seen approaching. The others decided on flight and grabbed up their clothes, but my brother and I stayed at our posts. It was a mistake. The gang didn't bother Micky much, but they put me through a humiliating and degrading hazing. I don't think I resented the boys who had done this to me as much as I did my brother, who had witnessed my degradation.

I was rather mean to my brother. I took a malicious delight in subjugating him, giving him orders, and making arbitrary rules for him. For instance, during the mile walk across the prairie to the lake I would make him stay two paces in the rear, and I inflicted upon him many sadistic tricks.

I ran with a gang who stole pigeons. This was usually a daytime operation. We would sneak into a back yard, climb to the loft of the barn, snare pigeons roosting there, put them in a sack and take them away to divide them. Then, by pulling a few feathers from their wings so that temporarily they couldn't fly, and by feeding them, we accustomed them to staying at our barn instead of where they really belonged.

As an adult, I don't think I have too much tolerance for flip kids. But I ought to, because I spent two or three years of my life heckling instructors and rebelling against authority in general. We had a nice effeminate young man for a Sunday-school teacher, and I remember demanding from him proofs of the stories in the Bible and proofs of God's existence, until finally he was driven into such a corner that he claimed that he had not only seen an angel but talked to one. In school, I was a lost soul. I didn't know the reason for being there; I didn't know what I was studying or why I was studying. Since I was such a lackluster scholar, I tried to shine in other departments. I dressed in odd outfits just to cause a sensation; I asked constant, needling and impertinent questions; I showed off for the class and was frequently sent home.

Finally I decided to run away. A friend of mine, a dumb, good-natured boy named Clix Matthews, was going down to Wheatley, Colorado, to pick potatoes. You could make big money down there—as much as four dollars a day. I decided to go with him. He was to come by before daylight the next morning and throw pebbles at my window as a signal. Then I would sneak out by climbing down a pillar of the porch and we'd be off to Colorado and gone forever.

My luggage was one of those old-fashioned telescope bags,

and I put my things in it and hid it under the bed. I went to sleep early and awoke to find Mama sitting beside me. She was very quiet and soft, though usually she was firm and determined. Her need to fight life, to educate her children and improve the conditions of her family, over no matter what odds, had made her rather grim. But at this moment she was tender. She said, "I know you're going to run away. I missed your things. It makes me very unhappy. I've tried hard to make a loving home for us all. But if you do want to go, then you mustn't go unprepared. You must take warm things because down where you're going, it will be cold this winter. You need woolen underwear and your overcoat." I explained my plan to her. "Well," she said, "tell Clix you'll come on a later train. You can meet him down in Colorado. Just give me time to get your things together so that you may leave properly."

The next morning, in the dawn's early light I leaned out the window and told Clix that I'd be down on the train that reached there in the afternoon and made plans to meet him. True to her promise, Mama prepared me for the trip. My clothes were assembled, and the telescope became heavy with winter underwear and my overcoat. I kissed all the family goodbye except for my father, who was not at home, and took the train for Colorado. When I arrived, Clix was not at the station, so I went to the agency where he was supposed to be employed and inquired for him there. They didn't know where he was; they didn't even know who he was. After walking the streets looking for him, I finally gave up, went back to the station, found a train that would reach Cheyenne that night and returned home. The prodigal, rather shamefacedly, knocked on the door and was admitted. No one gloated; they were all very glad to see me.

Shortly after this I was suspended from school for some further breach of discipline, and it was decided that I should be sent to Kearney Military Academy in Nebraska. This turned out to be very good for me. I recommend military academies as a cure for rebellious adolescents, especially if they have a wonderfully understanding headmaster such as Harry N. Russell, who was in charge of KMA.

Kearney Military Academy is a mile or so from the town of Kearney, and it is on an absolutely flat plain. In Cheyenne, you could see mountains in the distance, but at Kearney you could stand on the Union Pacific track and see it go off in a straight line over the horizon, east and west. The institution itself was primitive; two-story wooden buildings, wash basins in each room, hot water at the end of the hall, an outdoor privy. But the man who ran it sent every boy away a better character.

Kearney was not exactly a reform school, but it was close. Most of the boys there had had troubles at home. A few, however, were from well-to-do parents who had gone on trips and needed to board a boy. Or perhaps a mother had died and the father didn't know how to bring up his son. I studied there for a year and a half, and I can't think of anyone I admired or really liked except for Captain Russell. I had many companions but no real friends, no one that I ever wanted to see again once I had shaken the dust of the place. Today I have only the kindly memory of this good man who helped to make me a better boy.

The place was run like an English school. Everyone was called by his last name, and good manners were part of the discipline. We were taught to be clean, to be polite, to respect the rights of others and to stand up straight. I can't really remember whether I learned anything academically there or not, but I suppose I went through classes in the same old fuzzy condition.

Upon my arrival at the station, I was met by a couple of the students with a horse and buggy in which they drove me back to the school. I was entered at midterm, so found myself at some disadvantage among boys who had all grown to know each other. No one was exactly hostile at first, but no one was very friendly either. I knew that I was on the spot.

We lived by the bugle: reveille, inspection, breakfast, room inspection, drill, school, drill, play, and so on. There were bugle calls for everything, and we marched to and from all important events. My favorite bugle call was Tatoo, which was played as a signal for us to go to our quarters at night. And, of course, everyone loves Taps. There's no lovelier sound when you're tucked in your lonely bed, in your own room, away from the stress of other people, than Taps floating through the night air.

I got off on the wrong foot very shortly after beginning my life at KMA. After dinner one night, some of the older fellows suggested a snipe hunt, which was accepted with enthusiasm by the others acting their parts. I kept a straight face and went along with the joke, but when I had been planted in my spot by the creek I quickly left my post and cut back to the Academy. When the others returned to await my humiliation, I was sitting there on the steps to greet them. They laughed it off rather sourly and then about a week later gave me a fine hazing. I was taken from my bed and dumped into an icy creek. Two days later, I couldn't walk. I tried to crawl downstairs in answer to the bugle, but had to give up and was taken to the infirmary, where I was said to have rheumatism as the result of the hazing.

After I got off the sick list, I was accepted as one of the gang and things went better. I don't mean that I became an adjusted student, I didn't; I was always in some trouble or other, but I was one of the boys.

Punishment at the Academy was dished out in the form of demerits. If you had dirty fingernails, dirty shoes, a crooked tie or a sloppy uniform at inspection, you got a demerit. If you were late to class, failed to salute an officer, were rude, or negligent in your studies, you got a demerit. You paid for these demerits by walking guard duty, a punishment to which I did not particularly object. With a rifle over your shoulder, you walked up and down along a certain prescribed line. I spent a great deal of time in this fashion, but I like to walk and to be alone, so I would fancy myself on some romantic errand or would just let my mind drift off into any fantasy it pleased.

One day when I was walking across the yard I met "The Redneck," our adjutant, and he said, "I hear your mother is a Christian Scientist." I didn't know what a Christian Scientist was; I hadn't the faintest idea of what he was talking about. But when I went home for summer vacation, I found that he was right. While I was away, my mother had accepted this new doctrine, and indeed had been healed of both her neuralgia and her rheumatism. My brother and sister had also been helped in minor ways, so I was told. I resisted this new and unorthodox religion, but my mother assured me that among other things it would make me a better athlete. With this golden apple held out before me, I decided to give it a try.

We were not to be a family group for long. It had been planned that everybody except me was to go East to visit my grandparents. I was to have my heart's desire and work on a regular ranch, a big ranch. One of mother's new Christian Science friends was the wife of Judge Carey, who owned the CY outfit. This time I was to go there and work not only for my board but for some money—not much, but enough to pay my carfare.

I had some trepidation about the initial stages of this venture, but Mama, as always wishing to make us strong and independent, told me to be businesslike and write the ranch a postal informing them of the time of my arrival. The foreman of the CY Ranch received a postcard stating, "I shall report for work on the train which arrives at 7:10 P.M. on June 20, 1900. Yours truly, G. F. Abbott."

In the late afternoon we reached the little station, a shanty in the midst of a vast prairie. I disembarked with my suitcase and stood on the platform waiting. There were many men around loading buckboards with goods which had come on the train. I kept waiting for someone to ask me if I was the new arrival, the son of the friend of the wife of Judge Carey, but nobody paid me the slightest attention. The ranch hands had begun to get into their buckboards and drive away when in desperation. I spoke to the foreman. "Oh," he said, "I was expecting a man." Mama's advice to be businesslike had nearly caused her eldest son to be left standing by himself on the lone prairie.

I got in with the men and was driven across the plain about ten miles to the headquarters of the ranch. When I was assigned a place in the bunkhouse, one of the men said, "Who's going to bunk in with the new boy?" I didn't quite comprehend what this meant, but I knew from the laughter that it was something evil. Actually, that was the only time I heard a joke about pederasty from any cowboy. Perhaps, because there are always women around—the rancher's wife and the foreman's wife to cook for them and take care of them when they're sick—they don't get that feeling of isolation which comes to certain other groups of segregated men. They have lots of jokes, however, about sheepherders. A sheepherder and his dog will be with his flock away from all of his companions for two months or more, and there are many bawdy jokes about his seeking solace with his little charges.

One of the cowboys who had recently been in Cheyenne remembered having seen me there. "Hey," he said, "I know that kid. I seen him in a blacksmith's getting a pair of spurs made for a fighting rooster."

"I know you too," I replied. "I saw you coming out of Big Rose's place." A whoop of laughter greeted this and I found myself inadvertently started off on the right foot.

The first night there was a square dance in the bunkhouse. An old fellow came in with a fiddle and played "The Arkansas Traveler" and "Pop Goes the Weasel," the violin held against his hip while the men danced. Some of the men tied handkerchiefs around their sleeves to signify that they were the girls.

Before I left Cheyenne I had wanted to buy a pair of high-heeled cowboy boots, but Mama had vetoed this. She argued quite logically that if I had shoes I could wear them when I came back in the fall and returned to KMA, but if I had boots I would have to throw them away once I left the ranch. On my first night in the bunkhouse, I traded my shoes for a pair of high-heeled boots. The cowboy got a good pair of shoes a little too large for him, and I got a very old pair of boots a little too small for me. A disaster; not only did they make my toes permanently crooked, but they wore two sore spots on the sides of my feet that remained the whole summer long. The boots were, however, good for my spirit; I felt like a cowboy. I still have the scars on my feet made by those boots that summer, and somehow or other, I'm proud of them.

The CY was a big ranch, many times the size of Mr. Allen's. There were twenty or thirty cowhands employed, many of them specialists doing only one kind of work. There was a big reservoir on the place and the irrigators were in charge of letting the water flow through the ditches to the alfalfa field, then flooding each part in turn. The foreman had a son named Buck who was about my age, but though I had had a summer on a ranch, I was no match for Buck. I was allowed only to ride the well-broken horses, whereas he could ride the broncs. He could break horses and could throw a rope as well as most of the men. He treated me distantly and with veiled contempt.

In the West, strangers are always dropping in. You could ride all across Wyoming and Montana and never have to buy a meal. All you had to do was ride up to a ranch house, where you would be made welcome, bedded and fed. One day a young fellow came along who had been a soldier in the Boer War. He was a cockney and a great showoff. After supper, he did some card tricks and then out of his saddle bags he produced a set of boxing gloves and invited the men to fight with him. He would parry their blows, dance around, stab them lightly in the face, and in general show off his superiority. One of the men thought it would be good to see me get a pummeling and suggested that I take on Buck. Now experience is a great teacher. Buck was much stronger than I, but he'd never seen a pair of boxing gloves, whereas I, a city boy, had often boxed and knew something about it. I can't say that I whipped him decisively, but I more than held my own, and I think was raised in the respect of my associates.

I had many jobs on the ranch. They started me out riding fence, but soon they found out that I was not very thorough. I was too dreamy; I rode along the fence but I wasn't thinking about where the barbed wire was loose. I was letting my mind wander into the future, when I would be a noble poet reciting my verses, or a great soldier leading my army. Eventually it was decided to shift me to the alfalfa field. I was put to work driving the loader. Our gang, the ones who were working in the alfalfa field, moved their headquarters from the ranch home to the scene of action. We slept in sleeping bags and our only cover was tents.

The mowing machines had three horses, usually unbroken ones. A machine is so heavy that the horses cannot run away with it, and it proves to be a fine way to take the spirit out of a fractious brute. Another set of men drive the rakes, and the rakes bring the alfalfa up to the loader which throws the alfalfa up on the stack. As it grows bigger, the men stand on the stack and arrange it so that it will be solid and well drained for the winter. The loader is a strange contraption. The part that receives the alfalfa is a flat rake about ten feet wide that lies on the ground; pulleys lift this up and throw the alfalfa onto the stack. The horses pull the fork up moving forward and they let it down by being backed up.

My job was to drive the horses. If one drives them too fast, it hurls the alfalfa at the men who are on the stack, and the driver is rewarded with curses and a few appropriate comments upon his shortcomings and those of his ancestors. After a while, I grew skillful at the job, and like every manual exercise, it was great fun once you got the technique of it.

Horses have an instinct for time, the same instinct which made me wake up before my alarm went off. We always quit work at five-thirty, and at five twenty-seven they would begin to whinny. As animals they are not very bright, but they can tell time. After all, some of the dumbest men are better at knowing when it's time to knock off work than the bright ones.

When the alfalfa was all stacked for the winter, we moved back to the bunkhouse. The ranch was being run by Robert Carey, who eventually became Governor of Wyoming, as was his father before him. I admired Carey, a handsome, pleasant man, with well-cut clothes and English boots. He was dressed differently than the cowhands, but he was not a snob. Once his mother came to visit the ranch and she asked to see her friend May Abbott's boy, so on this gala occasion I washed myself up, slicked my hair back and went to dinner at the big house.

One evening the men went swimming in the reservoir. Cowboys are wonderful on horses, but they don't know much about water; most of them can't swim more than a stroke or two, if that. They presented a rather ridiculous figure, these heroes of mine with their turkey-red faces and their white, white bodies. I excited their admiration by swimming across the reservoir and then I gave an imitation of the helldiver and disappeared beneath the surface to come up on another part of the water. By the time the summer was over I had in one way and another improved my status in the cowboy world. They didn't think I was such a bad kid after all.

The time came to go back to Cheyenne. At each station I got off and strolled up and down the platform in my high-heeled boots, wondering if the natives were impressed, feeling like a young cowboy on his way to take a look at the big city. Finally the long, hot train ride was over. Why, the old town hadn't changed so much. I swaggered up the street to our house on Capitol Avenue. My boots hurt, it was true, but they felt like Mercury's wings. I was eager to see my family and to be the center of things as I told them of my adventures.

. . .

Back at KMA, I got in trouble again. I joined a melon-stealing group one night after Taps. Just as we were making our way into the melon patch, lighted dimly by a silver moon, I heard a faint rustling and a man stood up before me with a gun. We all turned and fled, but I banged straight into a barbed-wire fence. As it turned out, the "man" was only one of the other students who had so successfully hoaxed us, but my collision with the fence was a disastrous one. I had been wearing my new uniform and it was cut into so many jagged pieces that it seemed impossible to ever get it repaired. It was also rather a difficult matter to explain to the authorities.

Quite a lot of gambling went on at school. We played Fan-tan and Twenty-one. At first, I got taken, and I suspected there was a little cheating. Working diligently in the privacy of my room, I learned to pull a card off the bottom of the deck, and although I wasn't very nifty with the pasteboards, I could get a face card where I wanted it—on the bottom. With this secret weapon I retrieved my losses. My passion for gambling lasted all through school; I thought it was the most exciting thing in the world. But since then, I have no interest in it at all—I think it's a bore. It's perfectly evident that it is no way to make money, and it certainly is a stupid way to *lose* money, so why bother? I sometimes make a bet because I have to, or even play roulette to pass the time, but I couldn't care less about it.

I loved football. I wasn't big enough to make the first team, but I played on the scrubs, and I looked forward to football practice above almost everything else. I also discovered another talent which stood me in good stead. Every week there was a drill-down; we stood in line with our rifles at our sides, the commanding officer gave the orders and we executed them. When fault was found—a finger in the wrong place or any mistake—the cadet was taken out of line until finally there was only one left. As a reward for excellence in drill, this man was then appointed Orderly for the next week. Among the Orderly's duties was the collecting of the demerit cards from the box in which they were posted and delivering them to the Commandant's office. On the short trip from the demerit box to the Commandant's office, I would extract about three-quarters of my demerits, leaving just enough to keep things looking normal. In this fashion I saved myself a great deal of walking and was never detected. My proficiency in drill had a profit motive which made me invincible; I succeeded in winning the right to act as Orderly every other week, which was as often as the rules permitted one to capture the honor.

Another talent I discovered was that I was a good dancer. This was part of the school curriculum, but I thought very little about it until at the final ball of the year I was flattered to discover that all the older boys were coming around and asking me to sign up to dance with their girls. I could hardly believe it; I had never really been in demand before.

One day a new girl came to work in the kitchen. I think she was a foreigner, and I remember that she looked very defenseless and red-cheeked and soft and weak and helpless, a girl who smiled because she wanted you to like her, not because she was happy. One night one of the boys got a ladder and climbed into her bedroom window. He was followed by nine others. Who stopped the procession I don't know, but the culprits were detected. The girl disappeared, and the whole school was abuzz with the snickering excitement. Curious as I was about sex, and much as I would have liked to know what it was all about, it never occurred to me to wish that I had been one of the boys to climb that ladder. I only felt sorry for that poor, helpless girl and wondered what had happened to her.

However, I never felt sorry for my superior officers. I hated them and was a constant thorn in their sides—a sort of one-man trouble spot. I thought that Captain Glover and Lieutenant Gray had received their promotions because they were rich boys, that I was still a private because I was without pull, and I resented it. It is easy to understand how officers get shot in the back in a war. I don't approve of it, of course, but I understand it. Once I was promoted as far as temporary corporal, but inevitably I got into some trouble and had the honor taken away from me. I left KMA as I arrived, a lowly private, but I think I was a much better individual.

My last act at KMA, and the thing which gave me the greatest pleasure, was an ignoble one. I stole Lieutenant Gray's baseball shoes. This was risky because if my baggage had been searched I would have been in great trouble, but I got away with it. At Kearney I boarded the train which was bearing the rest of my family back East, our first stop being South Bend, Indiana, where we were to visit a relative. The guilty spike shoes were among my belongings. I put them on and ran proudly up and down the street in front of the house. A great elation flooded my soul. My spike shoes seemed to be gashing the lieutenant's face as I ran along. It gave me a great sense of well-being.

The train was taking us back to Hamburg to live with our grandparents for a while. We children were kept in the dark as to the real reason for this. We knew that Papa had changed jobs several times, but that didn't particularly interest us. The cold facts were that he had lost his government job and then had gone into several adventures in promotion: get-rich schemes in mining, oil, and the like, all of which had turned out disastrously. Finally my grandparents had persuaded him to bring his family home while he got a fresh start. He had got a job as salesman for a big flour company back in the East.

Papa had been a successful drinker for a great many years; in fact, it was said that he was able to drink any man at the Interocean Hotel under the table. But gradually he ceased being a good drinker and became a drunkard, and now, as I learned later, he drank so much that he was unreliable.

Tensions awaited us in Hamburg. My mother was forced into the false position of being supported by her in-laws instead of by her husband. In turn, the in-laws felt that since they were paying the bills they had a right to have more to say about what happened. This included such petty details as to how much butter should put on bread, but the main cause of contention was religion. The fact that my mother had become a Christian Scientist was a slap in the face to them, a humiliation. To think that someone related to them should ascribe to such an outlandish creed, should disgrace the Abbotts, pillars of the Methodist Church, should go down on Sunday to worship in "that hole."

The Christian Scientists in Hamburg were a small, valiant group of some twenty or thirty men and women. One man was an important Buffalo lawyer, but the balance of the church were inconspicuous members of society. What hurt my grandparents in particular was that the Thurstons, who lived next door, were

Christian Scientists—and the Thurstons were considered to be absolute cranks. They were said to have come from a wealthy family; and at any rate, their house was full of fine, old furniture, many pieces of which were moved over to my grandparents' house as the result of money lent and in payment also of doctor bills. They were out of step with this world; Mrs. Thurston had no friends and Mr. Thurston was a dreamy old man who went to Buffalo in some menial capacity and came back every day on the train. The children were the brightest kids in school, but they never played any games nor mingled with the others. They were what was known in the vernacular of the village as dubs. The Thurstons once had a great scheme for making a lot of money; they were going to raise silkworms in their attic. As a financial enterprise, it was a failure, but biologically it was a great success. They never could quite get rid of the silkworms.

The village regarded this little band of Christian Scientists with amusement and contempt. When people believe in their cause, however, this fortifies their will power and dedication. My own attitude toward all this was passive; I went to church there because my mother wanted me to, but I didn't welcome the ridicule. I learned how it feels to be a member of an outcast group. Togetherness is easier; it's more fun to belong to the gang.

Another religious factor complicated our situation. The Reverend Peter Thompson, an Englishman and a widower with three children, had been assigned to the Methodist Church in Hamburg. Reverend Thompson was a small, meek, self-deprecatory man, inclined to cater to his parishioners, flatter them suitably and kiss babies in the approved style of the time. One thought on first contact that he was too gentle to have any convictions, but if you talked to him, you found out differently. I had some theological arguments with him and I learned that you couldn't get into heaven until you were a Methodist. His two younger children were lackluster, but his eldest child, a girl named Dorothy, was bright and aggressive. When later in life, as a famous columnist, she wrote rather dewy-eyed articles about her father, who had inspired her to love Shakespeare and the classics, I was amused, because I could remember that he forbade her *Quo Vadis* because he thought it was a dirty book, and that I had smuggled it out of the library for her to read secretly. At any rate,

Aunt Eliza, who seemed long ago to have withered on the vine, was courted by the Reverend Peter Thompson. As a minister he needed a wife, and he also needed a mother for his three children. Neither was a job which would appeal to the more attractive members of his congregation, but Aunt Eliza was more than willing. Since she was an ardent church worker, and since she would, by small-town standards, eventually come into quite an inheritance, Mr. Thompson put on the blinders, so to speak, and married her for her money and to give his children a mother.

This happy event was not, as they say, in the bag at this time, and the conduct of the Abbotts from the West seemed likely to jeopardize the wedding bells. Papa, however, was doing better financially and had sold a whole carload of flour.

I entered Hamburg High School in the fall. It was exciting to see the fellows kissing the girls in the cloakroom. This was a new world to me, an almost unbelievable world. I didn't get to the kissing stage myself until sometime later, but I was agog with excitement. Also I was now a big boy, or bigger than the other boys in the class. My nickname in Hamburg was Big Abbott, to differentiate me from my brother, and I could compete successfully in athletic events. We had football, hockey, baseball and track teams, and since there was very little competition, I made them all. I was only an adequate athlete, but I was a frightfully enthusiastic one.

I was never really popular in high school; I was too mouthy and opinionated, too bossy. But by sheer aggressiveness, I got myself elected to important jobs. I was, I remember, the captain of the football team. We played games with the other little towns nearby. I remember once when we were going to play in East Aurora the bus broke down, and we had to walk the last five miles to the game. On the first play, I found my mouth full of blood and hair and discovered that I had broken off a front tooth on an opponent's head. A week later I had to have the nerve extracted. To those who now want to go back to the good old days, I say emphatically that I don't want to go back before novocaine —and this was before novocaine, at least in Hamburg—for to have a nerve extracted without benefit of that drug was a harrowing experience. The dentist shoved a wire into the root canal—I felt it going up and up like a hot poker, through my tooth, through my cheek, my eye, and out the top of my head. O Progress, I thank you for the needle and the high-speed drill.

Hamburg High School also had theatricals, and I turned out to be the best actor in the school.

We had some distant cousins, rich ones, who lived in Buffalo and had a summer place down on Lake Erie. Olive and Ted Abbott were quite the swellest people I had ever met, and when they invited me down for a weekend I was paralyzed by this high society. Everyone knew how to behave but me. I was amazed at the way the young men would put their hands on girls. There was a giant swing on their place, and the boys would grab the girls by their waists, push them up into the air, even run under them—all this accompanied by much shrieking and gaiety. I tried to do my part, but it really seemed to me so obscene to take hold of a girl by the waist that I could hardly bear it.

One of the boys played a mandolin, and at night we sat on a screened porch and sang songs by the light of the moon. The popular song at that time was "Hiawatha," and there was a parody which we all sang.

> Oh, the lady of the house
> Found a louse on her blouse
> Did she catch it
> Well, I guess she did.

After this daring number, there was a good deal of wicked laughter and knowing glances at one another. We danced too, and here I was all right, except that once they all stood aside and applauded when I was dancing with a girl and I stopped dead in my tracks. She was furious and hissed, "Keep dancing!"

That fall, 1904, I went back to school and continued the same old routine, a secret life of dreaming about women, continued excitement and enthusiasm for athletics, and the same old fuzzy attitude toward my studies. My mother's life now became complicated with an illness. Of course she would not have confessed to this "error," but she had to ask us to slow down when we walked with her, and soon she admitted that she thought there was something the matter with her heart. Aunt Anna, who hated Christian Science even worse than my grandparents did, tried to get her to go to a doctor, but for a year or so Mother stubbornly tried to "work it out in science." Eventually she was forced to return to materia medica and a surgeon removed an obstruction from her uterus and cured her in one simple day.

It's a puzzlement. When Mother knew nothing about this science of the mind, she was cured of two diseases which the doctors had failed to remedy. But then after she had made a great study of it, it was necessary to effect a cure by the material remedies. There is no doubt in my mind that people get cured of diseases by Christian Science. They also get cured by medicine; and most of all by miracles through surgery. But the best cure of all is nature. And who is to say what is responsible, which is cause and which effect?

In an abandoned room on the top floor of the Hamburg High School there were some old rusty fencing foils whose buttons on the points had been broken off. One day a couple of us started to fence. When my guard failed, I instinctively put up my hand to ward off the weapon, and the foil entered my hand between my first two fingers and came out three inches further, at my wrist. With bravado I dismissed this gruesome wound and started to fence again, repeated the same mistake, and this time the foil went through the fatty part of my thumb and out the other side. I decided that I was not D'Artagnan.

The Christian Science Church had a little reading room which the members took turns in tending. On that afternoon my mother was there on duty, and when I appeared with my wounds she gave me *Science and Health* to read and began to treat me. I had a very sore hand, but no infection developed. Was it luck, or God, or was I in good health? I don't know. Another time I ran a nail through my foot without any disastrous results. I was so unreligious by nature that I did not enter into the spirit of things as fully as the rest of my family. They all made a success of it. And as far as I can judge by looking at the happy faces of people coming out of a Christian Science church, a great many other people have as well.

That fall my father lost his job. By this time my brother and I had learned that the cause of Papa's trouble was his drunkenness. There were a few rows, for in adversity Grandma's mother love was aggressive and protective. Momma made a decision: she would move out. Since she had no money, she had to go to work again as a teacher in the third grade of the local school, and she rented a flat over the meat market uptown. She offered us our choice: we could come with her and live in this semi-squalid condition or we could stay with our grandparents. We all went with her, and of course this was an added humiliation to the Abbott family—it said to one and all that G. B. Abbott had failed and that his wife was leaving him and working as a schoolteacher.

I had had many different jobs since coming back to Hamburg. In the berry season I worked at the canning factory, and once I was a house painter for a couple of weeks. But my really big job was when I went to work in the summers for the Lackawanna Steel Company. They had a plant in Buffalo only half an hour away by trolley. I was taken on as an assistant electrician—twelve hours a day, seventeen and a half cents an hour. At the end of every two weeks you worked for twenty-four consecutive hours and were shifted to night work for two weeks.

My first job was cutting wires off little armatures. Nobody showed me how to do it; they just gave me the equipment and turned me loose. Later I was assigned as a cable-splicer's helper. The power that ran the plant was conducted by giant cables carried underground through conduits, and at appropriate intervals there were manholes where the splicing was made to join them together. I had been told to get down into one of these manholes and push cables over when I heard a voice, and looking up I saw the wizened face of a little old man with big mustaches. He glowered at me. Then in a thick Danish accent he said, "Vell, for Godsakes, look at the big feets on de boy. Vell, dey come handy in for pushin' de cables round." It was my boss, Jules Nelsen, the cable-splicer—a wonderful character about whom I later wrote a play called *The Man in the Manhole*, which won a prize at Harvard.

Jules abused me but he liked me and we became friends. One of my jobs was to go to the storehouse and fetch supplies. I would always stop behind the freight cars on the way back and practice lifting exercises with the lead sleeves, the casings which enclose the spliced cable. My goal was to be able to lift eight pounds from my shoulder straight up with one hand.

The Lackawanna Steel Company was a dangerous place. It

was said that they killed a man a day there. Probably this was an exaggeration, but it was certainly true that a great many workers did die violently. Coming to work on my second week, I saw a Swedish rigger hit by a trolley car. His body burst open, his guts ran out into the dust and his face became like a waxen image in a store window.

I myself had two or three narrow escapes. Once when I tried to jump one of the little trains running through the plant on narrow-gauge tracks I missed my footing and was dragged along holding on by one hand. In the other hand I had an oil can that I was taking back to Jules, but I didn't have sense enough to drop it. Luckily they stopped the train before I fell under. The engineer addressed some very uncomplimentary remarks to me, but I was so glad to be alive that his tirade sounded like a paean of praise. On another occasion, when I was sent up to fix an arc light on an unloader on a rainy night, I nearly fell into the ore pit below. There was no one else around, and I saved myself by hanging onto the slippery iron work and finally pulling myself back onto the narrow steel grading.

Jolly pranks were played on the greenhorns at the steel plant. Jules could stick his fingers into boiling solder without getting burned, and he would invite you to do the same. The trick was to wet your finger first; then the layer of steam caused by the hot solder protected your finger until you pulled it out. But not knowing this, the novice was badly burned. Another good joke was to tell the Hungarian workmen that if a man urinated on the gantry track it would cure gonorrhea. The gantry track carried some two hundred and twenty volts of electric power, and of course water is a conductor, so this was especially good fun.

Different nationalities did different work: the Swedes did all the rigging; the Poles made up the labor gangs; the Hungarians and the Czechs and Germans worked in the foundries. The Polish labor gang was like an ancient Greek social organization. It had one old man, a sort of Nestor, who was always called Starry; then there was one strong man who was the boss, one funny man, and one scapegoat. Each man who played a role had the same name in every gang.

The night shift was more difficult because I never learned to sleep well during the day. Our little back bedroom was pretty hot in the summertime. Mother would pull the shades and I would go off into a kind of half drowse, always conscious of the sounds of the village: the cries of children, the crowing of roosters, the hammering of something far away, and the whistles from the canning factory. Then, feeling that I had not really been asleep at all, I would be awakened by my mother's kiss and her soft voice saying that it was time to get up. Or sometime she would just sit on the bed and sing to me. Mother sang a great deal in her lighter moods or when she was working around the house. They were always the same songs—as far as I know, she never learned any new ones —the songs of her childhood such as "Can She Bake a Cherry Pie?" and "Ta-ra-ra-boom-der-é." I would get up and go to the bathroom, the table would be set, my lunch pail would be packed, and after a brief goodbye, I'd be off.

Sometimes I grew very sleepy on the night shift. One night I was waiting for an order to be delivered to the storehouse when I dozed off standing up and only awoke when I fell over on my face. One Fourth of July I had just finished working a twenty-four hour shift, but instead of going to bed I went to the celebration in Hamburg. Maynard Bentley and I won the three-legged race, and then I went to bed at five o'clock that afternoon and slept for eighteen hours. It was the best sleep I have ever had in my life.

My father's drunkenness grew worse. He would be off on one of his trips and come back all cut up. He lived at the flat with us when he was on his good behavior and went back to his mother's house when he wasn't. One day when he was packing to go on a trip, without looking up he said to me, "Don't ever touch a drop of whiskey as long as you live." I said, "I won't," and that was the only time we ever discussed the subject of alcohol.

Sometimes when I took my girl up the stairs to the ballroom at Kopp's Hotel to a dance, I would hear my father's drunken voice in the barroom haranguing his pals. He always held forth; he was an authority on all international and national topics. Once I defied him physically. He was having some angry words with my mother and he told me to stand aside. I said I wouldn't, and since I was bigger and stronger than he, I won that eye to eye battle. But it left a resentment between us which never healed. I didn't hate my father for being a drunkard; I hated alcohol, which made him a drunkard. When you walked by a saloon in Hamburg, you smelled beer, and even today the smell of beer symbolizes saloons to me. I have a greater aversion to it than I have for the smell of whiskey.

This same year, 1906, was a year of great tragedy for me. I had been graduated to the stage of intimacy with the other sex that it euphemistically referred to these days as necking. Usually this took place not with your friends but with strangers. A couple of girls would come out from Buffalo and walk around our streets. Maynard Bentley and I would follow them. Eventually we would pick them up, pair off, and after due process of courtship—technically very harmless—we would see them to the trolley and they would return to Buffalo. Maynard was a smoothie; he always handled the approach, and always took his choice of girls. I was perfectly happy with my subordinate role.

In the spring of that year I had a job as a night telephone operator. My cot was put alongside the switchboard and if anyone called after twelve o'clock, it would waken me and I would make the connection. As a switchboard operator, I did quite a lot of eavesdropping, and I was amazed at the ease with which my friends called up girls and established an intimacy with them. One day I called a girl, who we shall say was named Gladys, and giving the name of one of my friends, bantered with her quite recklessly. It was so easy that I soon called her in my own name and made a date with her. For some reason there was no one at home and I took Gladys to our flat. After considerable wrestling around, I suddenly lost interest and took her home. The next day I began to wonder what had happened; it had all been such a frenzy that, unbelievable as it may sound, I wasn't quite sure. I talked to Gladys on the telephone, and she wasn't sure either. A few weeks later, however, she called me to say that something had happened, that she was alarmed, and that I was to get in touch with her in a few days. When I called, a very stern mother wanted to know who I was, and I hung up quickly. Gladys reached me the next day to let me know the worst. The old country joke was not just a joke—it was a terrible reality. I had knocked a girl up; I had gotten a girl in trouble, and worst of all, one whom I really didn't like, a girl for whom I had contempt.

I went back to work for the summer at the steel plant without knowing what was going to happen. In the next few weeks I learned what hell is like. There were no thoughts of sex now, only of self-reproach, guilt, and of fear of the consequences. I had saved up three hundred dollars toward my college fund, and I was prepared to withdraw that from the bank and run away if necessary. I was fully determined that if anyone came to me and said you've got to marry that girl, I would take my money and disappear without a trace. One day when I returned from work, she was waiting at the trolley. Everything was all right; a local doctor had taken care of her. The weight was lifted. Gladys suggested that it would now be appropriate for us to go out together. But men are stinkers; I wanted to forget the whole mess. I disappeared from her life.

At the steel plant I had a new job as a crane operator. A traveling crane is a giant bridgelike affair running on tracks at the top of the building. The operator has three levers: one to make the crane run up and down the building, one to run the carriage on the bridge back and forth, and a third to lower and raise a big hook. My job was in the foundry, where sometimes the machine lifted delicate moldings that had to be set down gently. As a new and nervous operator I jerked the hook up too abruptly and cracked a molding. The foreman shook his fist at me and rushed over to climb the iron ladder on the wall which would bring him up to where he could get at me. He gestured for me to bring the crane over, which I did, but in my nervousness I didn't stop in time. I would have crushed him had he not swung back and squeezed between the ladder and the wall. When I finally got control of the machine and backed it up to let him aboard I expected to be fired but the man was so happy to be alive that he didn't say a word. Eventually I became very handy with the crane and took great pleasure in the skill of its operation.

I began to think seriously of staying on at the steel plant for a whole year instead of going back to school, in order to save money for my college fund. Things were not going well at home. My father was now definitely one of the town's drunks, and I had seen the humiliating spectacle of him weaving down the street on his way home in the middle of the afternoon. Mother refused to have anything to do with him until he gave up drinking. My grandmother fought for him like a she-tiger for her cub. We were always being threatened with disinheritance because we wouldn't side with him, but we stood for principle rather than money and never wavered in our loyalty to our mother. In fact, I overdid the vigor of my loyalty and was cruel and heartless toward my father. I remember once hearing myself say to my grandmother, "I wouldn't pick him out of the gutter."

Micky and Isabel went back to school and I continued to work. They reported school news to me, the most exciting of which was that they had a new English teacher, a girl just out of the University of Rochester named Ednah Levis. On Sunday when I was home and they were talking about her I said, "What does she look like?" My mother said, "There she is now," and I went to the window and saw a plump, rosy-cheeked young woman with dark brown hair, walking between two of the local girls. My mother said, "A rose between two thorns," and it seemed an apt metaphor. At that time, of course, I had no idea I was going to marry her.

The principal of the high school urged that I come back and graduate with my class. He was a University-of-Rochester man and he thought he could get me a scholarship there. School had been in session about two months when I re-entered. Miss Levis, the new teacher, helped me make up my lost work in French by special sessions with me each morning before school started. Finally I caught up with the class and the meetings ceased. Ednah told me afterward that because it made her life feel so empty she knew then that she must be in love with this obstreperous student. It was such a ridiculous idea to her that she was embarrassed by it.

It was now decided that I would enter the University of Rochester in the following year, 1908. As penance for my recent sin, I had kept away from women and worked harder than before. I would never have dared think of Miss Levis in a personal manner, but when one of the other boys took her out to some affair it made me frightfully jealous. On the next possible occasion I asked her and she accepted. We began to go for walks and to see each other more and more frequently. She told me a great deal about Rochester and what to expect up there.

One June night, sitting in the park, I kissed Ednah. She kissed me. We agreed that we would see more of each other in Rochester; she would go home to visit her family and I could come and have Sunday dinner with them. In those days one of the styles which women suffered from was a shirtwaist with a high collar supported by whalebones. One of these whalebones had come out, causing a chafing on Miss Levis' neck. When I helped to adjust it my heart beat, my blood raced; I was dizzy with the exhilaration of the touch of her moist neck.

How much can a man change his character? My experience at this time makes me think that under certain conditions it is possible to alter oneself to a great extent. When I was about to go to a strange city and spend the next four years with people who did not know me, I went into conference with myself and decided that I would try to improve; that I would try to become somebody else. There would not be one person at the University of Rochester who had ever seen me before or who would have any preconception about what sort of person I was. I thought that it must be possible for me to change. I was not really very proud of what I had been; I didn't like the character of Mouthy Abbott, the aggressive, argumentative disputant. I resolved to make every effort to become a more quiet type, to think before I spoke.

I even decided to change my name. Heretofore I had been called by my second name Francis, to avoid confusion with my father. But Francis was a girl's name, so I became George. Come to think of it, perhaps a psychologist could make something out of the fact that each of us changed his name on leaving home. My brother's name was McLaury or Micky; he changed his name to Burr, short for Burwell, his first name. My sister was called Isabel at home, and she became Polly in college.

As I started off for Rochester, I was filled with high resolves— not to be a good student or even a good athlete, but to be a more likeable fellow. To a certain extent I succeeded; at least I was generally liked at the University of Rochester, just as I was generally disliked in Hamburg High School. I don't say that the leopard's spots didn't show through once in a while, but they were tempered.

Part Two

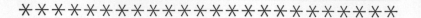

✳✳✳✳✳✳✳✳✳✳✳✳✳✳✳✳✳✳✳✳✳✳✳✳

IN 1908 ROCHESTER WAS—and it still is—more like a small town than any big city I have known. It seemed as though the people there were all of one kind. There was no slum, no depressed area, and no unassimilated block of foreign born. The industries there —optical works, cameras, dental equipment—had brought about an immigration of skilled German workmen, and whereas if you get enough Germans in one place you may possibly have a war, when you get just a small proportion of them you are likely to get industry, cleanliness, love of music, and a group of law-abiding citizens.

I could feel this atmosphere as I got off the train. It wasn't like Buffalo. It seemed a leisurely, pleasant place and when I asked directions, they were given in a cheerful, friendly manner. So I got on the trolley and started out for Prince Street, sitting there with my suitcase tucked under my legs, looking at the streets go by and feeling all the trepidation anyone feels when he is about to face new and strange things.

Finally Prince Street, turn to your left and there it was—the place where I hoped to spend the next four years, the place where I hoped to improve myself. I had a card telling me where to report for instructions, but I hesitated. I regarded my adversary with caution. I walked around it. The campus, set in the middle of the residential district, occupied about six city blocks. It certainly did not seem formidable; amid green lawns and big stone buildings covered with the conventional ivy there was no activity except for a few slow-walking professors or students, but I couldn't get up my courage to present myself. I carried my suitcase around the University of Rochester looking the place over. I made two complete circuits of the University grounds before I went in, and then of course, it was very simple. I was given a list of rooming houses and of possible places to earn my board by waiting on table.

I awoke in my boarding-house room, with its faint odor of other tenants and other days, waited for my turn for the bathroom at the end of the hall and made ready for the unknown. I pulled on my BVD's (no old-fashioned union suit for an up-and-coming collegiate type like me), put on my hole-proof socks which I had washed out the night before, shaved with one of those new inventions, the safety razor, parted my hair on the left-hand side, carefully brushed my blue serge suit (unaware of Marc Connelly's later dictum, that it would be better to have white cotton suits to go with blue serge tablecloths), and walked down the side street in the cool, clean, sunny September morning.

I felt like Sir Galahad about to seek the Holy Grail. But what kind of boy was I? Each of us, I suppose, is a different person to every other person. I am sure that my mother thought of me as a very fine lad who had, it was true, faced a few problems and had a few crises, but who had come through satisfactorily and was full of promise. My father, I am equally sure, regarded me as an almost unmitigated horror. Both my brother and sister loved me and idealized me and thought of me as merely shy—not the tough kid I thought I was.

When a man sits for a portrait he is seldom satisfied because he has a preconception of how he looks, a certain angle, and of course the most flattering one, which he has decided is *him*. None of us knows with any accuracy what he was like in childhood or indeed what his true character is in maturity. I cannot be sure of what I was when I entered college, but I do know how I felt. And that I shall try to make clear. I also remember some statistics about myself. I was six feet one and a half inches tall and weighed one hundred and seventy pounds, but I looked thinner because I was big-boned and rather pale. I had blue eyes and streaked blondish hair. Thanks to my military-school training, I carried myself well. My father was tall and erect too, but he swaggered. I was careful not to swagger.

I remember distinctly that while a part of me felt like Sir Galahad about to seek the Holy Grail, there was another part which felt that I was a small-town outsider about to face a lot of city slickers. I had great unease about the future but no fear. I had confidence that though I might be subjected to some onerous trials, I would come through in the end—I would show them. I had shed that disagreeable, aggressive character, Francis Abbott, back in Hamburg, and now I was that sterling young fellow George Abbott.

The formalities of entering college being over, undergraduate life commenced. The freshmen seemed keyed up as they gathered in little knots on the steps of the main building, some greeting old friends, some forming new acquaintances, and nobody paying much attention to the new and improved Abbott. Whereas I had been a leader in Hamburg High School, I was now nothing. This nothing was exaggerated by the fact that there were others who were already leaders. About half of the students at the University of Rochester at that time came from the local high school, and naturally it evolved that the leaders in high school continued to take charge of things in college. The glib talkers, the well-dressed, the assured ones, held the center of the stage; the unknowns, the grinds, the quiet ones, bided their time. Shallowness sometimes outshines depth in the early stages. And the rich boys always have an edge over the poor boys. For many years this obvious injustice made me unreasonably prejudiced against the rich, but when I became rich myself, the prejudice somewhat abated. I have now become very tolerant about people's undeserved wealth—or indeed any other attractive quality which may fall to them. Some people are born rich, some with good looks, some with brains, some with personality, and some with humor;

and whatever these qualities happen to be, it is foolish to quibble or to worry about the injustices of the world. It's part of the man; what he does with it is another matter. To carry the thought a little further: if in later years you are liked or admired because you are successful in your profession, it is foolish to speculate how people would feel about you if you were a ditch digger. It is much more practical to accept your assets without cavil and to enjoy them, and to grant the people who happen to have been born rich or handsome the same privilege. Actually, what Toynbee tells us of nations is equally true of individuals. It takes trials and problems and difficulties to sharpen the wits and toughen the character—and the rich boys are often denied this.

The sophomores were gathered on the steps of an adjacent building, and soon it became apparent why we were there. We were to have a clash with the sophomores. This was tradition; this was what might be called the opening get-together. I welcomed it. Physical activity was just what I needed, and as soon as the melee started and I found myself facing a boy of about my own weight it was a great release to have a practical outlet for my excitement. I slammed him on his back in short order. When I let him up, he introduced himself and invited me to a Deke rush. My friend seemed distressed at my lack of sophistication when I confessed that I didn't know what a Deke rush was. He explained to me that it was an invitation to come to the Delta Kappa Epsilon fraternity, to look it over and, by inference, be looked over. I had to tell him that I couldn't afford to join a fraternity. But he insisted that I come anyway, and that night he called for me and took me to the Deke house, where I am sure I presented a very sorry picture as a tongue-tied hick from a small town. They did not invite me to join them.

As we all know, memory is a tricky thing. Generally speaking, I have a bad memory—names of people, plays and books escape me. Sometimes when I try to think of an actress for a certain part, her face is before me, I can remember the plays in which she has appeared, but I can't remember her name. I finally am saved only because Celia Linder, my secretary, who has been reading my mind for twenty-five years, is able by some skillful legerdemain to deduce who it is that I am talking about. In my case this inability to think of names has, I am sure, a psychological cause. When I first started to read books I could not pronounce the unusual names, and when I first began to meet people I was too self-conscious to remember who they were; in rebellion I decided subconsciously to be eccentric and not know any names at all. It's quite a handicap, but I have found that when it is necessary I can overcome it. If I make a speech or go on a radio program, I concentrate on the problem and rattle off names with assurance.

Recently my brother started to talk to me about our childhood. Episode after episode was clear to him but struck no spark at all with me. When I went to my fifteenth college reunion I had a similar experience. Strange men came up to me and addressed me as "Abbey"—a name I had forgotten had ever been mine— and recalled events of the good old days. They seemed to be talking about someone else; it was all gone from me.

Yet I am convinced that somewhere in the back of the brain is a marvelous microfilm which records every act and every thought of our entire being. A strange experience along these lines once happened to me. I was in a hospital recovering from an operation and for several days was kept under sedation. In this weakened condition, with my guard down so to speak, scenes from my childhood flooded in upon me. For hour after hour these forgotten happenings plagued me in great detail—not vaguely but clearly. It was oppressive and painful, and I was relieved to find that when they took me off the dope I returned to normalcy; the past was again blocked out.

At any rate, my freshman year remains a flux of impressions, but for no accountable reason a few details stand out clearly. One scene in particular has kept coming back to my mind. This scene has played itself over and over, yet as far as I can judge it is completely meaningless and unimportant. In case there's a good psychiatrist in the audience, I will relate it.

I waited on table at dinner time, but sometimes I got my lunch at a cheap restaurant called Regan's, and there I once ran into another freshman named Gurley. He was no small-town boy like me, but a city fellow, very smooth, though nice and friendly. I thought him to be the height of sophistication because he told me that in reply to the question on his college questionnaire, "What daily exercise do you take?" he had written, "Lifting cups and saucers down at Regan's." He told me that was being rushed by the Psi U's and that he was very enthusiastic about the wit of a fellow named Sommerby, who was also being rushed. I never lunched with Gurley again; I never knew him well; I never knew Sommerby well. They both left school after their freshman year. How is it that a man who can't even remember Maurice Evans' name can have total recall about these two obscure contacts of the past. Could it be snobbery because of the Psi U's? (Ednah Levis was a great admirer of the Psi Upsilon Fraternity; she considered them the real elite. Because of her remarks I had come to regard them as an exalted group with whom I would in all likelihood never have any personal contact.)

Another person I have often thought about was Goodsell, the big guard on the football team. We waited on table at the same boarding house and got to be friends. He was a fierce-looking fellow with dark, menacing eyebrows; but at heart he was a gentle soul, too kind to take advantage of his strength, and timid about the ways of the world. Goodsell was going to become a Baptist minister; after he finished college he planned to attend a theological seminary. He didn't seem to look forward to this profession, but he was so fearful of the competitive world that awaited a college graduate that he chose the ministry because of its security. Goodsell's innocence would have interested Kinsey. He was shocked when he learned from me that married people took off their clothes when they went to bed. He thought that they always wore their underwear.

But the main thing I remember from my freshman year is that I gained confidence. The world became a better place; people became more friendly. I shed my feeling that many hands were turned against me and acquired a new confidence in myself and in the future. Much of this new assurance came from the fact that I had now not only the influence of college, but also of Ednah, who came to Rochester each Sunday, ostensibly to visit her mother, but actually because of me. I would spend most of that day with her and we would talk and talk. Our conversations covered a wide range of subjects but always returned to that most interesting of all subjects: me.

"College," said Professor Esteys, the principal of Hamburg High School who had been instrumental in getting me the scholarship at Rochester, "is a four-year period in which a young man is going to flounder around trying to find himself in any case, so he might just as well spend it in school trying to learn something." This seemed to me exactly the right attitude. I didn't think of college as a place where I would become educated; I thought of it as a place where I should find myself; where I should make some progress in the world. I looked upon studies as an incidental part of this experience. My dreams of college were mostly concerned with football, dramatics and the extra-curricular activities.

During my freshman year I made progress in all these directions. In the first place, I found to my delight that the classes were much more interesting than I had hoped. Up to this time I had been such a haphazard student that my efforts to acquire an education were severely handicapped in many areas. I had slithered through elementary school by dint of a certain facility, without really learning any fundamentals. In college I did well in those subjects which required no previous technical foundation. English, for instance, was easy for me, but I foundered at advanced algebra because I had no idea what they were talking about—I had been allowed to get by in elementary algebra without any real comprehension of what I was studying. To this day I don't know what a square root is. By the same token, I had no facility in languages because I had no comprehension of grammar. I said the phrases, but I didn't know what they meant. Oddly enough, of all the subjects I studied the two that have given me the most lasting pleasure have been German and geology. German, simply because Professor Shedd made us sing the German poems, and whereas I can no longer speak the language, I can, in a small measure, sing it. Geology, because it made me conscious of the contour of the earth; wherever I go I find myself trying to read the signs of the past. It gives me great satisfaction to recognize an area where once a glacier ruled.

In those days a freshman could play on the football team, and as a substitute I got into the game occasionally. Once I invited my sister to come to Rochester for a game, and during the contest I was sent in to replace another player. Polly reported to me that as I ran on the field a spectator near her said, "Here comes Abbott—good figure." My adolescent life had been filled with envy of those boys who seemed to be assured and graceful instead of gangly and insecure. I used to look at myself in store

windows as I walked by, hoping to find some reassurance that I
wasn't really such a string bean. Once I was in college I gradually became too involved in other matters to give much attention
to self-scrutiny. The fact that I would be classed as a fellow with
a good figure had never occurred to me, and this anonymous
praise lifted my spirits more than seven Phi Beta Kappa keys
could have done.

Another event also lifted my spirits. Toward the end of my
freshman year two seniors whom I knew but slightly approached
me and asked if I would like to become a member of Psi Upsilon.
I was flabbergasted; I even suspected that they were joking.
Though I had found congenial friends among many of the Psi
U's in my class I had just taken it for granted that my role in college was that of an outsider. Flattered though I was, I knew the
idea was impractical, and I said that I couldn't afford to join a
fraternity. The seniors replied that they were aware of my situation and that they were perfectly willing to postpone all dues until after I had been graduated. I joined the chapter and moved
into the fraternity house, where I lived for the balance of my undergraduate days.

I got so much pleasure from this companionship and togetherness that it seems unfair to question the value of fraterni-
ties. But their appeal is snobbish, beyond a doubt. I had a year
of being on the outside before I had three years of being on the
inside, and I know what it's like both ways. Of course, it is natural
for the human animal to seek its own kind, associate with those
who are congenial; nothing can stop that. But those who join a
fraternity in their first weeks in college put up a barrier against
others whom they might learn to know. I am very grateful for all
the happiness my fraternity gave me, but I still feel a little guilty
about those who were denied it.

That summer, at the suggestion of one of the students, I
tried a new kind of job. It was the most distasteful work I had ever
attempted. I became a door-to-door salesman of aluminum cooking utensils. With your wares in a suitcase you go to a door, hide
the suitcase at one side, ring the bell, get in if possible, make a
demonstration and then a sale. Unfortunately, I'm not a good
salesman. I shrink from trying to make people buy something
they don't want. A true salesman glories in the fact that he can

make people buy his product whether they want it or not. I did
fairly well financially, but I dreaded every potential customer I
had to face, every doorbell I had to ring.

September finally came around once again, and once again
on one of those warm, clean, autumn days when everything is
shining with hope and optimism, I found myself on the trolley
headed for Prince Street. But this time in what a different frame
of mind! To return to college as a sophomore is one of life's great
moments. No tension now: what the hell, the juniors treat you
about as an equal; the seniors greet you in a friendly fashion; your
own classmates shout their warm hellos; there is handclasping,
back slapping, boisterous good spirits—and even a little benign
sympathy for those small groups of poor, frightened freshmen.

That year I became the regular right tackle on the football
team. Perhaps my Aunt Anna was correct in fearing that dime
novels would have an effect upon my character. Had I been
asked to name my ideal, my hero, I should have probably said
Robert the Bruce or D'Artagnan, but it would not have been the
truth. My real hero was Frank Merriwell. Of course, I had long
since ceased to read anything so trashy as *The Adventures of
Frank Merriwell,* but this shining American boy who went to
Yale—as well as to most of the other colleges in the country at
various times in his paperback career—stuck in one's imagination.
Frank was the pitcher on the baseball team—he could throw the
baffling double shoot, a curve which went both in and out. On
the football team he was right halfback. Please note that at Hamburg High School I was pitcher on the baseball team and right
halfback on the football team. These positions, I believe, were
achieved not by athletic ability as much as by sheer push. When
I came to Rochester, I couldn't play baseball well enough to make
the team, and I wasn't fast enough to become a halfback, so I
had to settle for a place in the line. Nevertheless it was exciting.
Wasn't I on the varsity? Didn't I win my letter?

Actually, college football wasn't as much fun as high school
football. Even in as small a college as Rochester, it had a smack
of professionalism. Until the season was over all your time belonged to the football coach. Two of our best players came from
some prep school in New England and were rather hard guys
who didn't mix much with the rest of the undergraduates. One

day a game was unreasonably delayed in starting, and during the next few days scuttlebutt revealed the cause. Our two athletes were under the pay of some enthusiastic alumnus who had not come through with the last installment on time. The noble boys were not going to go out and die for dear old Rochester until they got their money. If this kind of thing could go on in a college as small as ours, you can imagine what was happening in the rest of the country. And this was fifty years ago!

I loved the game of football and still do. Often in my daydreams I correct the mistakes I made when I was on the team or relive my few moments of glory. And nowadays during the football season I will be anchored in front of the television set getting a vicarious thrill.

Going away on trips was one of the high spots of football for me. There was something very exciting about the team gathering with their suitcases and venturing off to some strange city. People sometimes ask me if I ever suffered from stage fright. My answer is that the fear which comes to you just before your first entrance on the stage cannot hold a candle to the terror which comes to you as you stand waiting for the kickoff at the start of a football game. The good players are probably not as frightened as the bad ones; they have more assurance, therefore more confidence and more eagerness for the contest. By the same token, I think that, in general, good actors are less frightened than bad actors. This goes against what people like to believe: that there's something intrinsically artistic or temperamental about being nervous. In my opinion, this is false. The greatest stage fright I ever experienced was when I was a supernumerary in *Carmen*. As I stood in line waiting to pull the chariot on stage I wished that I were dead so that I wouldn't have to make the entrance. Luckily a wheel broke off and they took me out of line. I'll never forget the relief I felt. Both in football and on the stage it is the first plunge that petrifies. After the first moment a calm yet intoxicating excitement takes over, and unless things are going badly the terror turns into exhilaration.

In the winter, I played on the hockey team, which was more like a scrub aggregation than a college team. However, my main preoccupation in the winter season was dramatics. I had made good in this right from the start, and now in my sophomore year

I played the lead in the college show. Perhaps I was inhibited as a person, but I was not the least bit shy on stage.

In the spring this young man's fancy—since he could make neither the baseball team nor the track team—lightly turned to thoughts of getting his marks up to a point where he could return to college the following year.

That summer I had a job more to my taste. Through some Psi U brothers, I got a job as a swimming instructor at Camp Arey, a boys' camp on Keuka Lake. I went swimming, played softball, rode horseback, all things which I enjoyed enormously—and got paid for it.

The next winter I also had a new job. I worked at an Episcopal Church as a combination basketball coach and Sunday school teacher. The coaching meant that I was in charge of the recreation room in the basement of the church for three nights each week, and I was also assigned to teach Sunday school in the hope that the boys would admire me as an athlete enough to obey me as a teacher of the gospel. Unfortunately, I nearly got the rector of the church, a very quiet-spoken young man, into trouble because of my teaching. To make the Sunday school lessons interesting—and I felt that practically all the Sunday schools I had ever attended were incredibly dull—I decided to take St. Paul's journey around the Mediterranean and try to make it real and dramatic to the boys. To the best of my ability I translated the archaic language of the Bible into everyday experiences and language. One day an austere deacon-like type of man stood in the doorway and listened as I was conducting my class. Paul was about to leave the brethren of one community and go to another land, and there was a reference just before his departure to the laying on of hands. I told the boys that this was just like saying, "So long, fellows." The listener registered consternation and disappeared from the doorway. Shortly afterward the rector took me aside and pleaded with me to go easy on my interpretations. It seemed that my visitor had been one of the pillars of the church, financially speaking, and he had a very literal idea about the interpretations of the Scriptures and didn't think that any young Episcopalian should be exposed to such heretical talk. The young minister seemed to have no personal objection to anything that made the Bible come alive to the boys, but he was trapped; if he was going to hold his job, he had to please the deacons. Life must be pretty exasperating at times for the young curates of the world.

Junior year: more studies, more football. In the winter, the glee club went on tour and I went with them. I was not a singer but was what is called a "reader." I was the comic who came out and made funny speeches or recited poems by Eugene Field. On one trip I received word that my grandfather had died. My mother thought that I ought to return for the funeral. I could take a train which would get me there in time for the church service, and then by leaving immediately afterward I could return to the tour with the club in the next town.

People had already gathered at the old homestead when I arrived. There was a hushed air of excitement; the somber masks which people wore barely hid the fact that this was a dramatic event. When I was taken in to see my grandfather's body he looked very small and white and unreal. I took one quick, queasy look and then retreated to join my mother and my brother and sister, who had been allowed to seek seclusion in Grandpa's old office. We talked in hushed voices.

The carriages arrived, and we entered ours and started for the church. When one of us made a joke we all laughed and Mama had to push us back from the windows, alarmed lest our disrespect for the dead would be witnessed. At church there was the usual eulogy, and then a very touching thing occurred. It was announced that four of Doctor Abbott's old friends would sing his favorite hymn. They took their places—two weathered small-town businessmen in their uncomfortable best suits, with their big watch chains and scrubbed faces, and two buxom women in their corseted dresses and their funny hats. Probably they had all resented many things that Doctor Abbott had done when he was alive; probably they ridiculed his pretentiousness and love of glory, or gossiped about his big pension which he didn't deserve. But now he was gone, and they thought of him in another light. They remembered the young doctor who came to their village and attended the sick in all weather, who wore out four horses working night and day during the epidemic, who would drive as far as thirty miles to take care of a sick child. They remembered only his good qualities and were sad that he was gone. They sang—soprano, alto, tenor, bass—"Lead, Kindly Light." The church was very still. Surreptitiously I wept.

That winter, 1909, I began to think about being a playwright. Like most boys, I had been greatly disturbed over the problem of how to make a living when I grew up. I had thought a great deal about being a lawyer, but my mother's influence, as well as my own inclination, made me want to write. Mama had suggested that I try to be a journalist—it was a word that appealed to her. Now I began to wonder if I could write a play. Ednah encouraged me to try and recommended a very simple formula. She said, "Write four pages every day, whether they are good or bad, and see what happens." I disciplined myself to do this and in due course produced a full-length three-act play. It was ludicrously bad, but of course like any aspiring author I was unaware of this. I sent it to the Shuberts, who happened to be the only producers I had ever heard of. When it was returned to me, I was confident that some incompetent reader had failed in his duty; I think I even expected to seek him out and have him fired when I became famous.

But, having discovered that a fellow could write a play by will power, I now embarked on a more practical effort. I wrote a farce of a more-or-less topical nature to be performed by the University Dramatic Club. It was called *Perfectly Harmless*, the principal character was an absent-minded geology professor (our dear Professor Gilmore), and the plot was a set of clichés borrowed from the farce-comedies in vogue at the time. The situation most popular just then was to find some reason to dress a man up like a woman and then throw him into embarrassing complications. Perhaps I was preparing myself for a job I was to do many years later—the writing of the book for *Where's Charley?* In due time *Perfectly Harmless*, which I also directed, was a success with local audiences and my inclination to go into the theatre became even more pronounced.

I had always been drawn to the theatre. I can remember clearly the first play I saw in Cheyenne, and later in Hamburg I used to take the trolley into Buffalo, wait in line for the gallery to open and climb the stairs to sit on those wooden benches. In

Rochester I had remained a devotee; I had even tried to get a job as an usher so that I could get in free.

It was at this time that Edward Sheldon became my hero instead of Frank Merriwell. I knew nothing about him except that he was a very young playwright who was very successful and that he had taken Professor Baker's course in dramatics at Harvard. That seemed a very suitable thing for another successful young playwright to do, and I decided to try to enter. Each year the McDowell Fellowship gave six hundred dollars to the student who submitted the best play in order to help him through Professor Baker's course. I began to write a play to submit.

Then a couple of other things happened which showed a change in my attitude toward life. At the beginning of my senior year it suddenly seemed to me that football was a waste of time, that it demanded too much for what it gave back. I told the coach I thought I wouldn't go out for the team that year. Perhaps I just wanted to attract attention to myself—I am not sure what my motives were—but in any case, such pressure was put on me that I had to give up any idea of resigning from the football team. The other change was that I was nominated as president of the student body and was defeated by the narrow margin of five votes. But I didn't care; I mean, I didn't really care. In my mind I balanced all the drudgery, all the boring meetings and committees which would be part of that office, against the transient honor, and I was content. I was beginning to achieve a little objectivity about life and about myself.

In my senior year I had some scholarship problems, because quite consciously I had selected a rather impractical curriculum. I had thought that I didn't care whether or not I got a degree, that I only wanted to go to college. But as graduation time approached my mother urged me to get my degree; you never could tell when you would want some position in which a college degree would be essential. To do this, I had to take four years of Greek in one year. Professor Kendrick saw a good deal of me in my senior year. He was one of those eccentrics whom you read about—a man so enthusiastic over his subject that he seems a little touched. He would tell you in all seriousness that the Greeks were the chosen people and that it had been an inexplicable mistake when the Jews were given this title. I kept to myself any thoughts I had about the chosen people and agreed with him in his love of everything Greek. I loved Greek history, Greek achievement, Greek drama—the only thing I didn't know anything about was the Greek language. As the final examination approached I can remember spending beautiful spring days sitting in my room with a translation of Xenophon's *Anabasis* in my lap, hearing the sounds of gaiety outside, preparing for my final examination in the old way—learning the pony by heart.

That spring I submitted my play for the McDowell Fellowship. Also I was graduated, and I went back to Camp Arey for the summer, and that year there was a cute girl in a cottage across the lake from the camp. It would have been disloyal to Ednah for me to call on this girl, but I used to swim across the lake and stop there for a rest. In this fashion I was able to enjoy a slight flirtation with a clean conscience.

What I remember best about that summer is making a wager that I could swim across Keuka Lake blindfolded. To swim blindfolded is almost impossible; inevitably you lose your direction and go in circles. I had a secret plan, however. I would swim for a minute or two, turn over on my back and get the glint of the sun through my blindfold, then head toward the sun again, which I knew was coming directly over the cliff on the far shore. Eventually the sun disappeared and I knew I was in the shadow of the cliff. Shortly thereafter, to my great relief, I could feel bottom. The relief to the poor judges who had been trailing along in a rowboat was even greater; it had taken three hours.

I won a bottle of pop for that trick, but I didn't win the scholarship to Harvard. I decided, however, to go anyhow. Once more I was leaving home on what seemed an adventure, but I approached this one with confidence. After four years at Rochester, I no longer felt like a crude small-town boy. After all, I was a big man on campus. But the boys at Harvard were so much more polished than those at Rochester that I realized at once that I was not one of them. I liked Cambridge from the start; it was aloof but not unfriendly, and everyone minded his own business. It seemed a place to improve oneself, not just a rah-rah college. Nobody had to die for dear old Harvard. At Rochester they were always talking about tradition; at Harvard they didn't have to talk about it because they knew they had it.

Professor Baker was an inspiring man. He gave you no non-sense about inner meanings and symbolisms; he turned your whole thoughts and energies into the practical matter of how to make a show. If it was good, a farce or a melodrama was just as important as a tragedy. One of the things he kept hammering on was, "Get the greatest given emotional result from the given scene." Don't have the character just come in and pick up the letter and go, but have him pick up the letter, then *look under the bed* and go. We were assigned to write one-act plays which would then be read in class and subjected to collective criticism. One of the first ones I wrote was a little tragedy of farm life in which a son defies his father and takes a horsewhipping to pro-tect his mother. It was called *The Head of the Family*, and later it was produced by the Harvard Dramatic Club. On the second night, the actor playing the father lost his whiskers in the big whipping scene, and I later wrote what I remember as a very funny burlesque on this which we produced at Radcliffe College.

For my first few weeks at Harvard I had no friends at all; in-deed, I scarcely spoke to anyone. Then one night a knock came at my door, and the boy who had won the McDowell scholarship, a young man named William Fennimore Merrill, entered. Billy Merrill lived in Chicago. He was very sophisticated in cer-tain departments but very naïve in others. Brought up by four sis-ters and a mother, he was effeminate without knowing it. He was often embarrassed in public by men crowding against him, but he didn't know what it was all about. Once he revealed to me that he thought children were born through the navel. He was, however, a mature judge of music and painting, and through him I became aware of these arts for the first time. Though I never succeeded in generating much passion for painting, I did begin to appreciate and enjoy good music.

Merrill's manners were impeccable—uncomfortably so. Be-side him I felt loutish. He introduced me to some other rich boys from Chicago, and I thought of them as the tea-drinking set. Such a thing as stopping in the afternoon to have tea was unheard of in my experience; in fact, when I first joined the group I would not drink tea—I thought it was too sissy. They made me cocoa on that occasion, but later I relented and could balance a cup with the best of them.

There were two dining halls at Harvard, and I ate in the cheaper one. I happened to sit next to a man named Ralph Brewster, who became a friend. With Brewster there was no talk of the theatre, only of life and politics and people. He had a relative who ran a high-class boarding house on Beacon Street in Boston; every Sunday he would take me there and we would put away a gargantuan dinner which would see us through the next week. Many years later Senator Brewster visited me out on Long Island, and we took up exactly where we left off with no difficulty at all; we were as warm and close friends as ever. He talked to me about his plans for doing big things in the Senate, and after a pleasant weekend I saw him off at LaGuardia Airport, where the Pan American people had been kind enough to send a plane for him. That same year Senator Brewster got into a hassle with Howard Hughes and was made to look very bad over just such things as free plane rides from Pan American. I am sure that Brewster was a good and honest man and that any favors he took from the airplane companies were accepted without guile. All of us Yankees find it difficult to refuse a free ride.

For the last eight years I had been a violent exerciser and a big eater. Now the exercise was taken away from me—postgraduates are not eligible to compete in any sport at Harvard—but the eating habit remained, and I began to feel logy and stuffed all the time. I walked, walked, walked; whenever I went from Cambridge to Boston, I walked even if it was raining. My trips were mostly to attend the theatre. The Irish Players were making their first appearance there, causing great excitement and enthusiasm among the discerning, and especially Professor Baker's class. I aspired to write American folk drama, akin to the Irish folk drama, and I worshiped Sara Allgood. One day her panties fell off during a scene in *The Shewing-up of Blanco Posnet,* and she deftly kicked them into the wings and continued without missing a cue. How could you not adore such a woman? Being a slick fellow, my friend Merrill knew how to get letters of introduction to actors, and through him I was permitted to join several of the boys in entertaining various members of the Irish Players after the theatre. I am afraid I didn't contribute very much for I did not have the patter, but I was terribly impressed and excited. Years later out in Hollywood, when Sara Allgood had become a fat old

lady, I interviewed her for a part in a picture which I was making
and I reminded her of our meeting. She was polite enough to pretend to remember.

In Boston there was an arty little theatre with the silly name
the Bijou, which was operated by Mrs. Josephine Clement. The
Bijou offered a prize of one hundred dollars for the best one-act
comedy, and I won the contest with a playlet set in a steel plant,
the plot of which involved a Danish cable splicer and his assistant.

Socially my life had expanded a little and through an attractive boy whom I had met at the Dramatic Club I was invited to a
weekend at a nearby summer resort. The others were more or less
used to this sort of thing, but to me it was a very glamorous occasion. We were four boys and three girls; the mother of one of
the girls was there as a chaperone—we saw little of her. We
went swimming in the cold, cold New England sea, and we played
games and laughed uproariously at clumsy jokes just from sheer
exuberance. Now I was really living. In the evening we gathered
around the great fire and then finally we went to our separate
rooms and to bed. After a while there was a light tap at my door.
"Yes?"

"Here's an extra blanket for you," whispered our hostess.

I was paralyzed. "Just leave it there," I said.

In the morning she was pleasant, as a well-bred girl should
be, but cool. I felt disgraced. Joseph was thought a noble fellow
when he ran away from Potiphar's wife, but I felt ignoble. I was
right, and yet I felt wrong. My traumatic experience in high school
days as a result of sex had left me with a great fear; moreover,
I was supposed to be in love and to be loyal to another girl. Yet
such is man's code—the real code, not the pretended one, but
the one which exists when men are together, the one which obtains in their real thoughts and their stories—that I was left feeling like a graceless lout. And if that cute red-headed girl is now
an old lady somewhere surrounded by her grandchildren, I
would like her to know that I kept her out from duty, not from
inclination.

Before I had time for too much self-torment, a happy event
occurred. My playlet, *The Man in the Manhole,* was produced by
Mrs. Clement and was a success. So much so, in fact, that she of-

fered me a job as her assistant for the coming year, at a salary of thirty dollars a week. It was wonderful to solve the problem of the future, even temporarily, and I accepted. Leaving college was like leaping off somewhere into the dark and now at least I knew where I was going to land.

One of my courses at Harvard was a series of lectures by Professor Baker on Elizabethan drama. We were seated alphabetically, and so on the last day of the college year Abbott took his place as usual in the front row and put his notebook on the desk before him. Next to Abbott sat Agnew, a well-dressed, aloof young man from the Gold Coast (the street where the dormitories for the rich young men were situated). Abbott and Agnew had sat side by side for the entire year without ever exchanging a word. Agnew took copious notes, while Abbott, who was not planning to stay for the final examinations, took no notes. When this last lecture was concluded, Agnew turned to Abbott and said in a rather patronizing voice, "I beg your pardon, but why do you bring that notebook to class?"

"It's a *de*coy," said Abbott.

With no change of expression, Agnew replied, "Don't you pronounce it de*coy?*"

And thus Harvard added a little extra touch of culture to Abbott before it wafted him out into the great commercial world.

My job at the Bijou would not begin until September, which gave me time for one more summer at Camp Arey and for a visit home. In Hamburg an almost incredible event had taken place: my father had stopped drinking. He had not only stopped drinking, but as events turned out he had quit drinking.

In a small town like Hamburg everybody knew who the dipsomaniacs were, and they bore the casual title of village drunks. There were two or three of them belonging to what are known as the good families in town. Periodically they would go away and take the Keeley Cure, then return to Hamburg sobered and reformed, but the cure never seemed to last; the temptation to take just one more drink reasserted itself and the village drunk reclaimed his title.

My father had been persuaded to try the Keeley Cure. He did—and then he fooled them. He came back reformed and he stayed that way. He never took another drink as long as he lived. My mother assigned the credit to Christian Science. My grandmother no doubt thought it resulted from her prayers to a Methodist God. My own opinion is that Papa had reached the nadir, had sunk as low as he could get; he had experienced the ultimate in degradation and humiliation and he knew that he had to either reform or die. As soon as he was sober, and therefore no longer at the mercy of his heartless family, his mother, who had stuck by him grimly through all his vicissitudes, gave up the ghost. Mama took him back, and gradually as the years went by he became a respectable member of society. He went into politics, became a supervisor of Erie County and ran the Erie County Fair. Still later, he became the sort of man who was honored by the Firemen of America, The Knights Templars, and various Chambers of Commerce. He lived to be eighty-four years old.

When the summer was over, I returned to Boston, rented a small room on Mt. Vernon Street and took up my duties at the Bijou Theatre, where in due course I learned something not only about show business, but about music and morals. Mrs. Clement was a cross between Madame Pompadour and Hedda Gabler, a woman of great charm who, when in a bad mood, would cheerfully cut out your gizzard. I respected her and feared her. My job as her assistant was varied; it involved everything from running errands to writing sketches to be performed by the little stock company which she maintained. Later when she discovered that I had given readings in the Glee Club at Rochester she tried me out in this capacity, so I occasionally bolstered the program by doing a single.

One of Mrs. Clement's protegés was a young composer named Carl Wilmore, who acted as accompanist for the singers and the silent pictures and also wrote original music when called for. He and I were assigned to do some musical playlets for the Bijou, and we wrote shows for Christmas and Easter. For the future we were planning something much more ambitious: an opera (a new type of opera, of course), but that never got finished. Carl was a brilliant fellow and I enjoyed his company very much, but there was something a little strange about him. He kept scrutinizing sailors and commenting on their figures. Finally, when he realized that I was so dumb and square that I didn't understand, he explained to me that he was a homosexual. I knew there were such things, but I had had no contact with this world and didn't know what it was all about. I pretended, however, that I understood. Wilmore went on to justify his moral position by claiming that practically all the important men of history were homosexuals. He made no attempt to introduce this into our personal life until one day in the office, when I was sitting at the desk, he sneaked up behind me and kissed me on the neck. The revulsion caused by the feeling of that whiskery face against my flesh was so great that I reacted by slugging him on the side of the head. He was wearing a new derby at the time, and it got knocked across the office and dented. Carl was worried about his hat, but otherwise passed the incident off and never again tried to touch me.

A few months later, he was in the hospital. His ailment was shrouded in mystery, but I suspect that it was somehow connected with his sexual aberration. He asked me to visit him. The Bijou did four shows a day, which gave me time to go over to the hospital between shows. I would take my make-up off and put an overcoat over my costume. I was playing in a sketch in which my trousers were torn at the knee. At the hospital I found Wilmore very weak; he moaned a good deal and spoke in a whisper. On his death bed, so to speak, he asked if he could feel my leg. While I talked to him he put his hand through the tear in my trousers and held my calf. Almost immediately he relaxed and ceased his moaning and groaning. When I came next, he repeated his request, but on the third occasion the nurse called me aside and accused me of smuggling him dope!

"Fairies," the average man calls them with a sneer, or "homos"; around Broadway they will be referred to as "queers" or "gay boys"; more dignified men refer to deviationists or to abnormality; vulgar men have more vulgar words. But behind all this affected superiority there lies very little real information. Men are only little boys grown up, and they are loath to expose their ignorance about anything to do with sexual matters. Of course the doctors have their statistics, but the average man utters glib contemptuous phrases without any real knowledge of the extent of homosexuality or any sympathetic understanding of its nature. Psychiatrists are most aware and most helpful. The man, or less frequently, the woman who goes to him may not be cured in the literal sense, may not have his sexual drive altered; but what he can hope for is to be better able to live with himself, to shed a sense of guilt. In many cases, furthermore, there is a sufficient change to bring about what seems to be—with what compromises, I know not—a happy married life.

Most people think that homosexuality is a sign of decadence, that just because they are attracted to members of the opposite sex they are superior. But the average person is not a fact-facer, and the fact-facers know that homosexuality is universal; that it has been found in every civilization from the rugged mountaineers of the Himalayas to the ancient Greeks. It is rather startling to read Plato and discover that the chapter on love is not about women at all but about boys. Homosexuality is a disagreeable fact that we just don't want to face, and so we look the other way. But it does exist; and that civilization generally admitted to be the greatest the world has ever known was a homosexual civilization. When the ten thousand Greek mercenaries made their famous march through Persia, they gave up food and women before they gave up their boys. The great Epaminondas, whose genius finally brought about the downfall of the Spartan army, formed his elite troops from lovers who were dedicated to die for each other rather than to surrender. Read *Satyricon* and find what the man in the street was like in Rome. Or investigate the Caesars and find what it was like on a higher level. Go from Leonardo da Vinci, to Tschaikowsky, down to the slums of every great city. It is there.

Homosexuality exists everywhere. I don't know why—to most of us, women are so much more delicious that it seems a very bad choice. It is possible to understand how men who are deprived of women are forced by sexual drive into turning toward each other; male rape is so common behind prison walls that the underworld has a whole vocabulary of slang to cover the situation. But when men have a choice why should it happen?

Many homosexuals live a life devoted in one part to a wife and children and in another part to boy friends. Of course, some are obvious in their effeminate behavior, but many more show no signs of it whatsoever. And if you knew the truth about some of your heroes and your movie and stage stars, you would be surprised.

In one of my theatrical companies there was once a rugged and tough character actor, not in the least the type of fellow you would suspect of deviation. When we went to Boston on a tryout he brought along his pretty young wife. We opened on Monday night and settled down for the two weeks' run, but on Wednesday morning, Bobby Griffith, my stage manager, called me at seven A.M.

"Sorry to bother you so early in the morning, Mr. Abbott," he said, "but Character Man is in jail."

"What?"

"Character Man is in jail."

"For what?"

"After we left him last night he stopped in some bar, picked up a male prostitute, went to a cheap hotel, and made so much noise that the police were called."

"You mean that fellow is queer?"

"I guess so. We've got to go to the judge and see if we can get him out in time for the matinée."

With the aid of Mr. Cavanaugh of the Shubert office we were able to get the actor temporarily released, but he had to return to Boston at a later date to stand trial. One of Bobby's most difficult jobs was to tell the actor's wife what had happened. She then confessed that it was not the first time; that whenever her husband got drunk, his predilection for men—and always men of the lowest type—asserted itself.

We persecute homosexuals socially and legally. It is difficult to see how the public is in any way affected by private actions, or why the law cares what a man or woman does as long as it does not infringe upon the rights of others. Of course, when any-one tries to corrupt the morals of the young, either homosexually or heterosexually, he should be punished—and that punishment can hardly be too severe. We are too soft on the sexual perverts whose victims are children.

A mother who coddles her son and dominates him for too long can make a homosexual out of her boy, and a father who is too brutally austere can do the same thing. And a like result can

be accomplished by environment. I have seen a rugged young
country boy join a ballet chorus and then just because of the need
to conform, to be one of the group, become a mincing lisper in a
space of two years.

Returning from a tour on the road on one occasion, the leading man was telling me of the problems involved in leaving the
city because of his goldfish. I asked him why in the world he
wanted to bother with a goldfish. He said, "My God, a fellow has
to have something to love."

The Bijou was a good transition from the theoretical to the
pragmatic; it was an easy way to get my feet wet. But it wasn't
the real thing and I knew that I must go to New York and see
what would happen there. Actually, I had no doubt at all that
someone would buy one of my plays before long, but I had to
make a living in the meantime. Since I seemed to be a pretty
good actor, I decided that I would go to the great metropolis in
the fall and try to get an acting job. After a healthy summer at
Camp Arey, which had been converted from a boys' camp to a
girls' camp, I returned to Hamburg for a last visit home before
setting off to conquer New York.

In Eden Center, a small town near Hamburg, there was a
young man who was about to go on the stage—he hoped. Arthur
Allen had attended the American Academy of Dramatic Arts
and he briefed me on some of the problems confronting the aspiring actor. The time to look for work was at the end of August. We
came down together on the Lackawanna Railroad, and my first
view of New York City was from the ferry coming across the
Hudson. It was a sunny morning and the tall buildings, those
fingers of hope reaching up toward the sky, thrilled me beyond
description. No immigrant coming to the promised land could have
had a greater sense of ecstasy than I. I was here at last; the city
beckoned to me; the world was my oyster; I would succeed. I
was exalted.

Arthur and I shared a room at the Twenty-third Street
YMCA for three dollars a week. We ate in the cafeteria and put
our trousers under the mattress at night to keep them pressed. I
had a list of all the theatrical producers, and I walked around
each day asking the office boys if there was anything doing. The

procedure was nearly always the same. You would enter the office, wait your turn to approach some deadpan, indifferent office boy or older man or woman, and then ask if there was any casting today. The politeness of these receptionists was at a very low level, but it varied in some measure, reflecting the character of the big boss himself. If the producer was an overbearing type, then his underlings would be equally so and would take it out on the poor defenseless thespians.

While waiting in the reception room, you could listen. The actors all gossiped among themselves about possible jobs. If a juvenile told an ingénue that they were casting small parts at the Shubert office, you would steal out quietly and race over to the Shubert office. There you would see one or two familiar faces who had also heard this gossip, which of course was mostly false.

Actors are often great poseurs. They will pretend to have offers they never received and affect a superior attitude to compensate for the humiliating business of seeking work from office boys. An actor would tell about how he could have gone on the road, but George Tyler had asked him not to get tied up because he had a big part for him in his next play. Or he could have joined the Jessie Bonstell Stock Company, but Augustus Thomas was writing an important part just for him. Or an actress could have gotten a fine job except that she was too pretty and the leading lady was jealous and didn't want her in the same company.

A typical office was William A. Brady's. John Cromwell, who later became a first-rate Hollywood director, was in charge of the casting. Hopeful actors might wait for an hour, sitting, standing, until finally when the room was full, Cromwell would come out and we would all line up. He would go right down the line saying, "Nothing. Nothing. Nothing." And then once in a while, "You wait." Or if it was a friend, "Hello, Ed, sorry."

An actress might start to tell him of her theatrical experience, or an actor would start to say he thought he was right for a certain part. Cromwell would move right on without waiting for the end of the sentence, "Sorry . . . nothing . . . not a thing . . . sorry." Sometimes the actors would even take hold of his sleeve to delay him, but he would move impassively down the line until he had cleared the room. At the time I thought that he was cruel, but I know now that it was an act of self-defense. His heart would

break if he considered each case individually, and he had to protect himself. Also, I regret to say that the most pushy actors are
not the best ones. Later, when John became an actor, I directed
him in a show called *Gentlemen of the Press,* and he couldn't
have been a more agreeable fellow.

After I had been looking for work for a while I began to
think that the whole theatrical industry was a sort of false charade
—a game in which the producers pretended to have jobs just for
the sadistic pleasure of turning down the hopeful applicants, and
that the actors, poor deluded fools, were following some rainbow
that had no end. But I kept hoping, for there did seem to be a
chosen few who could get to the inner office. The casting director
would be dismissing the group when suddenly someone who had
worked for him before would enter. Then quite unexpectedly he
became a friendly fellow and called out, "Come in, Bill, Mr.
Blank would like to see you."

How I envied and resented those insiders. All casting in
those days of 1913 was done by interview, in the office. The system now in general use—and which, I think, I was the first to in-
novate: tryouts by reading for parts—was unheard of.

Day after day, for a month I was in this procession. My
money had run out, and I had to get a loan from my mother—
the first and last money that I ever borrowed in my life. I was beginning to think that I'd have to be a newspaperman after all, so
I went down to the *Tribune* and succeeded in getting an interview with the managing editor. He didn't hire me. I even thought
that I ought to go back to Boston, which had a friendlier feeling
toward me, for common sense told me I couldn't go on like this. I
had not had one token of encouragement of any kind since arriving in New York. I wasn't discouraged in my heart; it was only
that my mind told me that something had to be done. Still, New
York remained a magic city full of promise. I suppose that the
streets were as dirty and the people as rude as they are now, but
I only remember that for me it was the mecca, it was where I
belonged. Even during the long days of monotonous rebuffs, it
was still the magic city, and at night walking the streets alone all
my dreams were undimmed.

In that month of job-hunting in New York, that beautiful nostalgic month of September, I constantly felt a sensation of loneli-

ness mixed with hope, a mood of happy unhappiness so strong that it almost made me dizzy. What I remember most vividly was the sensation which took hold of me upon coming out of the city streets to a view of the Palisades. Standing in front of this panorama, I was suffused with sadness and loneliness, and with hope and confidence. It was as though something said to me, the God that made this beauty will make your life come out right.

These moods often translated themselves into music—that medium which expresses so well both sadness and hope. The sad-sweet stab of emotion which came to me in those lonely days of job-hunting in 1913 found music to fit it. Tchaikowsky's Fifth Symphony became my theme song, so to speak my scenario—what I always saw when I heard the music. It always made the same picture. A young man is alone in a city, sad and discouraged. He is walking through the streets but no one speaks to him; all the world is busy with personal affairs. He walks further, the houses become scarcer until finally he comes to a hill, he climbs up and up. He comes to the top. A great cliff is at his feet and spread out before him is the shining sea (here is where the French horn solo starts). Standing there, he is given new courage by the fresh, clean air and the beauty all before him. Everything begins to look better; he feels strong, able to face any problem (this is the beginning of the last movement). Walking back down the hill, he is happy, exultant, carefree; the same problems are in his mind but now he can face them with ease. The people seem friendly. He feels that it is a good world. He goes to his room and starts to work with fury and conviction, knowing that he will triumph.

On one of the last days I had allotted myself to do the rounds, I came to the office of William Harris in the Hudson Theatre. I had been there a few days before; the office had been empty, and I had been given a cold rejection. It seemed footless to go in again: but I felt that I must be thorough, that I couldn't skip any chance. When I went up the stairs I found activity, and I was even passed beyond the barrier to see Mr. William Harris, Jr.

He looked me over, and said, "Go down to the stage and report to Paul Dickey."

Down there I found a show in rehearsal, and a dynamic, athletic fellow, with a hooked nose and bright eyes, in charge of things. Paul Dickey was a former Michigan University athlete, co-author of *The Ghost Breakers* and the Pearl White picture serials. He gave me a quick appraisal and then assigned me a small part to read. It was a false scene with a lot of phony society people rushing about and being gay, and I was quite ill-suited to the role, but I gave it my best. Dickey didn't seem to be paying much attention. His troubles were elsewhere; in another scene of the play there were two drunken college boys, and one of the actors was wooden. The next thing I knew Dickey told me to try it. This was the kind of part I could get my teeth into, and I let go with enthusiasm. I got the job—and before the day was over I got even a better part. The actor who was playing the more important of the two college boys disappeared from the scene; I was told to read his part for the moment—and then to keep the role.

I don't think it is possible to be much happier than I was at that moment. I was set to come to Broadway in *The Misleading Lady*, starring Lewis Stone. It is true that there were moments of anguish mixed with the joy. One day in the midst of rehearsals a big blond man came in and talked to Dickey. I watched him in terror, thinking he was an actor who had come to get my part. Casually I inquired; it turned out that he was a stage carpenter. Though he was about forty-five years old and didn't look at all like a college boy, the panic and the fear that had been built up by that month of rejections was still with me. Actually, I learned later that the producer and director were congratulating themselves upon having discovered such a talented fellow.

William Harris, Jr., was a man of taste and of progressive ideas, but his father, who held the purse strings, was an old-fashioned producer with very rigid ideas about what made a success. One day in the midst of a love scene he came rushing down the aisle and screamed at Dickey.

"Wait, wait. Don't you know you can't have the leading man kiss the leading woman until the final curtain?"

On such inflexible rules had the successful plays of his generation been constructed. Owen Davis once told me that in writing his great series of lurid melodramas for the ten-twent-and-thirt, he had used the formula that before any sentimental line there must be two laughs to relax the audience. But changes in the theatre were taking place, as they always are, and though

Paul Dickey would be considered old-fashioned now, he was a radical and an innovator by the standards of William Harris, Sr. Dickey wouldn't have dared to write a play in which the lovers failed to get together at the end, but he was willing to have one in which they got together in a slightly different way.

Finally we took the train to Atlantic City. It was as exciting as going off for a football game. Dickey and I had become very friendly by this time; having discovered that I wanted to be a writer and that I was fond of athletics, he treated me as a kindred soul. At each station stop we would get off and hand wrestle or broad jump until we heard "All aboard!"

Atlantic City is a wonderful place to try out; you can go swimming. After opening night I was too excited to sleep. One of the characters in the play had delusions that he was Napoleon and he had a gag line, "Wellington must not reach Quatre Bras." All night long I thought I heard people in the street yelling this. In my delusion, the whole of Atlantic City was swept up in our success. It was indeed a success, but not so great as that. It opened in New York at the Fulton Theatre (now the Helen Hayes) and ran for a season. I got good notices for my small part; I was set.

After years of reading good and bad notices about myself, I have now become fairly indifferent to critical appraisal. Today I am a little contemptuous of people who are inflated by a good review or overly depressed by a bad one, but I should be more tolerant and remember the excitement which I felt because of the few kind words that were said about me in this first part.

The year 1913 was a very exciting one for me. I felt as though I had conquered the theatre; the rest was going to be easy. I was already accepted by the other actors as a successful professional, and I was sure that one of my plays would be accepted any day. My salary had been raised to a lordly forty-five dollars a week.

It wasn't all work. Tea dances were then in vogue, and I went dancing in the afternoon with a couple of girls from the company. We learned the Maxixe and sometimes we went to a movie. These occasions were strictly Dutch. The theatrical code permitted the women to suggest going out, having dinner, or going dancing to any of the men in the company because it was always understood that since they made just as much money as the men they would pay their own share. This arrangement suited them because of the freedom it gave them. Indeed, the custom was so general that if a man was seen paying for an actress's meals, or when on the road carrying her suitcase, the relationship immediately became suspect.

All this time I was writing. I never joined the other actors after the theatre nor felt the need of "unraveling"; I went straight back to the YMCA and was up at nine o'clock in the morning, pencil in hand. There was a rich boy in our company, a fellow named Graves, who wanted to be a producer. When he found that I was a budding playwright, he became interested in my output. I told him of a plot I was working on; he was all enthusiasm and urged me to finish it as soon as possible because he thought it would make a vehicle for Lewis Stone. Inspired by this practical possibility, I went to work and wrote an act each day for three days. When Lew Stone read it he pronounced it puerile, and I decided that perhaps I had better take more time in writing my next opus.

Ednah was now teaching in East Orange, New Jersey, and I went out there every Sunday. We had no idea what the future of our relationship would be, but for the present it was adequate. I was contented with life. I remember drawing up, à la Benjamin Franklin, a list of relative important things in life. It went like this:

1. Health
2. Work
3. Love
4. Play

This sort of naïve over-simplification appealed to me in those days—and to tell the truth, it still does. With the slightest encouragement, I will launch forth on a violent argument in favor of health. I do not think burning the candle at both ends casts a lovely light; on the contrary, I am of the opinion that it is a dandy way to get a nervous breakdown. How can anyone enjoy anything in the wide, wide world with a headache or a queasy stomach?

Secondly, those men and women who have not succeeded in finding work which they enjoy are to be pitied. They have missed the salt of life. I think I could have succeeded in some other line of work—law, for instance—but I am eternally grateful that fate

and my own inclination led me to the theatre. It is endlessly exciting to have a profession which seems like play, to have a job
which comes into your head with pleasurable excitement the first
thing in the morning and haunts you all day long. Even the theatre's vicissitudes are exciting; after all you can't have ups without
downs.

And who can live without love? Not just the love of one
woman, though I am not here to sell that short. But love of people: togetherness and the feeling of liking and being liked.

As for play, the theatre is again kind, for it combines periods
of great concentrated effort, followed by period of idleness. To
put on a show one must work literally eighteen hours a day for
six to eight weeks: then comes the time when you are entitled to
a change of pace—and the glorious feeling that you haven't a single responsibility in the world except doing what you like. To
conclude this sermon: if you can approach your work and your
play with exuberant physical vigor, you will enjoy life and it will
burn a brighter light for you than any two-ended candle ever invented.

If a statistician made a graph of the emotions and conduct of
actors, it would show a definite pattern in their reaction to success—and quite a different but equally predictable one to failure.
And generally speaking success brings out the actors' worst qualities and failure their best.

During rehearsal they are keyed to an emotional frenzy of
effort. If things go wrong when the show opens, if they find themselves in a failure, you will then see actors at their noblest and
best. They rally to the cause with bravery and no self-pity. When,
however, the play is a success, another characteristic appears.
They pay off their debts, they read their good notices, they
move to a better apartment, they become more important people
at parties and among their fellows, and gradually they acquire a
false perspective of themselves. To put it bluntly, they get
swelled heads; this is the time of problems. Producers in the old
days had a vulgar way of stating the case: trouble starts, they
said, as soon as the actors get the wrinkles out of their bellies. Actors aren't hungry any more, but their psychology is the same.
The new assurance makes some of them dissatisfied and demand-

ing. The business manager hates to go backstage because the
members of the cast will buttonhole him with requests for better
dressing rooms, raises in salaries, tickets for their friends, complaints about the publicity, or a dozen other things.

I was not immune from this contagion. This little part had
been a fine stepping stone for a talented actor, but now I was
ready for something bigger and better. Actors are always talking
over their careers with each other. I found my career a fascinating subject, and as spring approached I decided to do something
about it. I went to see William Harris to find out what dandy part
he had lined up for me in his next production. He had no next
production, I discovered, and apparently he had not given a great
deal of thought to my future. He did, however, offer me a raise if
I would go on the road with *The Misleading Lady.* All the actors
advised me that it would be much better to open in a new Broadway show. Also, on the strength of my successful entry into the
professional world, I was now able to obtain interviews with other
producers. Many of these men were cordial—they even went so
far as to say they'd like to have me with them sometime—but
none of them was able to offer me a part at that moment.

I had to make a decision, I had to choose between staying in
New York, jobless, or going out on the road for a year. And my
choice had to be influenced by another decision I was about to
make: I was thinking of getting married. I didn't exactly know
that I was thinking of getting married. I was approaching the
whole idea with blinders on; I was getting closer and closer to
the idea while looking the other way and pretending that nothing was happening. I'd been in love with Ednah for seven years.
Perhaps it was time to make a decision, but the situation wasn't
quite as simple as that. She was three years older than I, which
wasn't much; but she was a woman, not a girl. She had the staid
deportment of a woman. My friends married girls. It was an extremely unorthodox idea.

Ednah was a serious person—for a good reason: she had
worked all her life. She was one of a family of nine, a family full of
ambition and determination to improve itself. She had never gone
out with boys, she had worked hard at home, and as she grew
older she had to worry about her brothers; and finally she had
gone to college, where she became a Phi Beta Kappa student.

Her life had been made up of duty. It was a good and an unselfish life, but it did not always make her a gay person. She was smarter than I; she always knew how to spell the word, how to punctuate the sentence, how to finish the quotation. Yet, perhaps just because I was male, I was the dominating partner.

She had strange blind spots and prejudices. She couldn't understand music any more complicated than a hymn or a march; and Ednah was convinced that the people who went to the Metropolitan Opera House were all fakers who went there only because it was the stylish thing to do. She had violent prejudices against certain people in public life, because of their looks; she never trusted Woodrow Wilson, for instance, because of his jug jaw. She read poetry a great deal and could quote it. She knew a great deal about art and had good taste in interior decoration, but absolutely none as far as her clothes were concerned. She affected to despise dress and said she only wanted to be clothed well enough to get by in a crowd and that it was wicked to waste money on personal adornment. She was embarrassed and ill at ease with strangers, but with those she loved, she was warm, natural and as completely unselfish as a human being can be.

We drifted.

In those days theatres closed when the heat of the summer began. Ednah and I talked about what do with our vacations. I had paid back my debt to Mother and had saved some money, and I thought that this might be the time to take a trip to Europe. Ednah had also saved some money and thought she too might go to Europe, so we decided we might as well go together; then we agreed that as long as we were going together we might as well get married.

Suddenly the war scare in Europe began, and though we decided to stay in America, we went ahead with our plans to get married. One of the actors in our company owned a cottage up in Maine, behind Mt. Desert. I rented it from him for the summer. We went up to Rochester and were married in the home of Elmer and Florence Fisher, Florence being Ednah's sister.

I forget what kind of minister married us; I just remember that one of the children kept whimpering all through the service. I stood there feeling like a dumb ox going down the chute to be slaughtered. There was no escape, and I was sick with fear at this preposterous thing I found myself doing. The Fishers came down to the station to see us off, and Elmer, who was insensitive to my state of mind, had the bad judgment to shower us with confetti. I grabbed the box out of his hands, kicked it under the train and escaped into our Pullman, where the other passengers were polite enough not to stare at us. The Fishers stood outside the window waving and mouthing until finally the train tightened its muscles and began to pull out of the station.

As the night lights flew by, a feeling of peace and security gradually enveloped me. I was glad to be on the train with Ednah. The world looked all right once again.

Part Three

THE COTTAGE IN MAINE proved to be charming. There were hills in back of us, and in front was an estuary from the sea through which the tide ran in and out. We picked blackberries, took walks, dug clams, fished, read, swam in the cold waters and, best of all, were happy and in love. It is a wonderful thing for a man to leave the world of daydreams and enter the world of erotic reality.

It was a good summer and an uneventful one. We had no visitors, but we made the acquaintance of a few pleasant Yankee neighbors, strong characters who were hanging on in this land of short summers and harsh winters. There was a nice family of skunks who came frequently to dine on our garbage, and they brought their children. It was charming to see the mother skunk parading across the field followed by her file of little ones, secure in the knowledge that nothing would molest them, except of course foolish dogs and heartless automobiles.

My swimming excited some local approval. Ednah would get

into the rowboat and accompany me while I swam to the other shore and back. The fishermen living near us were impressed, because most of them had never learned how to swim. Each day they'd go out in rowboats on that cold, gray, belligerent Atlantic Ocean, perfectly confident that fate and a good sense of balance would bring them back again.

When we returned to New York I had a slight shock. Incredibly, I had supposed that we would go on living as before: Ednah in East Orange, where her job was, I in New York, where mine was. But during the three weeks in which the road company was being rehearsed, she made it quite clear that she planned to be in New York with me. We rented a room.

Sordid surroundings had never distressed me when I was single—they were all part of the things one had to put up with at the foot of the ladder—but when I had to see my wife in a sleazy rooming house, it distressed me deeply. It distressed Ednah too, but what distressed her still more was the fact that we were soon to be parted. The mere mention of my tour made her lower lip tremble, and tears would follow. I dreaded these scenes, and I hated the way we were living. I began almost to look forward to leaving. After all, going on the road was sort of an adventure, and heartless though it sounds, I was glad to be gone.

That fall and winter of 1914-15 I saw the United States of America on one-week stands, split-week stands, one-night stands, and in big theatres and little. The other actors went to good hotels; I stayed at YMCA's and saved my money. It seems to me that I have been in every public library in America. I didn't always take out books; often I just went to browse and feel at home in that atmosphere. I have always had a great weakness for lady librarians; they seem to be my kind of people. For a while the tour was all right, but as time passed I discovered that I could no longer so easily adjust to the celibate life.

Time passed, as it always does, and eventually I was home and officially the head of the family. Ednah had quit her job and rented an apartment, a fifth-floor walk-up, in Washington Heights on Seaman Avenue. It overlooked the Spuyten Duyvil, which flowed into the Hudson River, and it was almost like being in the country.

I did not prosper; it seemed as if some perverse fate were trying to drive me into another line of work. My bright entry into the theatre seemed to have evaporated, and I felt as though I were trying to fight my way out of a maze. I couldn't believe that no one wanted me. After all hadn't I made a big hit, hadn't all the other actors told me that my future in the theatre was assured?

The next two years were a time of disappointment, frustration and failure. Gradually I lowered my standards. I ceased looking for a new part in a Broadway show and started to look for any kind of job—anything, just to be busy, just to make some money. I played bits in vaudeville; I went on the road with a silly farce called *Some Baby;* I was a nubian slave at the Neighborhood Playhouse's production *The Queen's Enemies,* for a salary of thirty dollars a week. Many years later when I had become a success on Broadway, I met Miss Alice Lewisohn, who had been my boss at the Playhouse, and she related an incident which I had not remembered, but which sounds characteristic enough. Seeing me standing to one side looking rather lonely one day during rehearsals, she asked me what I wished to do in the theatre, and I replied without hesitation, "Write, direct and act." She thought it was very amusing to hear this upstart bit actor speak so confidently—particularly since I later translated these ambitions into facts.

One of my many jobs was working as an extra in the movies. This was before the Screen Extras Guild had made a business out of this bottom rung on the ladder. In those days each of us felt ashamed of having such a lowly job, and many were the face-saving lies to be heard as we hung around waiting for the next shot. Like me, most of the extras were hoping to be noticed by the director and to be promoted. But I regret to say that promotion came more often from pull than from ability. The picture industry has always been saddled with favoritism, nepotism and its consequent incompetence, but in the early days the situation was even worse than today. Those in power were there by virtue of having been first in the field rather than as a result of worth. Like the town bully who is at heart a coward, they were arrogant; they threw their weight around blatantly and were susceptible to flattery. Most of them depended on yes-men and on compliant women to bolster their shallow egos.

.   .   .

Young lovers wherever you are, young married lovers, young couples: would you like a recipe for connubial bliss, a recipe for mutual devotion and happiness? Be poor but ambitious; be struggling but undefeated; be a unit against the problems of the outside world. That bond of interdependence is a warm and comforting thing; you have each other and you have your future. Do not expect everything to be as placid as a millpond; a little turbulence is a healthy thing.

Ednah and I had our arguments, not only about the affairs of the world in general, but about our own small problems. I only remember one really violent outburst, and I think that was about Woodrow Wilson's profile. I remember that I became so exasperated at what I considered to be Ednah's intransigent, female, illogical stubbornness that I stormed out of the apartment into the night and walked the streets for a couple of hours hoping that the bigoted woman I had married would be worried over what rash step I might take.

Ednah and I were never bored with each other. We debated everything: art, about which I knew nothing; music, about which she knew nothing; politics, which is largely a matter of prejudices anyhow; religion, about which we had both shed all our prejudices; relatives, always a good controversial topic; morals, ditto; health, of which fortunately we both had an abundance; grammar, which she taught me; manners; deportment; personalities. We even debated about money, a topic which was entirely academic at that time.

An electronic computer would have toted up the fact that my gross income for these two years was two thousand dollars per annum, and would have deduced that I should get out of the theatre. My relatives reached a similar conclusion. Not much was said, but it was to be sensed. On one of my rare visits home my mother's promising son felt as though he ought to avoid her steady inquiring gaze. I bolstered my pride with stories of better prospects, some real, some false, but no one seemed to believe them—or even to be interested.

Of course, Ednah was even more distressed at my lack of success and my bleak future than I was. She cared for my sake, not for herself. She felt that the spectacle of a man of my brains and ability being at the mercy of office boys was all wrong, and she urged me to go back to college to study law. She offered to go to work to support me and argued that I could keep up with my main objective—writing—as a lawyer just as well as I could as an actor. But some deep stubbornness would not let me give up. As a result Ednah took a job. She had a brother, Robert Levis, who was a prominent New York lawyer, and she took a course in stenography and began to work in his office. Eventually she became his office manager.

What's it like to be supported by your wife? Not bad, not bad at all—provided that there is no shame. Since I was perfectly confident that this was a temporary situation, and since I was writing every day—quite unproductively, it is true—or looking for work—equally unproductively—I had no feelings of guilt. I didn't even wonder what the neighbors thought.

In the morning, Ednah would give me final instructions before she hurried down to the office. "Be here when the iceman comes; be sure to take the laundry out; put the bake dish in at five fifteen." If it was a day for job hunting, I would wait until eleven o'clock, when the theatrical offices were open, then take the subway downtown, do the rounds, have lunch at the Automat, and then, if there was a later appointment, go to the library and read until time for that. I spent a good deal of time on the top floor of the library at Forty-second Street. What a wonderful institution, what a haven for displaced husbands.

If it was a writing day, I would work until noon, get my own lunch, take a long walk and then work some more. As the time came for Ednah's return, I would set the table and get the dinner ready. I became rather fond of cooking, and to this day I consider my oatmeal muffins very superior. Ednah's hours were always unpredictable. You don't get the same consideration from a boss who is a relative as you do from a stranger; you're supposed to enjoy staying until seven o'clock to help get out that brief. Usually we ate in the kitchen, simply spreading newspapers on the table. Once my sister Polly and her husband dropped in unexpectedly, and I invited them to stay for dinner. When Ednah arrived I could see that she was terribly upset about something. After they were gone, she was furious; she was embarrassed, as only a woman can be, that my sister would think that she was the kind of housekeeper who put newspapers on the table.

During these two terrible years when I was in the doldrums as an actor, I kept my ego and my hope alive by writing. As my playwriting continued to be fruitless, I turned in my discouragement to other forms of writing. An agent peddled a number of my short stories, but none of them was ever accepted. Then I thought that perhaps I could be a songwriter, and I wrote some lyrics which I later showed to John Golden. He said that they were adequate: they rhymed, they made sense, but they did not have that extra something which made a song click. I believed him and ceased my efforts in this field.

No one offered to produce my plays, but many producers claimed to see merit in them, encouraged me to keep on writing and professed to be anxious to read anything that I might submit. This brightened my life to some extent, for though I wasn't necessarily convinced that my plays were good or ought to be produced, still I hoped. When one script was finally turned down by everyone, I would put my hope in the next one.

Looking back dispassionately, I can admit that the theatre was not robbed of any jewels by the blindness of playreaders. They all told me the same thing: "You have good dialogue and good construction, but the idea itself isn't interesting." That, I fear, is the story of my writing life. I was not a successful playwright until I took parasitical advantage of other people's ideas. All my success has been either in rewriting some piece which was created by another author, or in adaptations for a musical book of such standard works as *Charley's Aunt* and *A Comedy of Errors*.

Nevertheless, it was through my playwriting efforts that I made my most valuable contacts. It is too bad that merit alone isn't sufficient to get ahead in the theatrical business—or for that matter any other business—but it isn't. One doesn't necessarily need pull, but one needs contacts; one has to be known. The circle of people who were familiar with me and with my work gradually widened. For instance, in 1917, George Tyler gave me a small part in *The Ohio Lady*, and thus I met Booth Tarkington and Julian Street. When the play was abandoned on the road, Tyler put me in another tryout, which brought me into contact with George Kaufman and Marc Connelly, who were later to put me in a road company of *Dulcy*, where I was to meet two other people with whom I eventually was to write successful plays.

As so often happens, Kaufman and Connelly were exact op-
posites. The first was quiet, dry, introverted, a very witty fellow;
the second was expansive and extroverted. When George was
rehearsing a show he wanted to be alone, but in the same situation Marc wanted a crowd of friends around to watch him do
his stuff. Once Marc was rehearsing a musical called *Two Bou-
quets,* and as was his custom, he invited a great many of his acquaintances to drop in at rehearsals. George was walking down
Broadway when a friend stopped him and said, "How are Marc's
rehearsals coming?" "Fine," said George. "The balcony's fallen off
a little, but it's still crowded downstairs."

My contact with John Golden had been affected because he
had read my plays and considered that they had a future even
though my lyrics did not. He and his partner, Winchell Smith, had
produced a great success, *Turn to the Right,* the year before and
now in 1918 he suggested that I come and work in his office. He
said that I could learn something about the business and at the
same time be useful to him as an assistant. He was right. I went
to work as a combination office boy, assistant casting director,
associate playwright and protégé. Golden was a compulsive
talker, and since I was one of the best and most enthusiastic audiences he'd ever had, he poured out his opinions about acting,
writing, publicity, business and life. John was a very warm-
hearted fellow, and though he often referred to himself as my father, my salary was only fifteen dollars a week. A father who has
had to struggle his way up is often of the opinion that hardship is
good for the son too. John was always exposing the pretense in
people, although he himself was the bunko artist of the world.
With his grand, hearty manner he would utter a piece of flattery
that would make you blush, but it was all part of the game and
he often mocked himself.

Years later, after Winchell Smith had died and Golden was
struggling along with what he called "clean" plays (which were
never well received by the critics and only passably accepted by
the public), he told me about how he got a good review from
Dr. Cadman, a minister who had an important radio program in
Brooklyn. He said, "I invite him and his daughter to the first
matinée. The poor old bastard never sees any shows but mine, so

he thinks they're great. Then I send his little girl a box of candy at intermission."

John liked to be associated with important people. He palled with the mayors from O'Dwyer to LaGuardia and back; and later Mrs. Roosevelt lunched with him at Sardi's once a week. He charmed them all and he charmed me; and though his reminiscences were probably more exciting to the layman than to people in the theatre, in those days I listened avidly.

Golden, in addition to handling the business of the firm, was working with the playwright Austin Strong on a future production to be called *Three Wise Fools*. Mr. Golden was one of those rare theatrical producers who got to work early in the morning. In fact, his routine was quite untheatrical. After being in high gear all day long, he suddenly collapsed right after dinner and went to bed at about nine o'clock. Full of energy again the next morning, he would drive in from the country, stride into the office and exude boundless vitality all day long. Well in advance of his dramatic entrance, we would hear him coming up the stairs, his big voice issuing orders or comments. Usually he was cheerful. He would give one quick look at his mail and then sit in the barber's chair which he kept in his office. His first conference of the day took place while he was being shaved. Next, having dispatched his press agent and business manager upon their respective tasks, he would settle down to the interesting part of the day's work: seeing actors, working on a new play and, above all, pontificating.

In addition to my job of listening to anecdotes, philosophical pronouncements and business dicta, I sometimes interviewed actors. But my most important and interesting task was serving as assistant playwright to Austin Strong. Golden felt that Austin Strong was lazy and that the rewriting of *Three Wise Fools* was not progressing as fast as it should, so in order to shock Mr. Strong out of indolence—and also perhaps with the hope that the office boy might come up with a good line or two—he set me to work writing scenes. Naturally, I attacked this assignment with vigor; if he wanted a scene, by God, he'd get it, and I would be back from the typewriter with my offering within two hours. Then my work would be criticized and passed on to Austin, and though it was more of a goad than a contribution, one or two of my lines were still in there when the play was produced, and thus I had for the first time the satisfaction of hearing my words spoken on a Broadway stage.

Before this happened, however, Winchell Smith returned from the country and preparations were made for rehearsals of *Lightnin'!* Golden thought it would be good experience for me to work as an assistant stage manager under Winchell. Again he was right; it was an invaluable school for a young director.

Winchell Smith was a quiet, unobtrusive, laconic man, who could enter the theatre without being noticed. His only interest was in what went on behind the footlights. Everything else was in his partner's, Golden's, province. I recall the first time I ever heard his name mentioned. An old stage-door man was talking about the different directors he had watched. "He's the best," he said, "the best of them all. When Winchell Smith gets through explaining a line to an actor, if he can't get it into his head, he'd better go back to driving his truck." That was Smith's greatest quality: he was crystal clear. There was no posing, no nonsense, just "this is how we do it." Ruth Gordon told me once that when she was rehearsing for a road company of *The First Year* she began to experiment with a line which was one of the biggest laughs in the show. Winchell said, "No, no, dear. If you've got lines that don't go, then you can fool around with them. But when you get lines that do go, just say it, dear, just simply say it."

Smith was only angry at me once. I was sitting beside him holding the book while he rehearsed a scene. Some perverse bit of immaturity made me want to show off, and I began to turn pages back to the first act as if I were looking up something. I think Smith sensed what was going on, for he turned and snarled, "What are you fooling with the script for? Watch the scene." A few minutes later he spoke kindly to me to show me that there was no lasting enmity.

Shortly after we tried out *Lightnin'!* in Atlantic City, where it looked like a success, the United States declared war against Germany. I had been brought up on stories of my valiant soldier ancestors. In the American Revolution one of them didn't know he was wounded until he found his boot full of blood; another fought at Quebec in his stocking feet. No conflict since the inception of our country had been without an Abbott until the Spanish American War, and I had always secretly resented the fact that my father had not upheld the tradition. Now here I was, the right age, the right temperament to be in the conflict, in good physical condition, and without even the excuse of having important work on the home front. At the time I had a romantic attitude about the war, and I wanted to go to officers' training camp. Imagining myself in a handsome uniform giving orders, I wished with all my heart to be part of it; but I never did enlist. Ednah implored me to wait until I was drafted; and my draft number turned out to be all that a wife could desire—I would not be called for a long time. Furthermore, I must confess that while part of me wanted to go to war (or to be more truthful wanted to wear the uniform), another part of me was loath to give up the chances in the theatre which now seemed to be opening up.

Also, just at this juncture, I had a particularly tempting offer. The malignant fate which had kept me out of work for so long now changed. I got a job with David Belasco in a play called *Daddies,* starring Jeanne Eagels, the wonderful actress who made such a sensational hit in *Rain.* The play was about a group of bachelors who had agreed to adopt war orphans, and I was the one who got the triplets.

By general agreement Belasco was the most important man in the American theatre at this time. He had been an innovator of the spectacular play as well as the realistic ones, and he had developed most of the great female stars of the previous decade. He had created a legend about himself; to work under Belasco was the ambition of any actor, and for someone like me, who aspired to direct and to write, it was a stroke of good fortune beyond any hopes.

Not only was Belasco a spectacular man in his work, he was spectacular in his personal life. To start with, he always dressed like a Roman Catholic priest. Why this flamboyant theatrical man chose the somber garments of the church, I could not guess. But he was never seen except in a black suit and reversed collar. He had a shock of white hair, a pale face, a rather unhealthy skin, and burning black eyes under bushy eyebrows. His legs were too short for his body, and he was pudgy, soft-looking—even fat. He moved with little steps, hesitantly. He had the air of a man who had difficulty making contact with the outside world. Stooges from his office accompanied him everywhere. If you met him on the street, his secretary would whisper your name to him before you reached a greeting point. His voice was soft, almost inaudible, and what amounted to a speech defect made him stress his s's so that his sentences were a long series of hisses.

Belasco developed one fine male star, David Warfield, but all of his other great successes were with women. He nearly always fell in love with his protégées and treated them solicitously—and with great jealousy and possessiveness. He never trusted them, and constantly called them at odd hours to check on their whereabouts. To the end of his life he was always in love, and there was someone in love with him. Belasco wasn't very attractive as a man. As a house-painter he wouldn't have appealed to a young woman but to stage-struck actresses, as a great figure in the theatre, he had glamour. (And fortunately for the older men in this profession, most actresses are stage-struck.)

In those days there was no Actors' Union—the hours of rehearsal were limited only by the will of the producer. David Belasco willed them to continue a very long time; in fact, he had lunch served in the basement of the Belasco Theatre so that we wouldn't go out and let our minds wander from the business in hand. Some actors considered this constant surveillance an imposition, but I gloried in this intimate contact with the great of the theatre. I listened hungrily to all their stories and quips, for sometimes the lunches were very jolly.

When there was some particularly difficult problem to be worked out, Belasco would keep us there for dinner, and we would work on into the night. Like the lunches this didn't bother me a bit, but John Cope muttered, "I get goddamned sick of hanging around here watching the old man think." And that's exactly what we did; we would sit by the hour while he looked off into space or muttered quietly to the actor concerned. He spent most of his time with Miss Eagels; the men's parts in this particular comedy were much easier, and he had very little to say to us. One incident will illustrate how Belasco approached a scene. When he told one of the actors to squirt soda into his highball at a certain point, John Cope said, "Aren't you afraid that's going to kill the laugh on my line?" Belasco got very intense. "This-s-s

play is-s-s about bachelors-s-s" he hissed. "I'd rather have the
s-s-sound of that s-s-soda than a dozen laughs-s-s."

Jeanne Eagels' part was really a phony; she played an innocent English orphan of sixteen, a synthetic sappy role that was
quite unsuited to her, and I think she realized that Belasco had
sweet-talked her into a job that was not good for her. Probably
she had accepted the assignment in her awe of the great maes-
tro's name rather than on judgment; at any rate, she seemed a reluctant and uncoöperative actress. Belasco didn't quite dare
bawl her out, so he vented his anger on the ingénue, Edith King.
This hapless victim had to endure long tirades and generalities
about the art of acting which were really directed over her head
to our star.

One day I heard the stage manager say to his assistant, "Oh,
oh, look out, he's got the watch." I tried to find out what this
meant, but they brushed me off. Later that day during rehearsal
Belasco grew angrier and angrier, and finally in his rage he took
out his watch and threw it on the floor. Subsequently I learned
that this was a prop watch which he brought along whenever he
wanted to create a good scene. I was also told that in one of his
other plays he had become so exasperated by an actor's continual
stupidity that he grabbed a fire axe and chopped the scenery to
pieces. It was a very effective spectacle which electrified the cast,
and only the stage manager knew that he had decided on the
previous day to change the set and that a new design was already
being constructed.

Daddies opened, and while the comments on its artistic
merit were qualified, its commercial success was undoubted. The
critics, as is their custom when dealing with popular stars, gave
praise to Miss Eagels. But realizing her part was phony, she knew
she wasn't good in it, even if the critics didn't; and hardly had we
opened when she began to make efforts to get out of her contract. Mr. Belasco disappeared; once the show opened we never
saw him. I think that he too was disappointed; the play was a
potboiler and nothing more. Also, he had made two mistakes
about Jeanne Eagels: one in casting her for a starry-eyed, innocent sixteen-year-old girl, the other in presuming that she would
fall in love with him.

Jeanne became friendly to me, and always addressed me as

Kid, treating me as a harmless junior. She was a creature of moods, strange and aloof most of the time and with most people. But at other times she would come into the theatre wearing a warm expansive aura and would talk to me with considerable intimacy. She talked about two things: music, which she loved, and men, whom she hated. She gave me the impression that men had wronged her and treated her cruelly and that her life work was to get even with them. Obviously she didn't consider me a man— I was sort of a sometime pal.

One of the tactics Jeanne used to persuade the management to cancel her contract was to be sick. One matinée when she was playing a scene with the leading man, she seemed to grow fainter and fainter. Finally she stopped in the middle of a line. The actor whispered, "What's the matter?" Jeanne gasped, "Water," and he rushed obediently off-stage. But while he was gone, Jeanne suddenly remembered that Winifred Fraser, an English actress, was having her customary cup of tea in the wings, and when the leading man returned with water, she said, "No, tea." So the order having been changed, he rushed out and got her a cup of tea. In due time, she won the Battle of Belasco, and he let her go.

In the meanwhile my draft number was getting closer and it began to look as though Abbott would soon be at the front. Wishing to be ready for promotion when the time came, I took advantage of some military instruction which was being offered at the Sixty-seventh Street Armory. Each day at five o'clock officers took us in hand and taught us some of the fundamentals. I marched and counter-marched with other potential draftees, feeling silly as I called out "Halt" or "Advance, friend, and be recognized."

But I never got a chance to make use of this preparation. During a matinée, word came backstage at the Belasco Theatre that the Armistice had been declared; the city was celebrating, and there was dancing in the streets. After the first act I did not need to be on stage for another forty minutes, so I took off my make-up and rushed out of the theatre. The main celebration was on Fifth Avenue, and I pushed my way down there. Indeed there was dancing in the streets, traffic had ceased and delirious people had taken over. A French sailor stood on a taxicab making a

speech which no one understood, but which all appreciated; a be-
jeweled woman was hoisted up beside him and she too made a
speech. Strangers threw their arms around each other; girls kissed
men in uniform. Church doors were wide open for thousands of
those whose emotions carried them therein.

Later I was to see the end of World War II, but as an explosion of pent-up feelings it did not compare with this first orgy
of emotion. It was a false armistice, but the real one followed
shortly—then suddenly there was a calm. The salt went out of
life; existence seemed flat; there was no excitement in the air.
The newspapers were hardly worth reading—they seemed flac-
cid and pointless. Instead of our big victories in the Argonne Forest, one read about the speech by Senator Blah. Even a spectacular murder up in the Bronx was dull; after all, we were used to
reading of a thousand murders each day.

When spring came, I began to look around for a good part
with which to follow *Daddies*. But my two practically jobless
years and the fact that I was now a married man made me cautious about throwing over a good part, so when I found nothing
and the management offered me a big raise to go on the road the
following season (plus thirty dollars a week to tutor the four children in the company), I decided to accept. Before a contract
could be signed the Equity Strike occurred.

Before Equity, the actors had practically no rights. They received no pay during rehearsals and they could be rehearsed indefinitely, or fired or stranded at almost any time. I knew that
their cause was right and, though I was not as fanatical as others,
joined the fight. Of course, the small actors were the ones who
needed protection, and many of the big stars who sided with
them did so out of conviction rather than self-interest. One group
of stars formed an independent organization to rival Equity—a
sort of company union. They called it the Actors' Fidelity
League and the other actors called them the Fidoes.

George M. Cohan was the most important person in the Fidelity League and the bitterness toward him by the majority who
were loyal to Equity was intense and lasting. Sometime ago when
Oscar Hammerstein tried to raise money for a statue of Cohan in
Duffy Square, he found that the people of the theatre gave him

neither enthusiasm nor money. To many actors Cohan is not the author of "Over There" or "Yankee Doodle Dandy"; he is still the traitor who double-crossed them in the strike.

There wasn't much comprehension of the other side's point of view from either group; it was a very emotional affair. The biggest hit in town was still Winchell Smith's play, with Frank Bacon in the leading role. Bacon could be said to be a Winchell Smith product; Smith had lent him money in the early days, given him small parts, written better parts for him and brought him along until finally trusting him with a star part. When the strike came, a bus rode up and down Broadway with all the cast, including Frank Bacon, aboard and a big sign on it saying *"Lightnin'!* has struck." Winchell, a quiet and tolerant man if there ever was one, never forgave Bacon and treated him coolly for the rest of his life.

The big strike meetings were always a bizarre exhibition; the phony elegance of some old Shakespearian actor would be followed by the coarse illiteracy of an uneducated union business agent. Nobody knows what actors are like until he sees them in the mass. Each one of them is an individual, but when you get them all together there is one common denominator: they are emotional, irrationally emotional. One minute they will all be screaming and shaking their fists; two minutes later they will be giving a rising vote in tribute to some gray-haired actor who has been on the stage for forty years.

Finally Equity won the strike. I was elected deputy of my company and we went out on tour. Once again I continued my economical way of life, living on the thirty dollars I was paid for tutoring the children and saving the one hundred and seventy-five dollars I received for playing the part.

As always on my trips on the road, everything was delightful at first, but gradually my thoughts turned to my beloved wife and then to the female of the species in general. As the tour of *Daddies* came to its close, the pressure became something of a torment. Finally it was almost over; we were on the train coming from Cleveland to Washington for one last week when I was offered a big temptation. One of the women in the company grew very warm toward me. I did not like her—she was a silly, sloppy woman—but at this stage my boiling point was low and she was, after all, a woman. I feared that I would not be able to resist the temptation I knew was coming, and how could I go home to my loving wife with such a black thing on my conscience? I decided on a reckless extravagance. When we got to the station in Washington, I disappeared from the group and caught a train to New York, first sending Ednah a wire that I would be arriving later that night. At five A.M. I rang the bell to our apartment. No answer. I knocked; no answer. I rang louder and longer; no answer. I beat on the door violently—to hell with the neighbors! After ten minutes of this, I heard Ednah's timid, sleepy voice, and after I had convinced her that it was really me, she opened the door. Perfidious Western Union had not delivered the telegram, but I was finally home and everything was right once again.

When I returned to Washington I found that no one had missed me. Cool, impervious and happy, I played out the week.

After *Daddies* closed, my good angel Paul Dickey appeared again. He had finished a new comedy, and he had written a part especially for me. *The Broken Wing* was a hit. In this comedy one of the actors, Joseph Spurin Calleia, played a Mexican peon, and as he went about his work he hummed a little song that he had composed. One day Calleia told me that many people had admired the tune, and that if I would write the lyrics we might be able to get it published. I wrote them and Harms published it, but not many copies were sold at first. At that time, I certainly could have used the money, but later on, when I didn't need it, the sheet music began to sell and I made as much as two thousand dollars a year out of "Adelai." I might add that my words were perfectly horrible.

To join or not to join a theatrical club was the husband-and-wife topic in those days. Some of my friends were members of The Lambs and The Players, and it had been suggested that I ought to affiliate myself with one of these organizations. It was what happened to important actors; it seemed to be the thing to do.

Ednah voted vigorously and persuasively against it. She argued that as a writer nothing could be more stultifying than letting the narrow, parochial outlook of the actor affect me; that it was important to keep in touch with people outside this limited world and not to get more deeply involved in it; that actors sat around and talked about themselves and their triumphs and failures until their careers assumed an importance all out of proportion to their value.

I decided that she was right, and I still think that she was right. Not that actors shouldn't have clubs where birds-of-a-feather may get together; it is simply that for the writer or director the performer's point of view is too limited and subjective; he must keep himself more aloof to achieve perspective and to be able to interpret the world for everybody, not just for the theatre.

My wife fought another battle which she did not win. We had saved some money and we differed radically about how to use it. Ednah was inherently conservative; she thought the savings bank was the only place for our hard-won capital. I was more of a gambler; I wanted to make our little money grow at a greater pace. Like millions of other Americans, I had been awakened to the possibilities of the stock market, and I had already begun to investigate them. My many hours in the library had included reading much on the subject of finance. I discovered that it was not such a complicated matter; making money merely required a cool nerve and a little common sense. Rothschild had told anyone who would listen just how to do it: "Buy cheap and sell dear." All the other authorities were in substantial agreement; you could make money if you bought stocks when everything looked terrible and sold them when everything looked as if it was coming up roses.

The debates between Ednah and me on the subject of finance were vigorous, protracted and sometimes emotional. She accused me of reckless, heedless financial idiocy; I accused her of wanting to put our money in a tin can and bury it in the ground, a policy which I contemptuously labeled as "ash-can finance." Despite my wife's protests, I earmarked part of our savings for speculation.

In a bull market I began to buy five- and ten-share lots. Going home on the subway I would open the paper to the financial page. It was wonderfully exciting to read that AT&T had gone up three points and that effortlessly I had just become thirty dollars' richer. I spent some time in the customers' rooms with the other Wall Street operators watching the slow progress on the big board, and I read all the various dope sheets and watched the

Babson Graph showing you how to judge at what state the market was.

Suddenly there was a bear market. An inventory sale at Wanamaker's store triggered the downward trend; then it became general. There were some long faces around the old home, but I wasn't too discouraged even though it appeared that I had lost the family argument. I felt that my blue-chip stocks were safe and would come back, and also that there would be a chance to pick up some bargains in a falling market when the right time arrived. It arrived. Things looked awfully black; now was the time to see whether I was a man or a mouse, whether all this reading I had done was to be translated into action, whether I was to be a contemptible theorizer or a courageous doer. Ignoring my wife's despair and prophesies of disaster, I went to the brokers to buy. Though the market was still falling, I bought five shares of General Electric at one hundred and thirty-five dollars. By the time I reached home that night it had gone down to one hundred and twenty-five dollars. The next day I bought five more shares, and it went down to one hundred and fifteen dollars. The next day I bought yet another five shares.

By now my speculation money was exhausted—but so was the market; it didn't go much lower. And a good thing. Ednah was pregnant. In our home there was some somber fact-facing. In how many American homes does this dialogue take place? "I think I am." "Well, are you sure?" Then the trip to the doctor, the certainty and finally the acceptance of the new situation— half-glad, half-sad.

Ednah hated to give up her work at the office. She enjoyed that part of her life, not for the money—we didn't need that any more—but because it gave her companionship, a sense of usefulness and of having something important to do. Moreover, she was calmly and unswervingly convinced that she would die in childbirth. She had only one last deathbed request: since she was to be with me only a few months longer, she asked me to spend this time with her and to accompany her to Rochester, where she was going to have the baby at her sister Florence's.

I agreed and gave up all thought of acting for the next few months. We went to Rochester; Judith Ann Abbott was born in Rochester, and Ednah was delighted to find that she was still with us. In fact, in those first weeks after the baby was born, she was beautiful; she had grown thin and this, combined with her new happiness and that aura motherhood seems somehow to endow women with, gave her a madonna-like loveliness.

Everything was all right with the world too. The stock market had gone up, just as Rothschild and I had thought it would. I made enough in the market during those months of idleness to pay for the birth, the trip and my vacation in the most painless of ways.

Back in New York I decided once more to take a job on the road. Perhaps this was because I felt the need of added security in my new role as a father, but more likely it was my desire to get on the good side of Kaufman and Connelly, who had offered me a part in the touring company of *Dulcy*.

Lynn Fontanne, who had been a hit in this comedy during its Broadway run, was the leading woman, and playing opposite her was that talented actor, James Gleason. The play was to be directed by the stage manager of the original company, a quiet, self-effacing young man named Howard Lindsay. Later he developed one of the biggest voices in the theatre and became anything but self-effacing.

It was an interesting tour. Gleason and Lynn Fontanne were fascinated by each other. This, I hastily add, was a purely mental affinity—both had great charm, but neither understood the other. Gleason was a thorough professional, a witty Irishman with very little sense of humor. Lynn was a hoyden, a fey girl who exaggerated her eccentricities because they were charming. A typical scene between them took place one night as they were standing in the wings ready for an entrance. Out of the blue Lynn made a statement like "all policemen wear red underwear." Jimmy told her that this was ridiculous. When she insisted he screamed, "I ought to know—I've got a lot of relatives who are policemen." Lynn smiled at him patronizingly and shook her head. "No, Jimmy," she said, "you just haven't observed. You don't know. They all wear red underwear." Gleason turned white with rage and stalked away while Lynn smiled happily at having won the battle. A few hours later they were friends again.

Gleason was trying to write plays just as I was. In collaboration with Dick Taber he had written a show called *Is Zat So?*, which was going the rounds. We talked about working on something together and finally started on a show later named *The Fall Guy*. The first draft was finished during the road tour of *Dulcy*.

In the company there was a quiet, intelligent and attractive girl named Ann Preston Bridgers, from Raleigh, North Carolina, who was anxious to do something good in the theatre. After finishing *The Fall Guy*, I went to work with her on a show about a little Southern coquette named Norma. We thought it would be a comedy, and we wrote one version of this play with that intent, but when we got to New York and had a little perspective about the play, it was obvious that it didn't work. Reluctantly we put it on the shelf. Two or three weeks later Ann called me and said, "I know how you could make a nice tragedy out of the show if you wanted to." When she explained her idea I saw its possibilities immediately and agreed to write a rough draft. In three weeks I had a show which was not far from that eventually produced under the title of *Coquette*. We both felt that it was good but probably too tragic for commercial success. Ann helped me to polish this draft, and then we put it aside again.

David Burton, in Gilbert Miller's office, had been one of those who had encouraged me for a long time. He had once said to me, "I know just what you can do and I'll have a good part for you before I'm through." Now he kept his promise. I got the part of a roistering cowboy—Tex was his name, folks—in a comedy called *Zander the Great*, with Alice Brady as the star. This was a very definite turning point in my career. I was good enough in the role to be selected as one of the ten best performers of the year, and I made a sufficient impression so that from then on I didn't have to look for work. Jobs came to me.

They say that all comedians want to play Hamlet, and there is a germ of truth in it. The actor is impatient with the success he has had and wishes to achieve something of a different kind, either tragic or comic. In my opinion, this desire accounts for the popularity of repertory in the acting profession. The repertory theatre gives the actor a chance to play many kinds of parts. Because it has developed many fine actors, it is held in esteem, but actually it cannot compete artistically with the commercial play in which the actors are picked for their particular skills in the parts needed. In plain words, type-casting is the best way to cast a play.

I had relished the few sentimental moments which had come to me in the part of Tex. Now I was quick to accept a serious part in a serious play by a new and very serious playwright, Maxwell Anderson, who was an editorial writer on the New York *World*. The play was written in blank verse, and the language was very daring indeed for those times. I was greatly excited by it all. One night after dinner, when I was telling Ednah of the day's rehearsals, I acted for her the moment when Frank Shannon yelled at Beth Merrill, "You whore, you bitch." As my voice rang out in the quiet of our apartment, Ednah held up her hand in horror. "Please," she said, "the neighbors."

White Desert was what might be called an artistic failure. It raised Maxwell Anderson's standing as a writer, but it left him just as poor as before. However, he was now definitely committed to the theatre; he could only think of the time when he would give up newspaper work for playwriting. We became friends during rehearsals, and when he found that I was an aspiring author, he suggested that we collaborate on a show he had in mind which would have a good part for me. It was to be about the Hatfield-McCoy feud. Of course, I was flattered and agreed.

At this time I received an offer to take the leading part in a new play, *Hell-bent fer Heaven*. My role was that of a Southern mountain boy, and the management, wishing me to have an authentic accent, offered to pay my expenses to go down to Boone, North Carolina, and listen to the local dialect at first hand. I suggested to Maxwell that he come along with me and that while I was absorbing the accent we could also get atmosphere for our play. I paid his expenses out of the money allotted to me for the trip, and we both lived parsimoniously and tried to work for a few hours every day. We made little progress, but we had long intimate talks about life, its problems and its frustrations. On the surface Maxwell was a stolid, scholarly man, but inside he was all romance: he wished to ride a white steed over the mountains and carry off a beautiful maiden as much as the next fellow.

Full of grits, greens, corn pone and mountain accent, we returned to New York City, where Maxwell resumed his distasteful task of writing editorials for the *World* and I reported for the first rehearsal of *Hell-bent fer Heaven.* What a difference it was to come into first rehearsal feeling confident, and how pleasant to take my place among the others with assurance—to know that as an actor I was somebody.

At the lunch break I met a man who was going to play a big role in my life during the next few years. Mr. Klaw, the producer, came over and said, "I want you to meet our press agent, Mr. Jed Harris." I looked up and saw a young man of medium height, with glittering black eyes and a large nose. He seemed to be wearing a slight sneer, and with his head stuck forward and his shoulders hunched a little high, he looked something like a bird of prey. Somewhat contemptuously, he asked me for some facts about my career and some pictures and then said he'd talk to me later.

The next time I saw Jed I was on the train going to Asbury Park for the tryout. I was looking out the window, dreaming away, when I became aware of someone sitting behind me. Jed leaned over and said he understood that I wrote plays. He was going to be a producer; in fact, he had already coproduced one play which had been a failure; of course, it wasn't his fault—his partner wouldn't take his advice; he didn't know whether to call himself J.E.D. Harris or Jed Harris; he had just been doing the publicity for a comedy called *Applesauce* and he had invented the phrase "applesauce on every tongue"; he hated actors—they were stuffed shirts and stupid—but of course I was an exception, I was a writer; the kind he hated most were those handsome Arrow-Collar leading men who affected an air of superiority and pomposity, but who were really people of neither taste nor wit.

We discussed actors. John Barrymore was the greatest. Holbrook Blinn was good too, and Richard Bennett. Some actresses— Laurette Taylor and Florence Reed—were very good, and there were young ones coming along: Katharine Cornell, Helen Hayes, Tallulah Bankhead. Jed discussed my acting too. He criticized it and told me that he thought I was a fine actor but that I was in danger of getting into bad habits. For instance, I was so anxious to seem natural that I broke my speeches up and sometimes made little indecisive sounds between the words. This was all right if not carried to excess, but if I didn't put myself on guard it might become a mannerism. I realized immediately how right he was. This was a smart fellow, not afraid to tell you the truth about yourself.

We talked about playwrights. Eugene O'Neill had good ideas but very little gift with language; his words were wooden. Kaufman and Connelly were skillful but superficial; Philip Barry appealed to the snob element but had no substance. As for directors, Belasco had flair but was false; Winchell Smith was true but had no flair; Winthrop Ames had taste but no guts; Augustus Duncan—who was directing our play—was incompetent. When we discussed managers he picked them off and enumerated their faults one by one. Everything he said seemed full of excitement and truth. I was fascinated, exalted. I had never known anyone who talked so brilliantly about the theatre and the people in it. His ruthless criticism of everyone, including me, was stimulating and exciting. The day which had brought this remarkable man into my life was a big one. I wanted to get my plays before him as fast as I could, to hear what wise and penetrating things he would have to say about them. He no longer looked like a bird of prey; he looked like an eager young genius.

When we got back to New York, I let him read *Coquette* and *The Fall Guy*. He thought *Coquette* was a good piece of writing; in fact, he praised it highly but said that its subject matter was too tragic to make it a good commercial prospect. It would be a fine play to produce after a fellow had a hit and plenty of money behind him. He was less kind about *The Fall Guy*. We had written it in two sets; and he suggested that we change it to one set and cut some of the shopworn, sentimental situations. When I relayed his suggestions to Gleason he agreed that they were valid but refused to have any contact with Jed. It is ironical that Jed, who later falsely claimed that he had made great contributions to my scripts which he produced, should have received neither credit nor money for the good work which he did on this play.

Hell-bent fer Heaven opened, was a hit, and later won the Pulitzer Prize. I enjoyed playing it, even having to eat an immense slab of cherry pie every night. Among the phoniest things in the theatre are the eating scenes. We so often see dishes brought on stage, a lot of food displayed, a few passes made with a fork which somehow never quite seems to reach the mouth, and then the table cleared. I was realistic about my eating, I trained for the part; I ate no dessert during the run of the play, and as a result that Horn and Hardart cherry pie looked pretty good by nine fifty P.M.

Stage mothers carry on relentlessly under a cloud of ridicule and suspicion. They are often a pest, but not always. Many are selfish, but some are well-intentioned; when it comes to the children of the stage, they are a necessity. These parents are sometimes doltish parasites living on the talents of their offspring, but they are also sometimes doing the wise thing for the child—using an opportunity to put by funds for his future. It is the stage mother of the full grown and fairly successful actress who causes the most anguish. Practically all of this breed wished to be actresses and failed. They have encouraged their daughters to choose the theatre so that they can now live vicariously the life which was denied them. They fight vigorously and relentlessly for the daughter's success, not only because they want her to get ahead but because it gives them satisfaction to be a force in the theatre. In general, these women care nothing for the play; in fact, they hardly see it. They have no perspective, and therefore scarcely any judgment. They poison the girl's mind and make her suspicious and intractable: the leading man is upstaging her; the ingénue has a better dress; the character woman has a better dressing room; the director isn't letting her make the entrance the way she should; she ought to have a curtain call all by herself. Such, people say, are the stage mothers. I must confess that much of this is hearsay. I have had very little trouble of this kind, and I don't anticipate it in the future. We are all expendable, including actresses whose mothers cause trouble, and life is too short to spend it in intrigue and bickering.

Some of the men in the theatre old enough to look after themselves also have mothers with whom they are entwined. But generally these mothers wish to be involved in the personal and social life of their sons, rather than in their business, and thus, pose no problem to the actor's professional associates.

Stage wives are something else again. I heartily approve of them. Benjamin Franklin once said, "A man has three friends: an old wife, an old dog and ready money." A great many actors have wives not old in years, but old in reliability—married long enough to feel permanent—whose advice they have learned to lean upon. A wife who may not be very bright in other respects somehow becomes a wiser person in the role of a fact-facing and truth-telling helpmate. Most actors' wives seem to realize that their husbands' success is bound up with the play's success, and to look at the whole endeavor with a point of view which is not as limited as that of the average actor. The atmosphere backstage is often artificial; it becomes a phony world, and its inhabitants need friends who love them well enough to tell them the truth. Wives are the ideal deflaters.

My own wife offered me advice about the next project in which I was interested. *Lazybones* was a play by Owen Davis, to be directed by Guthrie McClintic, and I was excited by it. Ednah read it and told me it was trash. It is difficult for an actor to judge a play in which he finds a good part for himself—he can't see the forest for the trees. I thought this was my great chance— the character I would play was on the stage practically all the time. He had sentimental and melodramatic scenes; he started in the first scene as a young boy and ended up in the last one as an old man. I was hooked. It was really claptrap, but I didn't know it.

At this time I was feeling very pleased with myself and was not in a mood to absorb readily the suggestions or opinions of others. I remember that during rehearsals I argued with Guthrie McClintic about his direction even to the point of bad manners. Why he had decided to do the play in the first place I don't know; he seemed to be quite aware of its weakness. Once I overheard him discuss the end of the second act with the producers, at which point the heroine dies. Someone suggested that McClintic have a setting sun behind her as this event took place, and in his pained, troubled voice Guthrie said, "Yes, or a summer snowstorm."

Probably the best acting part I ever had came to me next, in the Theatre Guild production of *Processional*. The Guild was in its heyday; it produced boldly and made many innovations. *Processional* was an expressionist play by John Howard Lawson, later one of the unfortunates to be in trouble with a Congressional Committee and to pay in prison for his Communistic convictions.

I was the leading man. June Walker, one of the cutest little ingénues you ever want to look at, was the leading woman. Playing a newsboy was Ben Grauer, later the well-known announcer, and Harold Clurman, Lee Strasberg and Sanford Meisner played members of the Ku Klux Klan. Not type-casting. I played a radical organizer who was hunted by the Ku Klux Klan and blinded by soldiers—it was that kind of play. It was also very poetic, and John Golden ridiculed it. "When a man can't create a real love scene, he writes vague talk about the stars just to cover up his incompetence," he said. Philip Moeller, who was the director, wasn't very good, but he was artistic. It was a success.

While I was enjoying being a high-brow actor in *Processional*, the miracle occurred: *The Fall Guy* was to be produced. I was to have my first play on Broadway. It all happened because Jimmy Gleason was now a big shot. His farce, *Is Zat So?*, had been produced by the Shuberts and was such a tremendous success that he was now in demand both as an actor and playwright. Any show in which he was a collaborator could get produced. I argued fruitlessly that Jed Harris deserved the right to do the show because of the use we had made of his advice, but Gleason would have no part of him. In his success, Jimmy had become autocratic; he was still a nice fellow, but his word was final. It was arranged that the Shuberts would produce *The Fall Guy* and that Gleason and I would direct it jointly. However, since his role in *Is Zat So?* would keep him very busy and would prohibit his going on the road with the tryout, it was assumed that I would do most of the work. I made arrangements with the Theatre Guild to leave the cast of *Processional* in order to take up my directorial assignment.

A new director is at a disadvantage—he's on trial with the actors. He's not quite free to do everything he wants—he has to please people. Ernest Truex was the leading man and he was tolerant of me, but there were certain places at which, as an established star, he would draw the line. He didn't, for instance, want to have some young squirt of a kid telling him how to make an exit. The important stars of that time considered the director's control over them to be strictly limited. "If the performer doesn't know his job well enough to get off-stage without the help of the director, he better get out of the business. If they can't trust me to make an exit, they better get a new boy." In such details a star was very conscious of his dignity; to control him too much was to imply incompetence on his part and to infringe upon his rights.

Of course, since those days of 1924, the status of the director has changed considerably. At that time directors sometimes did little more than steer the actors into their positions on stage—to function as traffic cops, as it were. When he was directing *White Desert*, Brock Pemberton didn't even do that. He said, "Just pretend it's a room and find your own positions and we'll see how it works out." In many cases, the detail of acting was supposed to be the performer's business. Even the great Belasco didn't bother much with the coördination of little things between the actors.

In this first assignment of mine, I had to compromise, and I was frustrated by this inability to express myself fully. I longed to go deeper into the action, to control the whole stage, to make everything fit like a jigsaw puzzle, but for the moment I had to content myself with half-measures.

The Fall Guy had a promising opening in Atlantic City, but before I could begin to enjoy the feeling of success, troubles developed. Every tryout has some potential trouble hidden in it, a crisis which threatens to disrupt things and to cause anguish to all concerned. When the play is going badly this is understandable, because there is an obvious need to change—though there may be great difference of opinion as to what the change should be. But even when things go well some conflict, some clash of personalities usually develops.

In this case it was really trivial. The Shubert office, which had operated our play on a sort of absentee landlord basis, suddenly became interested in the project. And how do you express your interest in a new project? Why, you change something. So somebody or other back in the Shubert office decided one of the actors should be changed. I didn't think so. I was threatened; I was told that it wouldn't do me any good in the profession to obstruct people in power. Looking back on it today, all this is trivial, but at that time, being inexperienced in such matters, it was harrowing. I knew that I had to fight for my show, but I felt alone, far from home, standing defenseless against the greatest theatrical syndicate in the country. I refused to change the actor. I telephoned Gleason, and he stood by me. We stuck it out; we kept our man. And we proved to be right; when the play opened in New York, not only was it a success, but our actor got good reviews. *The Fall Guy* wasn't a smash, but it was a hit and at last I had achieved the ambition which brought me to New York in the first place. I was now a playwright, and I was getting royalties for my efforts.

Prosperity affects different people in different ways. Jimmy Gleason transformed his whole life. He seemed to feel that he had now tapped a well which would never run dry. He had royalties from *The Fall Guy* and *Is Zat So?* which had several companies playing on the road, as well as his actor's salary. He and his wife Lucille really let go—they had a town house; they had nine servants; they had gold plate. Then Jimmy went to London with *Is Zat So?* and although he was receiving both salary and royalties from the London company, his expenses were so great that he had to send home for additional funds. *The Fall Guy's* revenue was important to me, but it was just a drop in the bucket to Jimmy. If he could have foreseen the future, he might have been a little more cautious, because he never was to have another hit. When his money had evaporated, Gleason went to Hollywood and spent the rest of his life out there giving fine performances, for the one thing he never lost was his acting ability. I am sure that if I had ever asked Jimmy if he regretted spending his money so lavishly he would have replied, "Not for a minute, what's money for? Something to sit on? It was great while it lasted. I'd do the same thing over." After all, while it seemed a reckless destruction of his resources from my point of view, from his point of view his behavior was perfectly normal. He had always spent everything he had; he just kept doing the same thing—the only difference was that he had more to spend.

I was more cautious. My whole training and environment made me so; I had been schooled by my mother on such Calvanistic phrases as "A penny saved is a penny earned," and "A fool and his money are soon parted." I had been taught to despise people who used money to keep up with Joneses or to be a good fellow and to buy popularity. Ednah was even more conservative than I, but for very different motives from my mother's. These two women who influenced me so strongly both advocated the most rigorous will power in planning for the future, but while

Ednah was a dyed-in-the-wool conservative, my mother was in
fact a radical. She advocated saving not as a virtue in itself, but
as an end toward getting money to spend. In her youth, Mother
had hoped to go to faraway places, to have fine clothes and a
beautiful environment, and when it became obvious that these
things were to be denied her, she hoped that some of her children would have them. My mother was strongly against smoking
or drinking because it was harmful, not because she thought it
immoral. Conventional morals didn't concern her; once she told
me that she saw no harm in gambling if you could afford it. With
Ednah, saving was a natural instinct. Actually, she was perfectly
happy as she was; she didn't want anything else that money
could buy. I think, in fact, that she instinctively dreaded that our
life, our tight little Arcadia, was going to be invaded and destroyed by our new prosperity.

There was still another reason for me to be cautious. The
fate of those theatrical people who had made quick money and
then ended up with nothing was always before me. It was before
all of us on the Great White Way; and we all knew or gossiped
about performers who had sold their houses and were now existing by borrowing from friends. Or we would see some former
headliner going down Eighth Avenue to the delicatessen with a
girlfriend who was supporting him. Then as now, in the ranks of
the extras at the motion-picture studios were the faces of former
stars. Even the supposedly wise money men, the producers, were
victims of this quixotic business; such successful and prosperous
tycoons of that era as Charles Dillingham, Al Woods and George
Tyler were to end up penniless.

So the Abbott household was not greatly affected by my new
affluence. However, we did move to an apartment at 112th Street
and Riverside Drive near the Horace Mann School, where we
planned to enter Judith when she became five years old.

We were living in the Jazz Age, but we didn't know it. From
day to day I was not aware that this period of life was any more
frenzied than it had been ten years before. I had never been in
a speak-easy. Everybody talked about them and about bathtub
gin and bootleggers, but those things were all outside my ken. I
believed that liquor was poison and that if it could be abolished
it was a good thing. And I believed in obeying the law; I felt

strongly that if educated people flouted the law they encouraged the great mass of people to do the same thing. It seemed to me that the social structure of the times was rotten—but then in various ways it always had been, so this was hardly new or startling. Women's clothes did seem bizarre to me; the sack dresses with no waistline were like a parody of a female, and the fashion which outlawed breasts and made girls ruin their figures for life seemed an abomination. But after all, these styles weren't as silly as the hobble skirts which had preceded them or the corsets, bustles and ponderous clothes of another time.

Altogether, during the fabulous twenties I was involved with my own small trials and triumphs. These were exciting days, not because of any Jazz Age hysteria but because of professional opportunities. The chances which I had been looking for all these years—to write, to direct, to work in the theatre—now poured in upon me in abundance. I seized on every opportunity that came my way; I was compulsively unable to turn down anything. In the next two years I was to work on nine plays either as a director or a writer or both. The play-doctor accepted almost every case that was offered to him.

John Golden was delighted by my success and was anxious to find a part for me through his office. When I told him about the Hatfield-McCoy story which Maxwell Anderson and I had started to work on, he liked the idea, but wanted to eliminate Anderson from the picture and get Winchell Smith in his stead. By this time, Maxwell had started writing with Laurence Stallings an army play which was to be *What Price Glory?*, the biggest success he was ever to have. In any case, Maxwell was glad to get a little ready cash and to be rid of his obligation to finish the play with me. Golden paid him fifteen hundred dollars for his rights and it was agreed that I collaborate with Winchell Smith.

In retrospect it seems to me that neither Winchell nor I was the right author for this idea. We made it into a show, a melodrama, whereas its only hope was to be treated in a more important way—to delve deeply into the causes of feuds and hatreds, and their footlessness. Of course, I was delighted to be collaborating with a man I so admired, but the work proceeded desultorily. Each day I would go down to the Astor Hotel, where

Winchell was staying, and we would talk about the story line, but there were many interruptions. I don't believe that, in his heart, Winchell had any real enthusiasm for the job. Although I tried to pump a great deal of excitement into my own approach to it, I don't believe I did either. Our conferences were sterile and uninspired. They were, however, enjoyable—Winchell always served an elegant lunch and usually invited three or four amusing people—I liked listening.

Finally Golden suggested that the authors repair for a week to Winchell's country home in Framingham. In this charming environment I had a pleasant week, but my collaborator was anything but industrious and I was uninspired. If nothing came of our talks Winchell would suggest going to the club for lunch. There he would get in a card game with some of his cronies and be lost for the day.

Winchell's wife was a sad woman whose tongue became very thick by eventide. Winchell said, "Yes, dear" to her on all occasions. If she asked him to come home at a certain time, he would agree instantly, but would return only when he pleased. If she called him in the middle of a game at the club he would go to the phone and say, "We're coming right away, dear," then come back and resume the game. I think he realized that I disapproved, because one day in a mood of candor, he explained to me what he felt. He showed me an old scrapbook; there was his wife—a very pretty girl. He told me about the back bedrooms she had shared with him and the hardships they had gone through together when he was struggling. That was all; he let me draw my own conclusions. And they were, of course, that while he would never desert her, he felt that no good could be done by sacrificing his life completely, so he achieved this compromise which seemed to salve his conscience.

In the fall of 1925, *A Holy Terror* was produced. Smith was ill and so the responsibility reposed on Golden and me. John believed that scenery and lighting had nothing to do with the success of the show; therefore we used second-hand scenery and the house lighting equipment. I did the lighting, directed the show and played the leading role. I wore a gun on each hip, was quick on the draw, trenchant of speech, and gay and courageous in tight places. In every way I was an outstanding Kentucky feudist,

but I'm afraid I wasn't much of a real character. The leading
woman was one of the new up-and-coming actresses, a Grecian
beauty named Helen Gahagan. I liked her; she was a straight-
forward, serious girl and very, very ambitious. We talked of our
futures and of life and art. She was confident that she would become a great opera singer, and indeed she later went to Europe
and devoted some years to that effort, but she ended up as a
member of Congress.

During the rehearsals of *A Holy Terror* I had been trying to
get the villain to fall off a fence naturally. It was about eight feet
high, and when I shot him I wanted him to relax and fall all the
way instead of clinging to the fence, but he was a little frightened
and hung on. To shame him into doing it right, I tried to show
him by example. Unfortunately I forgot that I was wearing a gun
on my hip and I received a deep bruise which lasted for weeks.
But there was another even worse pain: we failed.

In the meantime, I had begun work on something else, and
it now looked at last as if I should be able to repay Jed for the
help he had given me on *The Fall Guy*. I was writing a comedy
with John V. A. Weaver, the author of a volume of slang poetry
called *Love 'Em and Leave 'Em*, which had been quite a success.
When we finished the first draft of our play, which was about
some characters in a department store who talked Johnny's language, I showed it to Jed. He had only qualified enthusiasm for
the project, but he was so ravenous to get his hands on anything
that would make him a producer that he urged me to use my
influence to get the script for him. I gave Johnny a sales talk on
the virtues and brains of this talented tyro, and when he agreed
to go along with me Jed got the show. Now began the rewriting
and the casting. Johnny and I wrote; Jed and I planned. And we
talked. I admired his keen and flexible mind more than ever, and
we spent hours together every day. We planned our futures—we
were going to be partners: he was to be the business man, I was
to be the director, and together we would conquer the world. Ednah was never jealous of any woman so far as I know, but she was
jealous of Jed. She sensed how happy and excited I was to be
with him, how absorbed I was in our plans, and she felt like an
outsider.

During rehearsals of *Love 'Em and Leave 'Em*, a few flaws

began to appear in the beautiful fabric of my perfect relationship with Jed. They were only a few signs on the distant horizon, no bigger than a bad temper, another and less attractive side to my partner's character. I would be in the midst of rehearsals when I would become aware that Jed had entered the theatre silently and was sitting behind me. He would be in a foul mood, unshaven and unsmiling. If I ventured some optimistic comment on how well things were going—and I have a weakness for thinking things are going well—he would counter caustically. Later in the office he would apologize and turn on the charm. It wasn't his fault—his wife nagged him and he didn't get enough sleep—and he seemed almost a helpless little boy who needed and expected protection from his friends.

Again we went to Atlantic City and opened after the usual mechanical troubles. I thought that things went fairly well, but Jed did not agree. Business was not good so he was in a black rage, and I was made to feel responsible and even a little guilty. Among other things, he advocated that we change one of the important actors. As I have mentioned earlier, when things go wrong, everybody wants to change the actors. I am nearly always on the other side; I argue that if the show is right it could be played with a completely different cast, that it could even be played by a stock company and still be effective. The thing to fix is the script—not the interpreters.

Jed wanted me to go in and play the part which he felt was miscast. I disagreed with him; I didn't think I was right and I believed that the actor who was playing the part was right. We argued violently and acrimoniously. My state of mind grew worse and worse, and I began to wish that I had become a doctor or a lawyer—anything that would have saved me from this frantic and hysterical life. For the first time in my experience I had insomnia. I came to each rehearsal spent and listless after a night of sleeplessness.

Finally I telephoned Ednah and told her of my problems, and she came down to join me. With her arrival my troubles evaporated and disappeared—they seemed trivial. I talked things over with her and she substantiated my point of view. The next day I went to rehearsals relaxed and confident and made my decisions and stood by them. The play opened in New York and was a fair success.

The success smoothed things over. Jed was now a producer, his heart's desire, and I was the proud co-author of a second hit. All harsh words were forgotten, and again we became enthusiastic co-plotters for the conquest of the American theatre.

Next I directed a comedy for Laurence Webber, and once again I rushed in without consideration and again paid the penalty: the show was a failure. When Jed came to New Haven to see the production he was pleasant and helpful, but, of course, he was happy that it was not a success—he wanted my successes to be with him. His comments upon the show were astute; I felt that he was almost infallible, and I was eager to get back under his banner.

At this point I also was interested in finding a good part for a new actor named Lee Tracy. Jed called me one morning and asked me to hurry down to the office; and when I got there, he said, "If you will re-write a show I've just read, we'll have a great part for your boy Lee Tracy."

I read the script, a melodrama by Philip Dunning called *Bright Lights*. It was a confused script, full of wonderful characters and wonderful scenes, but there was no doubt about its possibilities. The main plot was exciting and topical, and with the exception of the ingénue, who was a bit sappy, the characters were fresh and true and arresting. The problem was to give the play order, and to me that did not seem difficult. It had proved difficult to others, however: the play had been read by nearly every manager on Broadway, and it was only because all the important producers had seen it that it finally came to a newcomer like Jed. The property was now controlled by its original author who agreed to let me collaborate, so Jed took an option and I started to work.

On the strength of Jed's success with *Love 'Em and Leave 'Em,* he had acquired a new partner, Crosby Gaige, who was to put up the money for the forthcoming venture—now called *Broadway*—but was not to appear on the billing. Gaige was a very personable gentlemen: poised, amiable, urbane. Socially, as theatrical producers go, he rated very high—almost as high as

Gilbert Miller—but artistically he was close to the bottom. He seemed to have no feeling for the theatre; in fact, I suspect that he got into it just to meet actresses. Gaige had two sidelines about which he was enthusiastic and well-informed: cooking and pornography. Some years later, in fact, he wrote a cook book which became a best seller. I spent very little time in his office and I never saw his pornographic library, but whenever Jed returned from a conference he usually had an amusing report on the latest acquisition.

Crosby's interest in our forthcoming production seemed to be passive; but when I wanted to change an actress who was not very good Jed confessed that she was Crosby's friend and that her presence was part of his deal. It cost a good deal of time and energy to get a performance out of her, but by the time we opened in New York she was acceptable.

A great many producers never really become professionals, to the end they remain talented amateurs. Crosby was a not-very-talented amateur who enjoyed the atmosphere and the glamour of the theatre but who didn't care to devote too much energy to achieve success in it. Therefore he was perfectly content to sit in the background and let an energetic man like Jed carry the ball. Although he had taste, he was too indolent to do much about it. He also had money, and when it came to money he functioned very effectively.

I was doomed to go through a couple of violent crises in the production of this play, but fortunately fate had given me a staunch friend and ally in the person of my new collaborator. Philip Dunning was a strong, patient, stubborn man. He was extremely handsome, tall and slightly stooped, with black hair streaked with gray, a black mustache and wonderfully kind brown eyes. Once having turned his show over to me, he backed me whole hog.

Broadway was destined to be one of the biggest successes in the history of the New York theatre, both artistically and financially, but none of us sensed this in advance. As is usual in the theatre, none of us could look back and say, I told you so. We never know. Sometimes things go well and you feel optimistic, but that is about as far as hopes go. Irving Berlin told me that his song "White Christmas" was written on short notice to fill in a needed spot in a picture, and that "No Business Like Show Business" was designed only as a utility number to cover up a scene change. When *Oklahoma* was in New Haven under the title of *Away We Go* Dick Rogers was very worried and asked me to come and see it. I found Rodgers and Hammerstein, Agnes de Mille and Lawrence Langner all feeling harried and insecure. I saw the Saturday matinée and thought it was completely charming. (I remember that I did make one suggestion—that they cut out "Poor Judd Is Dead"!) I did have the prescience to state that the show contained some of the best music that Dick had ever done, but I certainly did not realize that I had been watching an epochal production.

Broadway went well in its tryout in Atlantic City; in fact it looked so promising that the Broadhurst Theatre, which Aarons and Freedley had built especially for their own musicals, was assigned to us for our New York opening. Although during the negotiations over the lease the owners had several acrimonious debates with Jed about the contract, finally everything was adjusted. Our play was put away for the summer, and then Jed did a smart thing. He asked Phil and me to meet him one night in his office, where we would have no interruptions, and he said, "This show is going to get by no matter whether we improve it from now on or not. But it will be a much more important production if we eliminate all the cheap jokes. We don't need them. There is enough good comedy so that you can afford to throw out the stuff that downgrades the show." When we agreed he read the entire play aloud, indicating the material he felt should be deleted. It proved a canny thing to do and a very good way in which to edit a play; since then I have often used the same tactic.

Unfortunately, Jed's opinion that we had a fine show was not a steadfast one. In accordance with his character—one might almost say with his malady—he would plummet overnight from the wildest and happiest enthusiasm to the blackest and most miserable depression. His pessimism had mastered him when we took the train for Asbury Park to try out the show before coming to New York. I imagine that Crosby Gaige had been especially irritating. To Gaige's point of view, *Broadway* must have been a little too different and too radical in theme and treatment. I would guess that he used his influence to make it more conventional, more like the kind of show he was accustomed to see in the theatre.

At any rate, at this late date, Jed now suggested that we rewrite the last act. Phil and I disagreed strongly and, though the argument was long and violent, we stuck by our opinion. We both felt that it belonged and we refused to give it up. Jed's next criticism really stuck a knife in me. He wanted me to step down as director and be replaced by Hugh Ford. He explained that both he and Crosby felt that this man, who had more experience, was now needed. I was too flabbergasted to defend myself, but Dunning spoke for me. Phil had a very soft, warm voice and he generally spoke quietly. When angry, however, he became almost hysterical—almost inarticulate—repeating words over and over, and on that trip to Asbury Park he repeated quite a few words.

In retrospect I do not object to Jed's criticism on the ground of disloyalty; there is a loyalty to a play which supersedes even that of our friends. But I do censor his frightfully bad judgment. Had the change been made, the play would have been reduced to its lowest common denominator and been just a passable production instead of the smash that it turned out to be. We stood our ground, Jed was forced to retire from the battlefront and the tryout went well.

On opening night I sat in the balcony to be out of sight; I felt then—as I feel now—a great embarrassment at being seen on such occasions, a self-consciousness that amounts to a sense of shame, as though I were caught in public half-dressed. Also, I wanted to sit where I could go backstage quickly in case anything went wrong. But on this night nothing went wrong. The laughter seemed spontaneous; the applause was big. On opening night one is too tense to know whether it is the genuine thing or the claque —the friends, agents and relatives. By now I think I can tell the difference; there is a certain pure-gold ring to real enthusiasm that can't be duplicated by any number of well-intentioned actors' friends.

That night I hurried backstage between acts to tell the cast that things were going well. At the beginning of the third act, I began to be very sure that they were going well—as Lee Tracy made his entrance, spontaneous applause broke out which left no doubt that the people in front were telling him that he was great; I had never heard anything quite like it before. Then when the curtain calls were over and people poured backstage to tell us how good we were, they sounded as though they meant it. Sometimes it is difficult for people concerned with a production, who naturally are anxious to hear good things, to detect the difference between real and spurious praise. From long experience I have learned to suspect such phrases as "It's wonderful, darling," "I had a wonderful time," "Everybody loved it." I have found that if you are willing to pursue the matter further and say, "I'm glad you liked it, but I'm worried about that scene at the end of Act One; I don't think it's quite right," you are more likely to hear, "Well, I agree with you that there's a little something wrong there, but I thought the trouble was with the actor." John Golden always said that if you criticized your own play, you would usually find out whether others agreed with you or not.

But after *Broadway*'s opening night no one could be lured into critical remarks; enthusiasm was genuine. I felt confident that we had gone over well, and so, tired and happy, I took the subway home, to make my report to Ednah, who had preferred to stay home. Phil was going to wait up for the verdict of the critics. In those days the reviews did not reach the streets until two-thirty or three in the morning, and since there was nothing I could possibly do to improve the notices, I thought I might just as well wait until breakfast time to read them.

I didn't have to wait that long. At about five A.M. the phone rang; it was Phil. He had to tell me the good news. In a voice flooded with excited happiness—and perhaps also a drink or two—he told me of the full extent of our hit, and then he read me all the reviews from the morning papers. They were full of superlatives. No optimistic hope of mine had reached so high. Everything was perfect; *Broadway* was the hit of hits.

It is impossible to feel such extravagant, intoxicating happiness for every hit. I have not since been so emotionally overcome as by this first big success. Because I realized that it might never happen to me again I felt I must enjoy it to the full. For the next few days, I walked about in a faintly unreal condition.

Jed, who with the success of this show had become a rich man overnight, now embarked on other enterprises. He planned the production of a new play, *Spread Eagle,* which he engaged me to direct, and he gave Ann Bridgers and me a contract for *Coquette*. Life was almost too exciting to bear. I felt delirious— as though I had been inflated with pleasant oxygen and was not really touching the ground.

A few days later I touched the ground—with a thud. Jed took me aside and explained that Crosby Gaige had not realized that I was to get a percentage for directing *Broadway,* but had thought my fee was limited to two thousand dollars. He was terribly sorry, but on account of his partner there wasn't much he could do about it. I was stunned.

Jed was quite within his rights. We had no contract: I don't know that we had even discussed the deal. I, in my naïve way, had supposed that the fee which had obtained in *Love 'Em and Leave 'Em* would apply here—a very small royalty—one percent of the gross with a guarantee of two thousand dollars. I did, however, get the royalties due me as a co-author, and I had what was of much greater value—the prestige of a big hit. But I was not then as philosophical as I am now, and I burned with resentment at what I thought was a gross injustice by one who had been so close to me. A London company of *Broadway* was being planned and many road companies: I refused to direct them. Later Jed gave me five hundred dollars for each company if I would come in and give them a final polishing before they took off. To protect the play and to make five hundred dollars I agreed. Nevertheless, the schism was complete. We did business unsmilingly and with hostility—we were never friends again.

Jed now had new friends. He was lionized everywhere. He was on the way to being the boy wonder of Broadway. But even with his new and glamorous life absorbing his time and energy, I am sure that the quarrel with me must have torn him as it tore me. Psychiatrists say that some people like to suffer. Perhaps to lose one's best friends is a good way to achieve that; certainly the pattern of Jed's life was to continue in that vein. As the years went by, he had acrimonious disagreements with such other associates as George Kaufman, Thornton Wilder and Herman Shumlin.

While Jed was in the spotlight taking bows for our great success, Dunning and I were also in the line-up being given credit for our parts in it. New opportunities came to all of us. One could not be long depressed over a little financial matter with so many exciting things in the offing. Sam Harris sent for me, and when I arrived at his office I learned that Jeanne Eagels had asked him to get me as her next director. This was balm to my wounds. Mr. Harris told me frankly that another director had at first been assigned by him to do *Chicago* but that Jeanne had asked for me. I was delighted. The show was scheduled to commence rehearsals on the following Monday, but there were a few days' postponement to give me a chance to make changes in the script, and in the interval I worked with the author.

During rehearsals Jeanne was more nervous and high-strung than I had remembered her. She was taut and wary; I felt as though I were dealing with some unpredictable wild animal. But she was a great actress, and in contrast to some of our great actresses who have to mumble their words for a week or so to get the feel of the role, she was able to show her talent on the first day of rehearsal. The second day she was twenty minutes' late, the third day a half-hour late. I asked her to have lunch with me. When we finished eating, I said, "Jeanne, I want you to do me a favor."

She drew back, suspicious and tense. "What?"

"I want you to be on time."

"Oh, well, I couldn't help it this morning—I meant to be on time. I came out of the house on time but there was that man following me, and so I had to meet the car around the corner. Then the car went around the wrong corner and the man kept following me. And I had to walk all the way up to Seventy-second Street before I could get in. It wasn't my fault." She said this with such sincerity and distress that it didn't even sound odd to me. I have a one-track mind and I suppose I was only thinking of how to get her to rehearsals promptly.

"Well," I said, "it doesn't make any difference about today, but I mean in the future. If you'd be there at eleven it would be a favor to me, because I can't very well ask the others to come on time if you don't."

She looked at me blankly. "Why not?" she said.

The next day Jeanne was there ahead of me grinning like a little girl and hoping that I'd be late, but come Saturday, she was tardy again.

Jeanne had a man-servant named Tony, a big, heavy man with a little piping voice who was a sort of bodyguard who hung around the theatre to run errands for her. He told me that when Jeanne was married to Tad Coy, the great Yale football player, she used to like to see him box with their house guests. She took sadistic pleasure in seeing Tad beat up others. One day she thought she'd like to see Tony given the business; she insisted that he put on the gloves with Tad Coy. Tony didn't want to lose his job, so he played it very cozy and tried to box a defensive game; finally, however, he was stung by a blow which made him lash out, and he knocked Coy to the floor. In his little squeaky voice, Tony told me, "Of course, none of dem knew it, but I used to be de champion of de Pacific fleet. After dat Jeanie sort of respected me."

I asked Tony if he couldn't help me get Jeanne to work on time, but he became evasive. When Monday came we received word that Miss Eagels was sick. She was indeed, and she never returned to the cast. Her death was doubly tragic because it was so avoidable. If only she could have achieved a little inner peace and found some philosophy to stabilize her life, or some logic to give her control over that restless demon that drove her to all sorts of silly excesses. Her use of drugs probably accounted for the mood I found so inexplicable—but what accounted for the drug addiction? When people in the theatre prove difficult, you usually want to get away from them as soon as possible, but Jeanne Eagels' talent was so great that it was impossible to feel any resentment for her irrational behavior.

As my professional life grew so did my personal life. I made a few new friends, many new acquaintances. I joined the Harvard Club. One day Sidney Howard invited me to lunch and I found myself sitting between him and Frank Crowninshield at the Coffee House Club. I had no idea that I was there for inspection, so I was easy and natural. A week later I was invited to join.

I am not inherently much of a club member, but the Coffee House was an institution which I cherished from the start. It is a club of some three hundred members chosen from various professions in New York City. There are architects, writers, musicians, doctors, financiers, explorers and even a prize fighter. Between twenty and forty men show up for lunch each day and sit at a long table. No one needs to be introduced. The conversation is general, and shop talk is taboo. It is as easy and natural an intercommunication as I have ever found.

Then I joined another organization, the Artists & Writers Golf Club—a club without a clubhouse! A group of men who took trips ostensibly to play golf, but really just to get away from home for awhile. John Golden and Johnny Weaver were both members, and they invited Philip Dunning and me to join and to take the trip to Palm Beach which was then being planned. After due domestic consultation it was agreed, and off we went.

Taking a train has always been exciting to me; and whenever we go on the road with a show I still have that same feeling of excitement and pleasure, as if I were off to play football, as if something wonderful were going to happen just around the corner. Now I was off on a pure-fun binge, rich enough so that I didn't have to worry about the money, and conscience-free because I felt that I had earned the vacation. The day the train pulled into Florida, I was awake at daylight peeking out of my lower berth window to get my first look at a palm tree and hopping off at each station to get my first smell of the warm, tropical air.

We stayed at the Poinciana Hotel, since destroyed by a hurricane. Nearby, special tracks ran on to the Breakers Hotel, where the plutocrats parked their personal pullmans. Irving Berlin said, "I think it's wrong to keep private cars standing idle on those tracks. They should give them away to some poor family that hasn't got one."

Florida was wonderful. I couldn't play golf but I got some clubs and hacked around with the other thirty-five handicap boys, and at night I went to Bradley's and watched them gamble. Then Dunning and I met a couple of married girls on vacation whose husbands were up North, and we took them out dancing. When we called for the girls, my blonde looked at me and said, "You look like a detective." I couldn't think what she meant for a minute. It was my derby hat. I didn't know anything about Palm Beach or what one was supposed to wear; I just knew it was a swell place so I had brought my best hat.

I found that I didn't know how to dance any more. I had

been schooled in the waltz and two-step, but now they did something called the foxtrot that had a different rhythm. I was green, but after all, I was a successful Broadway character and the girls forgave me. After dancing we engaged a couple of those perambulators pedaled by an attendant (now extinct, alas) and went for a ride down the path that runs beside Lake Worth. You could smell the tuberoses in the gardens of the rich as we passed and see the swath of the moon cutting across the water. It was all very romantic. It was a taste, just a taste of something from another world.

Now I returned to work—not with Jed, but *for* Jed. I began the rehearsals of *Spread Eagle* in a belligerent frame of mind; I felt that I had been wronged, and I had a chip on my shoulder. Relations between my producer and me were strained; if he offered a criticism I was inclined to belittle it just on principle. The play was a passable success.

Tragedy sometimes comes into our lives so gradually that we hardly recognize it, except in retrospect. We fear things for ourselves or for those we love (the pain in the left side that may be fatal heart disease; why isn't he home yet—he's two hours late, he must have had an accident), and then happily it's over and the baseless fears are all quickly forgotten.

One day during an infantile-paralysis scare, our daughter Judy had symptoms that pointed toward that feared disease. Before we learned that it was a false alarm I suffered unspeakable tortures. I thought, if this child, this epitome of innocence, can be so stricken, I'll go out and blow up buildings. I was violently and irrationally angry at fate and at the false world that claimed there was a good God when such injustices could occur.

Ednah was never sick. She was one of those healthy creatures who loved to walk in the rain, never bothered to bundle up for the cold, never complained, never had any trivial ailments. Therefore, when I returned home to learn that she must go to the hospital for an operation, it was a violent shock. It was the kind of thing I couldn't believe. There was the possibility—we had to face it—that this thing might be malignant, but neither of us feared this much. It just couldn't happen to us; it was something you read about, because of course it did happen to others. I was like the soldier going into battle who knows that bullets will not find him. Ednah never learned the worst about this operation, but I did. Since she was required to go back for x-ray treatments, I think she probably suspected something. Success was hoped for, but we would have to "wait and see."

At the time I was collaborating with Dana Burnett, the novelist, on *Four Walls,* a tragedy, or perhaps a melodrama (the border between them is very fine), about the return home of a Jewish boy just out of prison. We needed for this role that impossible thing, an actor of power and maturity who was young in years. Muni Wisenfriend, a graduate of the Yiddish Art Theatre, was playing an old man in his first Broadway appearance and when I was told that he was really in his twenties I couldn't believe it, but an interview discovered him to be not only young but personable. How exciting theatre business becomes when you suddenly strike gold in this fashion. We engaged not only him but his wife Bella Finkle. The play was a solid success and launched Muni Wisenfriend, later to be known as Paul Muni, on the English speaking stage. It also gave Dore Schary, one of the supernumeraries, his start on Broadway.

My relations with Jed had worsened. The rift had been magnified, and now there was only undisguised animosity between us. We seldom met, and when we did it was to say violent things. However, he held the contract for *Coquette* and now planned to do it. I couldn't bear to work in the same theatre with him and I refused to direct it, so he engaged another director. Ann Bridgers and I had always wanted Helen Hayes for our play but had failed to interest her in the script, Jed now was more persistent and more persuasive, and she agreed to the lead.

When rehearsals started, Ann attended; I did not. Three days later, while I was working with the understudies of *Four Walls* I received word that Helen Hayes wanted to see me. When we met, she told me that the show was going badly, and that it was my duty to resolve my differences with Jed and to take over the direction. I told Miss Hayes that I would do so on one consideration: that Jed stay away from the rehearsals. She delivered the ultimatum and, I suppose, added pressure of her own. It was accepted. For the three weeks of rehearsals of *Coquette,* I never saw my ex-partner. Sometimes I was aware of a vague and sinister figure slithering among the shadows of the top balcony, but that was hardly enough intrusion to upset me.

Coquette didn't go well in Atlantic City. To use the actors' phrase, it was a bit heavy for the peasants. From there we went to Philadelphia, and though it had partisans, again it got a bad reception. I'll always remember Lee Shubert, who was supposed to be purely a commercial manager, expressing his unstinting praise and his confidence in this show. Jed, of course, was now in the picture again, and he reverted to his old tactics; there was some restless demon in that man that made him always have to seek changes. In a new script this could mean intelligent, constructive criticism, but when the play was further along his compulsion only hurt the enterprise. Once again I resisted him and we had harsh words, but we opened at the Maxine Elliott without the changes.

Coquette was a great hit. It was the weeping wonder of the world—I don't ever think I've seen so many people sob in a theatre as they did during this play.

From then on I saw nothing of Jed. Of course, I heard about him because he was now established as the Little Napoleon of Broadway, the darling of the critics and intelligentsia. He told people that he was the most intelligent, perceptive man in the history of the theatre, and a great many of his listeners were persuaded by his eloquence. He had almost persuaded me, and I found myself thinking, After all, the two biggest hits I ever had were with Jed. Perhaps he is the cause; perhaps his energy and impulse brings out the best in me. I said to Dunning on one occasion, "Do you suppose Jed is really as smart as he thinks he is?" Dunning considered the question for quite a time and then he said, "Well, the theatre was always here, he didn't invent it."

For several years Jed's star continued in the ascendancy. He produced such great successes as *Front Page* and *The Royal Family*, both directed by George Kaufman. Later there was *Our Town*. He charmed many, but he antagonized many. And before long he lost those who had been his greatest admirers.

My early admiration and fondness for Jed eventually turned into a wholehearted, uncomplicated hate. I wanted to smash him in the face—in fact, I often thought of doing just that. Then when

I pictured myself being hauled into court for beating up a man so much smaller, I would drop the idea. As I look back upon the really glorious halcyon days of our first friendship, I am full of regrets that we ended up in bitterness and recrimination.

Jealousy is an ignoble emotion. I used to think that professional jealousy was a peculiar disease of the theatre, but I have since observed that soap manufacturers, used-car dealers and others also suffer. However, because of the publicity which attends those who work in the theatre, our jealousies or energies are probably the biggest and best.

I was not immune from this affliction in those early days. I was jealous—particularly of Jed. I had that childish feeling of being unappreciated; but Ednah, for whom I have so many things to thank, was a soothing influence. She tried to persuade me that temporary credit didn't really matter, that what happened from day to day was relatively unimportant. That I should enjoy my work and let the chips fall where they may, that the doing was what counted and where the real happiness lay.

How glad I am that I was able to accept this philosophy, that I have been spared during the ensuing years from wasting time worrying about what the other fellow did or said. Oh, I do not claim that all vanity is gone, that it does not please me to be thought talented. But I think I have been able to put that emotion in its proper place. I could now ask for more grandiose billing, but I think perhaps it is caution not modesty that deters me: it is fine to be in big type for a hit but it is embarrassing for a failure. Besides it seems bad taste. To have a credit read "Entire production conceived and staged by John Doe" is ridiculous. It's like saying "Entire part of Mother played by Lizzy Flop." But, to confess the whole truth, when I see my name in lights and know that the producer put me up there because he wanted to, not because my contract demanded it, I am pleased. Thomas Jefferson once wrote a disgruntled friend, "Go on deserving applause and you will meet with it!"

Back in those days of the late twenties I was getting one credit which I didn't deserve. I was now considered the "play doctor" *par excellence.* I was a genius; I could fix anything. Unfortunately, I began to believe my own publicity and I tackled almost any assignment that was offered me. Thus, for a while I was connected with a great many indifferent plays that should have been allowed to die peacefully on the road. I have no doubt that I made them better, but it is one thing to take a script, rewrite it and recast it from the beginning, and it is quite another to go out on the road with a cast already selected by someone else, and in the limited time given you refashion it into a big hit.

Then in 1928 I went to Hollywood. Talking pictures had just begun, and I was one of those who felt that this medium was going to be important. I welcomed the chance to enter this new field, and when Paramount made me an offer I accepted. To break me in they asked me to do a short subject in their eastern studio. It was called *The Bishop's Candlestick*, starring Walter Huston, and since they liked it I was soon off to the coast to try my hand at a longer picture.

Al Capp says that Hollywood is the place where they give you the warm hello and the cold goodbye. And that for various reasons is what is likely to happen. You are greeted with enthusiasm, flowers in the room and a car at the door, and made to feel very important. Later, it is gradually impressed upon you that while there are certain things which may be artistically fine in the East, they don't go in pictures. You are made to understand that you are not writing for Broadway but for Oshkosh, and that if you don't want your picture to be an abysmal flop you had better heed the words of wisdom of those who know the business.

Hollywood has changed in many ways since the early days, but in other respects it is still the same. There is a kind of pretension and falsity woven into the texture of the place; it is the phony, phony land. People pretend to be richer than they are, more successful than they are, better fathers, better lovers, better friends —even better losers. They read the best books, listen to the best music, and make a great show of culture, but their real passion is the daily gossip columns. No big party is complete without the presence of one of the lady columnists. Of course, pretension and keeping up with the Joneses isn't limited to Southern California, but somehow it seems to be more *naked* in the picture industry. The actor, writer or director who comes to Hollywood is supposed to live up to a certain standard: to have the kind of car in vogue at the moment; to take a big house; to have a swimming pool; to entertain; to gamble for big stakes. Only a few non-conformists resist this pressure.

In 1928 Maurice Chavalier was the highest-paid man in Hollywood. He was getting fifteen thousand dollars a week, but being a frugal Frenchman he had no notion of spending it according to the local pattern. The studio heads were greatly embarrassed over the fact that Chevalier always drove to work in a second-hand Ford, and he heightened this indignity by parking the car across the way where it was free instead of paying a quarter in the regular parking lot.

B. P. Schulberg was the executive producer at Paramount. My work often brought me to the studio late at night and nearly always I saw a light burning in Mr. Schulberg's office. He had arrived that morning twelve hours earlier. I had once been tempted to try and make good in the executive branch of Hollywood; there was lots of money in it, and the competition didn't seem to be severe. But when I visited Mr. Schulberg in his office and heard the constant nagging detail which pressed down on him at all times, and when I saw the long hours that he worked, I decided that this was not the life for one who was interested in health, love and play.

My first picture—a farce called *Why Bring That Up?*—was shot mostly at night. There had been a fire at Paramount which had destroyed some of the sound stages, and therefore we had to work in the open a great deal and to choose a time when there was as little noise as possible to intrude upon the microphone. I worked hard and fast, and because it was new it was exciting. It all seemed very romantic to me, and as I walked home at five A.M., listening to the mockingbirds singing in the stillness of the first faint suggestions of dawn, I felt lonely and nostalgic and happy.

One of the greatest pleasures of success is the ability to reward those who have stood by you in the thin times which preceded it. Long before this I had repaid my mother the money she had lent me, and I could not, bromidic though it sounds, ever repay her for the love she had given me, or her faith in me, or the tenacity with which she had labored to make me a worth-while and successful person, but perhaps by giving security to the latter part of her life I contributed toward making them her happiest years. My father's reformation contributed another part. They were now living together in a small house that just fitted my mother's housekeeping needs, and they had a car which my mother drove with frightening assurance.

Their home life was not exactly ideal: like so many other homes it was a compromise. I am glad from a selfish point of view that my father married a superior woman, but I suspect that it would have been better for him had he married a docile one. My mother being a perfectionist was a bit of a nag—small things had to be just right. He never argued with her, but with long-suffering patience he would reply, "Yes, May." But once closeted in the privacy of his bedroom a different character would emerge. He became a lion. Unaware that the sound carried, he would hold forth commandingly. These violent fantasy scenes of his were never about his wife or his home but always about his other life. He would transport himself to the environment he truly loved—uptown, the club, the society of men—and his commanding voice could be heard laying down the law, pontificating about politics or giving somebody hell. At home he felt guilty, the man who must forever atone for the unhappiness he had caused: uptown among his fellows he was important, a Supervisor of Erie County, a man who was honored at banquets by Masons, firemen and Republicans.

My visits home were not a great success. Since nearly all my memories of Hamburg were distressing, I was uncomfortable there. My weak attempts to gain contact with my father during these years of his respectability were a failure; our former antagonism could not be entirely erased. He would try to talk to me about the theatre, but the theatre is a secret society which has its own language and cannot be communicated to outsiders. Willing though one may be to explain and to answer questions, the life which seems so exciting to you is dust-dry when said in words to the uninitiated.

Moreover, I still resented my father's constant desire to make a good impression on people, his political instinct to always butter up his friends. Walking down the street in Hamburg, he would whisper, "There's Mr. Kleinfelder across the street. Say hello to Mr. Kleinfelder." Such prompting only drove me further into my shell. Papa was proud of me because I was a success, but beyond that I fear I gave him very little satisfaction. My daughter, however, since there was no disturbing past to destroy the relationship, was fond of her grandfather and gave him some of the love I could not. They corresponded regularly and had an easy and affectionate way with each other.

My mother knew the score, but by this time she could not possibly have checked her impulse to criticize. Her sense of humor, however, never deserted her—and whether the crisis was large or small, some objective faculty stayed outside and looked at it with amusement. Apropos of her relations to my father, I remember an incident. My father, as Supervisor of Erie County, kept an office in Hamburg, but when he resigned, the office automatically ceased to have a function. Now, on the previous Christmas I had given them each one thousand dollars to be used for some frivolous purpose. I suggested a trip, and my mother took my advice. One day she said to me, "Would you like to know what your father did with his money?"

I said I would.

"He kept his office."

"What for?"

"To get away from me," she said, and we both laughed.

Mother hated growing old. I confess that I used to be embarrassed at some of her getups. She would arrive in New York for a visit with a hat that belonged on a girl in her twenties. It was almost grotesque to see her old face with slightly rouged cheeks and the rimless glasses looking out from under a rosebush.

What we wear and how we wear it may not expose our whole character to the observer, but it offers many clues. This is equally true of our faces, our speech, our locomotion and our handwriting (since having learned something about graphology I confess that I am a little worried about the way I sometimes cross my *t*'s! I find a symbol there of intolerance and impatience), and our choice in art. Even when my family was at its poorest, the pictures on the wall indicated my mother's aspirations. Once when I was at Leonard Bernstein's I was struck by the similarity of the pictures he had chosen. They were turbulent, modern. Many of them, to my inexperienced eye, looked like tortured guts. It occurred to me that he chose these paintings because in his heart he enjoyed confusion and emotional upset. Then I realized how different was the choice of pictures on my walls. I liked Chinese art—peaceful mountains and valleys. Once in Rome I entered an apartment which was different from any I had ever seen. It was beautiful; everything in it was perfect, but it was simple and peaceful because it was so uncluttered. I don't like a cluttered life and I don't like a cluttered room.

Like other American males, I often took my wife with me when I bought clothes. Once I selected a hat, the brim of which turned down all the way around, but Ednah vetoed it violently. She said it was "too Broadway," and so I ended up with a conservative Homburg. Many months later out in Hollywood, I added to my wardrobe from time to time and when I met Ednah at the railroad station out there her first words were, "Where did you get that hat?" I had all unconsciously acquired a new hat with a brim turned down all around. Something in me had craved that kind of hat; it was an exhibition of my desire to be a little more dashing, a little less conventional, and without any conscious intent it had found expression.

Manslaughter was the best picture I made because it had the most believable story. Claudette Colbert and Fredric March were superb in the leading parts. One of the scenes demanded that the heroine be photographed water skiing. We had a double ready to do this; since it was to be a long shot, no harm would come of this conventional subterfuge. But Claudette was jealous of her work and she didn't want a double. She said that she would learn how to water ski if he would delay the shot until the afternoon. Grimly determined, she spent hours in the cold water and hot sun, and when the time came she was ready and we didn't use the double.

People often think of actresses as pampered creatures with no particular force of character, but they have a will power and a resolution that is astounding. They are much more aggressive and violent in the pursuit of their careers than most of their male counterparts.

Then came the panic of 1929. In Hollywood, just as everywhere else, people stood around unable to believe the disaster which had overtaken them. I remember that my friend Johnny

Weaver was trying to run his small stake up to thirty thousand dollars before he took his profits, but the day before he planned to sell the collapse came, and by that evening he owed eleven thousand dollars. I was unaffected by the panic because I had sold out two years before. I had then watched ruefully as the market went up and up, but I had not succumbed to the temptation to buy in again. Because Ednah liked business and because I felt that she hadn't enough to do, I had turned over a large sum to her to use for real estate investments. She had taken second mortgages on new building developments. To her, the word mortgage had a pleasant, safe sound, while the word stock sounded evil and reckless. The sad truth turned out to be that the money put in second mortgages was all lost while that put in stocks more than held its own.

In the midst of all this I received an offer from Universal Pictures to work on *All Quiet on the Western Front*. Maxwell Anderson had originally been assigned to this task but seemed to be having some trouble with the picture technique or with Junior Laemmle—I never quite understood which—and now they were scheduled to start shooting without a script. I was paid a magnificent salary to rewrite the picture, and when it came out it had one of those baffling credit lines: "Screen Story by George Abbott, Adaptation by Maxwell Anderson, Dialogue by Maxwell Anderson and George Abbott." I wonder if I fought to get all that. I can't remember.

Just as I finished this job there came distressing news from the East. I had been aware that Ednah was not well—not from anything she said, for her letters contained no hint of trouble, but because one or another relative from Rochester always seemed to be staying with her. I did not know, however, how serious the situation was until her brother Arthur called me and said that he thought I ought to come home. I explained the situation to the heads of the studio, and they showed more heart than is generally attributed to large corporations by arranging immediately for me to do the work I owed them in their Long Island studios.

Ednah had not wanted me to come home. She didn't want me to see her in her present condition, and she was furious at her brother for calling me. The fact that I had been sent for furthermore alarmed her, for despite the worsening of her condition, she had believed the doctor's optimistic patter and thought that she would soon be well again. Now she wanted to know. That dread word cancer was not spoken in those days, and she said, "I want to know if it's that same thing. If it is and I'm going to die, then I have to make plans."

I went to the doctor and asked him to tell me the truth. He said, "No one can bear the truth. I've had a disease which I thought was fatal, and I know what I'm talking about. You can do no good and only harm if you tell her." From him I learned that Ednah had only a few months to live.

I don't suppose anyone knows what he would do in such a situation until it occurs. I let Ednah know the truth. I didn't say it bluntly; I didn't come right out with the flat statement, but the very fact that I did not give her a definite reassurance was a confession that her fears were justified. She knew.

The selflessness and nobility of this woman were now thrown into bright relief as never before. There was no self-pity, no thought of anything except what had to be done for those she was to leave behind. Ednah's sister Florence, who had four children, lived in Rochester, and Ednah felt that it would be best for Judy to be brought up with them. We would move up there as soon as possible, take a large house near the school, and install the combined families while there was still time.

Having made these arrangements, Ednah wished to protect Judy financially, and so we went to the Chase National Bank and set up a trust fund for Judy and a smaller one for me. This latter fund was necessary in case I should fall victim to some designing actress and be bilked of all my money. Ednah somehow had a picture of me—not shared by any of my other intimates—as one who was financially irresponsible, a sort of reckless gambler. The agreement with the Chase National Bank was an irrevocable one in which they handled the securities without any consent of mine. This proved to be a great mistake; Mr. Chase didn't do very well by that fund, and it shrank by over half in a very short time.

After we had established the new routine in Rochester, Ednah waited to die almost impatiently, for she hated invalidism. During this dreadful period I met many old friends and made new ones and saw something of life in a small city, from a point of view which, of course, had changed since the days when I was an undergraduate. I was surprised and a little dismayed at the amount of drinking the well-to-do people of Rochester seemed to find necessary, as well as by the fact that their conversation seemed to lean so heavily on dirty stories. There was very little freedom for adventurous souls in a city like Rochester. In New York a sex-minded husband can easily get lost, but in Rochester it is easy to keep track of where everyone is. Illicit sex among the upper classes seemed to be rudely handicapped; adultery was at a low ebb. As a consequence, steam had to be let off in other directions, and so one had to listen to a great many bawdy jokes, most of them humorless except for their shock content.

Ednah died. It was what she wished. She was so distressed at being a nuisance that she had wanted to be moved to a hospital where she would not inconvenience anybody. One night she said, "I don't suppose there is any after life, but if there is I hope I see my father there." This was particularly touching to me because I had seldom heard her speak of her father, who had died when she was a little girl. Then she grew worse, and her last words were a barely audible "To the hospital." She died as she lived—thinking of others.

There was no hysteria in the household and the children were temporarily kept ignorant of the death. Suddenly I realized that I hadn't seen Judy for a long time and I inquired as to her whereabouts. No one had seen her. After a search, she was located hiding in a closet on the top floor of the house. No one had told her, but she knew. She had gone off to hide and suffer by herself without tears.

Fifteen or twenty people, half-familiar faces, mostly women, stood beside the grave. Ednah's younger sister Elsie, who had come from Cleveland, was late. To relieve the tension I made a joke. It sounded crass and unfeeling, and I was ashamed of my clumsy ineptitude.

Ednah and I both had rejected the idea of any formal funeral. A minister appeared, of what denomination I know not, probably Lutheran, because Elmer Fisher played the organ in a Lutheran church. He read the Twenty-third Psalm. The hot salt tears began to flow down my face and into my mouth. My chest ached, my ribcase seemed to contract. I felt as if I couldn't breathe. I would have to gasp or choke; perhaps I sobbed, others were doing so, they wouldn't have noticed me. I was devastated not from a sense of loss, but from an overwhelming pity. Suddenly life seemed so futile, so unjust. To think that this good, good woman should be reduced to misery by a degrading and terrible disease as a reward for a life of unselfishness and self-sacrifice. It was more than I could bear.

Dust to dust. It was over. We went back to the house talking calmly and exchanging wan smiles. I regarded my daughter—she seemed all right. She was with her cousins and her aunt. It was best. I went for a walk to be away from them, and the world seemed very still. Finally the time came for me to take the train back to New York. I was glad to get away from this sad place. The goodbyes were finally over and I was safely under the blankets in my berth. The train went hurtling through the night, and I pulled the blankets around me like a shield, for I began to have a guilty feeling of great exaltation. There was a whole, new, different life waiting for me. The click, clack of the wheels kept saying, "You're free, you're free, you're free!"

Part Four

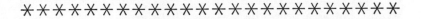

SOMETIMES FATE SNEAKS UP ON YOU. Sometimes a great change takes place in your life without the realization coming to you till long after the event. Sometimes, however, you are aware that a change is occurring. When I came back to New York from Rochester I knew that I was entering a new and different life. When I left Hamburg and went off to college, I had hoped that I would enter a new life. I planned with all my might to turn over a new leaf, to leave behind that trouble-making character, Francis Abbott, and become an agreeable fellow named George Abbott. Now, as I came back to New York, I had not planned to turn over any new leaf, but fate had done that for me. Indeed, it opened a whole chapter of new leaves.

I had left the city a domesticated animal; I had been traveling in double harness. Now suddenly I had no harness at all—I was absolutely free to go or come as I pleased. My new life started out prosaically enough. I moved into a modest hotel on Fifty-first Street and then reported for work at Paramount's Long

Island studio. Walter Wanger, a debonair and charming young man recently out of Dartmouth, was in charge. Though he was enthusiastic and eager to do better things in the picture medium, my first assignment was anything but avant-garde. It was a vehicle for Claudette Colbert and Fredric March called *Secrets of a Secretary*, it had been written by Charles Brackett, and I was assigned to work with him on the script and then to direct it.

I liked Brackett. Practically everybody liked him—he was that sort of person. He came from a background of culture and wealth, but as a friend he was simplicity itself. In fact, he was almost insecure. His father had wanted him to be a lawyer and he had gone through the disagreeable task of passing the bar examinations before turning to his real love, writing.

One day Charlie and I were discussing the possibility of losing all our money, of being wiped out—a subject which was discussed by a great many people in those days, for it was at the height of the great depression. I said, "If you lose your money, it doesn't matter because you inherited it, but if I lose mine, it's tough because I had to work for it." Charlie shook his head and wagged his finger at me. "Oh no, my boy, if you lose your money, you know you can make some more because you've already done it. But if I lose mine, it's a real tragedy because nobody is going to give me any more." I could see his point. Neither of us was wiped out, however, and Charlie, in the course of events, became one of Hollywood's top producers and writers and earned more than his father had ever given him.

I now began to enjoy a delightful phase of life which most men experience in their twenties. I began to go out with girls, to have dates. This was all new to me. In my high school days I'd had no money, and later my bond to Ednah had prohibited any such frivolity. Now, at the age of forty-three, I began to write down telephone numbers.

As I look back on it, it is a wonder that any girl went out with me. I was a puritanical and exacting escort. It was the day of speak-easies, but I wouldn't go near one, nor would I buy a girl a drink. I felt that since prohibition was a law, it should be obeyed; furthermore, I hated tobacco and it seems to me that I was always asking girls to move to the other side of the table so that the smoke wouldn't blow in my face.

Actually, in my heart, I still justify my bigotry. Laws should be obeyed. Not that prohibition was a good law, but that I do think the flouting of it by the leaders of society encouraged a lawlessness whose harvest we are still reaping. If it is all right to patronize a speak-easy, then it must be all right to operate one. The low-class citizens got rich furnishing liquor for the high-class citizens, and today their contemporary imitators are getting rich circumventing laws against narcotics or gambling. As for smoking, the reformers call it a filthy habit—and it is. Where this habit is concerned, all sense of neatness seems to be forsworn. If the banker, the statesman and the college professor throws his cigarette on the sidewalk, can you censure the Bowery bum for doing the same? It surprises me that intelligent people should be so infected by a passion for conformity that they themselves get involved in the ridiculous business of puffing smoke into their lungs. Even though they may have begun smoking in their youth in order to prove that they were grown-up, one would think that after a brief survey of the insurance statistics on the subject they would give it up in maturity. End of lecture.

Occasionally Charlie Brackett talked to me about a group of men and women who lunched at a round table in the Algonquin Hotel and who were known as the Algonquin Set. Charlie was on intimate terms with most of them, and his stories of their wit, pranks, feuds and friendships fascinated me. No matter what animosities divided them, Charlie told me, there was one person who commanded their united affection: Neysa McMein. Fame is fleeting and the public no longer remembers her name, but at that time every taxi-cab driver, every salesgirl, every reader of columns, knew about the fabulous Neysa. By profession she was an artist who worked in pastels, and she was the highest-paid illustrator in the country. But she was also, by avocation, a hostess at whose studio many bright and attractive people were drawn, and from which countless witticisms were reported to the hoi polloi. H. G. Wells was said to have spent a part of every day there during a visit to New York; it was in Neysa's studio that Charles MacArthur met Helen Hayes; it was there that Dorothy Parker dropped her most unkind cuts.

I was particularly interested in what Charlie said about Miss McMein because I had once met this famous woman. Before we went to Rochester I had attended a large party at the Coffee House Club and there sitting with a group of people I heard a woman say, "Look at Neysa McMein. She's just like one of her pictures." I turned and recognized the graceful posture of the pretty girls I had seen on the covers of *McCall's* magazine. I would not have recognized Miss McMein, although I did know that we had once met in the great confusion of a dozen people in Minnie Maddern Fiske's dressing room, but after a moment I summoned up my courage to go over and speak to her. To my great relief she was surprisingly cordial. She invited me to join her for supper. Even in the dim lights of the Coffee House Club I could tell that she was not as young as I had thought, but her way was soft and young and so was her voice. She had green eyes, a large mouth—then very much in style—and tawny molasses-colored hair. Though she was taller than the average woman, she seemed always graceful and almost fragile.

I told Miss McMein that I wasn't sure that she'd remember me. On the contrary, she reassured me, she had heard my name so much of late that she was getting bored with it. One of her models was in love with me. I was dumbfounded. Yes, she said, this girl had seen me in two or three shows, and she could talk about nothing else. What shows, I wanted to know, but here Miss McMein became a little vague. I was to discover as time went by that this charming woman often became vague.

She told me that her name was pronounced Neesa McMeen, not, as I had thought, Nasa McMine. She said that her real name was Marjorie but that when she was young she had named herself after a beautiful Arabian horse. Her married name was Baragwanath. She pointed out her husband, who stood across the room surrounded by a laughing group, a position which I was to discover was his natural orbit. He was a dark, handsome man whom one might have taken for an Italian or a Spaniard. Miss McMein also told me something of their life. They had a perfect understanding, and each went out without the other. For instance, she loved opera and he hated music; why should she inflict her taste upon him? She loved movies, she said, and then somebody came and took her away.

So now, many months later, I decided to call her. I feared that she was simply being kind to me before and that any attempt to intrude on her life might be met with a cold reception, but such fears were groundless. She invited me to lunch.

On the great day I arrived punctually and was shown into the big studio. Miss McMein was at her easel working, and on the stand in front of her stood a naked model. Neysa introduced me to Miss Naked offhandedly and waved me to a seat. I sank into the chair trying to act the part of a poised man of the world who was used to being around artists and naked women. I wasn't quite sure where one was supposed to look under these circumstances; I didn't want to avert my gaze, nor did I want to stare. The sky, which on that day was a drab nothing, became very fascinating and I gazed out of the window a good deal of the time. My hostess looked very unlike the chic woman I had met at the party. She wore an old blue smock smeared with many colors of the pastel with which she was working. There were also several unrelated smears on her face and even in her hair, and her hands were a mess. As I became acclimated, I discovered that the model was a pleasingly robust young woman, but I did wonder how the artist could get such long-legged pictures out of such a short-legged girl.

Lunch was announced. Neysa took off her smock, Miss Naked put on hers, they washed their faces, and we sat down. How exciting all this was to me. This small adventure into bohemia, this contact wtih the famous artist. Sometimes Miss Naked's robe would fall back a little, revealing too much neckline, which had a very sexy effect and made me realize the old truism that clothes enhance by what they conceal. The conversation was not earth-shaking but it was easy. The world seemed full of charm and I full of a great happy ego as I talked about myself and my work.

During the ensuing weeks I took Neysa to the movies two or three times. She had a childlike enthusiasm for motion pictures, no matter how bad they were. When I called for her, I would sometimes meet her husband. Jack would be going out for the evening on one of his dates. I felt uncomfortable with him, but he seemed perfectly at ease and talked to me in a friendly manner about the best places to take a date. He recommended one little club in particular—he referred to it as the cheaters' paradise. He was a man of the world, all right.

. . .

At Paramount I began work on another picture. It was called *Stolen Heaven;* Nancy Carroll, at that time a very popular star, was to have the lead. I remember the movie largely for two things: the Cuban orchestra and later the trip to Havana.

I had sometime before this seen a picture called *Hell's Harbor,* which had a Cuban setting and which portrayed a group of natives playing exciting music. The percussion instruments used were all new to me, the sound was new, and I thought of this music as some particularly delicious kind of jazz. When I had to choose an orchestra for *Stolen Heaven,* which was set in Palm Beach, I immediately set out to find one from Cuba. By this time I had learned that the rhythm which I liked so much was called rumba in this country—quite erroneously, I may say. Rumba is a very fast rhythm usually used for exhibition dancing, but there is also a medium rhythm called Son, a slower rhythm called Danson, and Dansonetta and Bolero, and the most charming Wahita. Then there is also La Conga, a rhythm which the slaves sang, pausing every fourth beat to pull up the chains as they plodded along.

The band in the picture was only a partial success because we didn't know how to dance to it. I asked the members of the orchestra to show me and they tried, but this was much too subtle a dance to be picked up so easily. As a result, our rhythms were authentic, but the dancing was a sort of bastard foxtrot.

Another chance to get acquainted with Cuban rhythms was soon presented to me. On their yearly trip south the Artists and Writers were going to Havana. Because of the depression, tourism had come to a practical standstill in Cuba, but now an energetic young reformer, a sergeant in the army named Batista, had thrown out the corrupt politicians and was going to institute great changes. He wanted the Americans to come there once again, and the Tourists Commission offered us incredibly low rates to bring our outing to their city.

On these trips the artists sometimes took their wives or their girl friends. One well-known writer took his two sons and his mistress on a trip, and there were various assorted relatives and secretaries welcome to go along if somebody paid for them.

Nancy Carroll had two girl friends who often visited her on

the set. One day, in the course of small talk, I suggested that they all come with us on the trip to Havana. They seemed interested in the idea, so I told them what ship we were taking, where we were going to stay and how much it cost. I dismissed their plans to go along as just wishful thinking, but when the Artists and Writers appeared at the dock to embark for Havana, there were the three girls. This, as you may imagine, caused great excitement among the middle-aged lads. Everyone wanted to meet Nancy. I was traveling with Charlie Brackett and Philip Dunning, and we had a conference. Should we fight off the wolves and stake out a claim on these girls, or should we let them be on their own? Phil said, "I think it's practical to let somebody else buy the champagne."

It was a great trip. We all stayed at the Nacional Hotel and were practically the only guests. These dignified men, these members of the intelligentsia probably feeling free from all convention for the first time in years, reverted to their boyhood and behaved like a group of sophomores on the loose. Everybody drank a great deal, and one of the chief topics of conversation was how much everyone had drunk. It was a subject of extreme interest, and somehow something that was supposed to be very funny. Eight married men fell in love with Nancy Carroll, who I may say conducted herself with great dignity throughout. There was jealousy and many bitter quarrels in her honor. One night Jeff Machamer broke down the door to the girls' apartment at four A.M. He had nothing serious in mind; it was just his way of showing that he was in there pitching. He had to pay for the door. On a slightly higher plane, Deke Aylesworth and Jack Wheeler put an eel in their bathtub and then placed bets that no one could get it out. A great many drunken artists fell into the tub, but nobody got the eel out until Montgomery Flagg remembered that in seafood restaurants waiters used a napkin to lift the creature out of the tank.

After three days of glorious away-from-the-cares-of-the-world unrestraint, we embarked on a little steamer for Key West. In the Seasick Regatta I will match that trip from Havana to Key West against the crossing of the English Channel any day in the week. We landed slightly green but happy, and took off for Palm Beach to finish the golf tournament, which, however, could only be an anticlimax. It was one of those trips about which we would never stop talking.

At the Long Island studio, *My Sin* by Owen Davis was waiting for me with Tallulah Bankhead as the star. This unique personality had been touted as the coming thing in the motion-picture world. She had already made two pictures for Paramount directed by George Cukor, but they had been a disappointment financially. Indeed, this was the fate of all her pictures; Tallulah's flamboyance and theatricality charmed the sophisticated world, but the bobbysoxers and housewives and folks out in the Middle West never bought it.

Tallulah's conversation was rough—she liked to shock, and she seemed to want everybody to think the worst of her. Each morning when I went to her dressing room to talk over the day's shooting she would be putting on her make-up wearing some flimsy thing which made her seem almost naked from the waist up. This was not intended to be alluring; it was simply sheer indifference. Tallulah was never coquettish in any way when we were alone, but on the set she would sometimes make quite a fuss over me. Once when the set was filled with extras waiting for the next shot, she came over and sat down in my lap and said, "I hope they all think we're lovers." But on another occasion she confessed, "I only fall in love with cads. I could never be mad about you, darling George. You're too reliable. I'd always know where you were."

Tallulah liked to take exotic baths. Once I went to her apartment to help pour a huge can of milk into the bathtub. In all fairness, I should add that I was not invited to stay for the main event.

My Sin was not a very good picture, and the next one which I was supposed to work on promised to be even worse. Since the studio had fallen behind in its schedule through no fault of mine, I asked to be released, and I suppose they thought it was a good idea, for they quickly agreed. I returned to Broadway to direct a farce called *Louder, Please,* by Norman Krasna.

When summer came, the Baragwanaths moved to Long Island, and Neysa invited me to drive out for lunch one Sunday. They lived in Sands Point in a beautiful English house of about twenty rooms. It was of white-washed bricks and vines climbed up the walls; there were giant oaks everywhere and little groups of dogwood clustering under them. I was shown through the house to the terrace, where Neysa sat alone having breakfast. It was a lovely sunny day and very still. The house, I learned, was full of sleeping guests; there had been a big party the night before. Then gradually the guests began to appear and the host himself, and the terrace became filled with talk and laughter. It seems that Jack's coördination was not at its highest peak when he had arrived at five A.M., and he had missed the garage door and wrecked the car. After lunch we played croquet. My first reaction to this game of my childhood was one of contempt, but I soon discovered that my sneers were premature. Instead of the little wooden implement which I remembered, I found in my hand a mallet that weighed about as much as a sledge hammer. I discovered that the balls too were different, that the distances they could be driven was great, that the boundaries were unlimited and that the wickets were narrow. I found, indeed, that I was a very incompetent player, an amateur among a group of professionals. This particular type of croquet, using English equipment, has since spread to Hollywood and a few other places. Each locality has some special rules, but in all of them strategy is the most important part of the game. It is not simply getting through wickets that counts; it is getting through wickets at the right moment. Like other beginners, I didn't understand this, and argued with my partner, Jack, that I should go through the wicket while I had a chance. I irritated him a good deal. I imagine we lost.

However, I did get asked back to Sands Point. I spent a couple of weekends with the Baragwanaths during the summer and participated in a life which was new and exhilarating to me. I had no desire to be in "society," but it was exciting to be able to observe it from the periphery. These people all knew each other and had many things in common, and while they were always scrupulously polite to an outsider, they could not always talk down to his level. Most of the time I sat silently and listened to conversation which might almost as well have been in a foreign language. You heard the words, but unless you knew the code, you couldn't comprehend. Among the initiates, however, there was not the slightest confusion as they spoke glibly of Maggie, Jack, Jock, Cobina, Babs, Sonny, Marie, Isabel, Fay, Madeleine, Lil, Dumpy, Joy, Dolly, Lurelle, Babe, Grace, Millicent, Herbert, Billy, Joan, Liz, Harry, Ted, Byron, Hope, Nicky, Baby, Mona, Dick, Ruth, Raoul, Sister, Brother, Jules, Hank, Laddie, Averell, Harold, and That Son-of-a-Bitch. The latter, of course, was in the White House. There were several Maggies and Maries, but no one ever seemed to have the slightest doubt as to whether the Tommy referred to was Tommy the polo player, or Tommy the piano player.

That winter Neysa decided to take a trip to the Mediterranean and Egypt with Alice Duer Miller and Mr. and Mrs. Paul Hyde Bonner. She asked me if I wanted to go along. Did I! Neysa was the ideal traveling companion—enthusiastic, romantic, imaginative, sensitive and urbanely witty and charming. Alice Miller, the author of *The White Cliffs of Dover*, was a cool, calm and aristocratic New England lady, well-informed, humorous and controlled. Indicative of Alice's character was the fact that she smoked exactly three times a day—one cigarette after each meal. We did not pick up the Bonners, whom I had never met before, until Naples. Mrs. Bonner was rich and social; her husband was handsome, affable, and not only social, for later in life he proved to be a worker by writing several successful novels.

In the winter of 1933 we sailed from New York on an Italian ship. The second day out I found myself itching, and when I reported to the ship's doctor it was discovered that some Latin parasites had moved in on me. All my clothes were sent to the laundry, and to assuage my feelings I was assigned to a royal suite of grand proportions. I decided that it was almost worth while being lousy.

We landed at Nice in a cold, drizzly spring rain, and had lunch with some friends of Neysa's. That evening I tried out my tango on Enrico Caruso's widow. Then on to Naples, where I looked out my hotel window and saw the real, live, authentic Vesuvius sending her glow into the evening sky. We visited that incredible proof of the past, Pompeii, where the little houses, little streets and little beds reminded us that the fierce, powerful Romans were actually very small in stature. It was hard to believe that these small people could defeat the giant Gauls with a sword and spear. But here they had lived; their chariot wheel-tracks were still in the pavement, and their drinking fountains still stood in the streets.

After crossing the Mediterranean we got on a little train for Cairo. The Semiramis Hotel there was clean and lovely. From my terrace I could see the pyramids in the distance. Suddenly a high wailing sound came keening through the air. I knew what it was, but I couldn't believe it—it all seemed unreal. In the distance was a mosque and high up on the minaret was a hooded figure walking slowly around and calling the faithful to prayers.

As our ship had approached Egypt the previous day, Neysa had discovered that there would be a full moon the night of our arrival and in one of her romantic moods had given us all the exciting news that we could see the pyramids by moonlight. From our little group, great cries of ecstasy went up. When we rode out after dinner, there they were, green and blue and mysterious, and just as I had imagined them. But the ecstatic cries of my companions seemed too much; their reaction was so extreme that it seemed phony. I found myself becoming the oddball.

For one whole week in Cairo I continued in a rebellious and unreasonable antagonism toward my fellow tourists. Perhaps I was unknowingly jealous of the Bonners, for I let myself believe that their enthusiasms for various tombs were insincere. Whatever the explanation, though I did my best to hide my sulkiness, I began to feel like an outsider; everyone was out of step except me. As I look back upon it, I condemn myself as all moody people should be condemned, because the week was filled with the most exciting and memorable incidents.

Neysa, the captain of our crew, planned each day. Paul Bonner, the secretary and contact man, paid all the bills, did all the tipping and collected from each of us pro rata at the end of the day. We were escorted everywhere by a handsome dragoman who had been engaged for the duration of our visit. We visited museums and tombs, which I found uninteresting. We went shopping, and my literal mind rebelled at the custom of haggling. It seemed ridiculous that you couldn't ask for a price and either pay it or walk away. But no, you had to sit down, have coffee, be told a price you knew to be excessive, offer less, and finally settle upon a sum which the dragoman had told us to hold out for. We drove out to the desert for a picnic. Bonner and I rode Arabian ponies. We all rode camels; let me tell you that camels give you a rough jouncing. One would think that these soft-looking animals with great padded feet would furnish a gentle mount, but they are the stiffest, most inflexible bumpers that I've ever experienced. Arab horses are something else. My early cowboy experience came in good stead here; I had a grand time showing off, careening around the desert to the admiration of all.

The handsome dragoman liked us so much that he decided to give us an unusual treat: he would introduce us into a real Egyptian home. We would be honored to meet his wife, who was not one of these backward women, but a modern. It was a clean house where the population explosion was already in force. A great variety of children about ten months apart in age were visible, but silent. The wife was unveiled, it was true. She seemed to be about thirty tired years of age. She had no teeth.

We went to an Arab nightclub and watched fat women demonstrate incredible control of their belly muscles, then listened to singers keening seemingly endless songs in high minor voices. The lyrics were apparently simple. After one woman had been singing for some fifteen minutes, I asked the dragoman what she had said. He replied, "She say it is nice day."

We spent an afternoon with a snake charmer. He took us to a suburb where there were some vacant lots, carrying with him an empty bag in which he said he would put his snakes if he were lucky enough to find any. We followed him about while he banged the trees with his staff and called to the snakes in what he said was Hebrew. Soon a cobra appeared which he taunted into striking again and again until finally when it became exhausted he was able to grasp it by the back of the neck and put it into his sack. One snake which he found was nonpoisonous, and he let it bite the back of his hand; it sank its teeth into his skin and worried its head back and forth angrily like a terrier with a rat. He found a scorpion which ran up a tree; when he called to it in his alleged Hebrew it stopped; when he banged on either side of it with his staff it remained immobile. Finally he dismissed the scorpion with another phrase and it ran on up the tree. I have no idea how much of this was fake and how much was real, but it was a great show.

The next part of our expedition was to be a trip up the Nile. We were to stop en route and visit ancient cities, museums and sites of interest. But my crankiness reached a climax at about this time and I told Neysa that I had decided not to finish the trip with them, that I would stay at the Semiramas Hotel and write while they were away. Fortunately, she was an understanding woman; instead of dismissing me as a difficult fool, she talked to me calmly and said that I must not think of doing any such thing, that I must not break up the party, that I must go along with them, that if I wished to stay on the boat and write, I could do so, but that I must not do anything so drastic as to leave the group. I gave in; in retrospect I suspect that I really only wanted to be coaxed.

We took a train through the desert for a few hours and began to feel the new heat of that barren country. Finally we came to a little town and rode through its streets toward the pier, and suddenly, over a rise in the road there was the Nile, lying below us—and at the dock lay a little ship with awnings out on the deck. I loved it at first sight.

I had read about the White Nile and the Blue Nile, but I had no preconception of the real Nile—the Dirty Nile, a great floating mudpie. Part of the charm of steaming up the Nile is that no man can chart it; the swirling brown water builds up new sand bars over night. Our ship, a dahabeah, was constantly finding itself aground on some unsuspected shallow and having to be pulled off by the crew going ashore with ropes or freed by the leverage of oars in small boats. During these exercises, the men always sang the same song, a lovely plaintive chant. In the middle of the night we would wake up and hear it.

Little boats with strange sails passed by, and robed women walking very straight with jars on their heads came down to the river to get water. It was all a scene from the Bible. The land on both sides of the Nile is green for only a few hundred yards, and in the distance there were always brown bare cliffs. Man-driven oxen walked endlessly around and around pulling water up and dumping it on the land. Sometimes the men waved to us, or if they saw the women they made a few obscene gestures just to show how virile they were.

The whole trip had the dreamlike quality of an idyl; time

seemed to pass endlessly and pleasantly. Abbott the tomb-hater had to reverse his attitude; he became the first to line up for all historic events. I should add that the tombs up the Nile are not like the petty ones around Cairo. These tombs were dug deep into the earth and always had something on the wall worth looking at.

Everything in Egypt looks better from a distance. The long line of women with jars on their heads is a thing of beauty from far away, but if you get close you find that the women are filthy, that the water they are carrying would poison anyone but an Egyptian and that flies are everywhere. The Egyptian fly is not like our evasive American pest; he cannot be brushed away. He just lands there like a heavy thing and stays. When they land on the babies' faces, the mothers don't bother to brush them off; they say that they will just be replaced by other, hungrier flies. It was impossible to go ashore without a fan, and it became obvious why Cleopatra always had a few graceful attendants standing nearby creating a breeze.

Our little ship was an interesting study in national traits. We were English, French and American, and because we were isolated in a floating world, the characteristics of each were accentuated. The English were independent, aloof and smilingly courteous and superior. The old ladies and gentlemen rode donkeys out to the ruins without ever asking for a helping hand. Once I offered to assist an Englishwoman of about eighty descend a ladder, but she politely let me know that she could take care of herself. The French, on the other hand, were parochial and clannish, and they seemed to have to help each other to do everything. To get Mama from our little ship out to the tombs was an almost hysterical event. Mama could not ride donkeys; she had to have a carriage, and it took many helping hands and much excited argument to get her in and out. The Americans were individuals, eccentric and varied. One fellow looked straight out of Coney Island, there were a couple of Midwestern businessmen with wives and cigars and lastly, there was us—rather superior people, I fancy.

On the last day before our return to Cairo, Neysa pointed out that it was just a month since we had landed in Egypt, that there would be a full moon again so we could see the pyramids once more. Cries of ecstasy arose all around me. But I wanted to go to an Arab nightclub, so I announced that they could include me out. Just before dinner there came a knock at my door. It was Neysa and she was crying. I tried to comfort her, and asked her what the matter was. "They won't go," she said. "You're right about them, they're just pretending. They don't want to go. They want to play bridge." Feeling noble, I accepted the role of true friend; I told Neysa that I would forego the nightclub and that we would visit her beloved pyramids together. Again it was beautiful, and as seen through Neysa's eyes, it acquired a double magic: not only beautiful, but weird, mysterious, like a scene under water. Then we walked further to see the Sphinx and sat in the sand looking through the green, silvery moonlight at that ancient enigma. There was a ridge of sand behind us, like a snowdrift, and all at once in the stillness I became aware that there was something in our rear. There was no noise, but it was there. We sat very still holding our breath. At last a shadow appeared. I had to turn. Two Arab soldiers stood watching us. In sign language, with much finger shaking, they told us that we were in danger and that we should leave.

The next night I had another eerie experience. The Bonners and I decided to observe some of the wickeder things in this wicked city. Reluctantly the dragoman agreed to arrange a tour. Neysa and Alice went off to play cards with Pearl White, the silent-picture star, who lived in a great house in Cairo and owned one of the biggest racing stables in the country. The Bonners and I were first led to a building and told to sit down while the dragoman went in to make arrangements. Finally he came back and instructed us to continue on alone; he could not go with us; it wasn't a thing that he was supposed to countenance. As we started up the stone steps on the outside of the building, lighted only dimly by Neysa's moon, we became more and more uncomfortable. There was no sound or light; my heart was pounding and my breath was short. I felt like a character in a Poe short story. When we reached the door both Bonner and I with old-fashioned Southern courtesy allowed the lady to go first—in fact, we fairly pushed Lily ahead of us. There were two women inside. We sat on a stone bench while they danced for us in the nude. They had mediocre figures, were bad dancers, and it all cost a great deal, as we discovered on returning to the dragoman.

The next day we set sail for Athens, and the grandeur that was Greece, saw one of the most ancient theatres in the world, stood among the Ionic pillars of the Acropolis and thought about Pericles. Then we came home. Originally we had planned to make Paris one last stop, but the simple fact was that I was homesick for Broadway. There was a cruise ship leaving Athens for New York, and when I decided to take it Neysa and Alice were apparently of a similar mood.

Most of the sight-seeing which we do in our lifetimes is soon forgotten. Not so with my trip up the Nile; it has never faded. The sights and sounds and smells of Egypt and the things we did on that trip have come back to me through the years again and again.

The theatre took over my energies once more. Dunning and I went to our office every day and made plans for the play we hoped to produce in the fall. Whatever I had written on the Mediterranean trip must have been abandoned; I have no memory of it and I assume that I must have thrown it away. A compulsion to write has often driven me to work on ideas for which I had no inner enthusiasm. My past is littered with abandoned manuscripts, and when I abandon them I do it thoroughly by throwing them in the wastebasket.

Now an event took place which radically changed my life. One day Neysa said, "I was talking to Woollcott last week. He asked what I thought of the idea of his coming out to Long Island and living with us this summer and paying us what it would cost him to live in the city. I talked to Jack about it and Jack said, no, he didn't think it would work, but why didn't I ask George."

I could hardly believe my ears—I had always regarded the Baragwanaths' Sands Point home as a place only to be visited infrequently. To be offered to share it seemed like all the Christmas presents in the world put together. And, indeed, that is the way it turned out. Neysa, practical about money as she always was, sat down with me and discussed the finances, and laid down the house rules. Each of us was to be completely independent. I was never to feel obligated to go with them anywhere; they, on the other hand, were not obliged to take me with them when they went out but would do so when convenient. We would give it a try, but if we found that we got on each other's nerves we would call it off with no rancor on either side.

When I moved out to spend that summer of 1933 with the Baragwanaths I turned out to be the man who came to dinner; I was to spend fifteen summers there. A great many of the richest and most attractive people in the country had built estates on the North Shore of Long Island. They lived a gay and pleasant life; there were parties nearly every night, and they all dressed for dinner. I learned that tuxedo was a dirty word and that I should refer to that garment as a dinner coat. I also learned many other things, and I studied with interest the morals and manners of these children and grandchildren of the strong, ruthless men who had made fortunes in the preceding century.

It was not a snobbish group. There were no climbers as in Newport, or phonies as in Palm Beach; instead the society consisted of a rather flexible clan of people who lived near each other and associated with each other because of friendship and similarity of background. The haves are always very suspicious of the have-nots, so naturally it was a reactionary group—That Son-of-a-bitch in Washington was out to get them. They were predominantly Republican, although Jim Forrestal, Stuart Symington and Averell Harriman later became prominent members of the opposite camp.

In general, the members of the clan were not well read or well educated, though most of the women had been to some sort of finishing school and knew a good deal about art. They spoke French and/or Italian and had good table manners. Most of the men had been to college, and they seemed very much like each other. The son of a wealthy family is apt to be just that. Unless some discipline or interest at home gives him a different point of view, he is apt to slide through school gracefully, row on the crew, become a dashing figure and get gentlemanly C's. I was shocked at the amount of bad grammar and mispronunciation heard in this circle. An odd, indicative thing occurred one day: a very social fellow mispronounced the word almond. It grated on my nerves so violently that I reacted without thinking and corrected him. He bridled, turned to me haughtily and said, "I get around." His instinctive defense was that he was socially acceptable: perhaps too there was an inference that I wasn't.

An eavesdropper would get the impression that these people had too much; they had homes not only on the North Shore but in Paris, Rome, Palm Beach, Nassau, Newport, or the Adirondacks, and everyone seemed to have a shooting place somewhere down South, or a ranch in the West. Nearly all the men had an office to go to; some did real work, some did token work. The women did good deeds for a socially attractive charity, gambled, and wore too much jewelry. One would think that a woman with a wrinkled neck or flabby arms or mottled hands would not wish to call attention to these defects, but the passion for ostentation was stronger than common sense, and oversized jewelry glittered everywhere.

Hospitality was a part of the code of good breeding—not politeness, but hospitality. Mrs. Rich Bitch would always receive you with cordiality and warmth if you were her guest. In fact, sometimes I would be under the impression that Mrs. Rich Bitch rather liked me—until I met her on neutral ground and found that she did not even recognize me.

Surrounded as these people were by too much of everything, it seemed ridiculous to have to listen to their fulminations against the New Deal. But their croakings of evil days to come were not as groundless as I thought; their way of life was doomed, and their big estates which seemed so permanent have already been converted into dandy little colonies of split-level homes. I don't mean to imply that taxation ruined them. It didn't, but it made their way of life so difficult that many of them compromised and discovered that they were just as happy with fewer acres. Others gave up their estates because suburbs gradually surrounded them and made their ancestral homes—ancestral for one generation—less attractive.

So far as I could observe, the Baragwanaths were the only people in this set who were not wealthy. They could not offer hospitality on the same scale as their friends, but they could offer something much better: wit, charm and humor. Undoubtedly Jack and Neysa would have been elected the favorite dinner partners on the North Shore, and unquestionably there was no house to which people preferred to be invited. An extra man was no problem in that environment, and the Baragwanaths took me with them wherever they went. I came to know their friends, and in a tentative way to be accepted by them. Some slight residue of my have-not days made me a little critical, but I kept any derogatory thoughts strictly to myself, and in general I got a great deal of pleasure out of this new and different circle.

The neighbors whom we saw the most were the Fleischmanns. Ruth, who had been a girlhood friend of Neysa's from Quincy, Illinois, and Raoul, who was the principal owner of *The New Yorker*, an experimental magazine in its infancy, lived in Manhasset, a couple of miles away. Before the Baragwanaths put in their own pool, we used to pile into a car with our bath towels and go over there to swim. It was always fun to go to their house; they were a witty and urbane couple. Unlike most members of the group, Ruth was able to make fun of herself. Once she told me of an incident which happened when she had spent some weeks in a hospital. She had always been a very pretty girl and, of course, she was pleased when many of her friends came in to tell her how well she was looking. But one day she saw the doctor's chart of her case; it read: Fleischmann, Ruth: middle-aged, slightly flatulent female."

Each July in Manhasset Joan Whitney Payson gave a magnificent party. It out-did Hollywood, and it was indescribably beautiful. As you drove up the winding road, there were lights in all the trees as far as the eye could see; lanterns twinkled way into the hills. Emil Coleman and twenty musicians made music for dancing in the big house, and if you followed the carpeted path with its little blue lights down to the swimming pool, you would find another band holding forth there. As all big parties should be, Joan's was always a costume party. The guest hiding behind his make-up loses his shyness and becomes wittier, brighter, less earthbound. The lights and music created an aura of beauty and good will. As the night passed, the dance floor would become less and less crowded and the older people would begin to leave. The summer dawn came over the hills dimming the lights of the lanterns in the trees, the celebrants crawled into their cars with weary, happy goodbyes and drove unsteadily to their various houses to take their sleeping pills. Afterwards the party would be the main topic of conversation for several days.

There were hundreds of transients who appeared and reappeared in all these houses: attractive couples from Philadelphia or Boston; friends from further out on the Island; relatives; and those who might be classed simply as hangers-on. In feudal days great families employed a jester to amuse the guests and ease tensions and the custom has continued. Nearly all of these wealthy people had a man who was a friend of the family, who was always around: an agreeable fellow whom everyone liked, a reliable fellow to escort the wife, a good-hearted fellow who would dance with the unattractive women and be polite by obligation rather than inclination. In an atmosphere where there was a good deal of malice, these always agreeable fellows were good company. They may have sung for their supper, but they did it so well that they did not degrade themselves.

If I had been completely honest with myself, perhaps I would have admitted that I wanted to be popular with the people of the North Shore, but some innate stubbornness made me cling to my own provincial character and refuse to make the proper effort. The women, I believe, liked me better than the men. After all, I suppose I was a potential rival—a new rooster in the barnyard. My attraction for the great social world was complicated by another factor: I knew my mother would have enjoyed it. Her often repeated admonition to seek the best, to resist the temptation to be a big frog in a small puddle, her dream of being surrounded by "superior" people and "superior" things, a dream which of course she never realized, fitted the life I was living. She would have had tremendous satisfaction in seeing me there, and part of the reason I was fascinated with it was because of her.

At this time there had been a great deal of publicity given to a play called *Twentieth Century*, by Ben Hecht and Charlie MacArthur, which Jed Harris had slated for production but which had been postponed and postponed. One day Phil Dunning told me that he heard that the deal with Harris was off and suggested that we try to acquire it. At almost the same time Billy Rose asked me to direct *The Great Magoo*, by Ben Hecht and Gene Fowler, and so I told Hecht that I would direct the play if he would let Dunning and me produce *Twentieth Century*. He said that he would be only too happy to do so except for the fact that they had no third act. He gave it to us to read, and it was agreed that if we could furnish them with a third act we could produce the play. So while Dunning retired to his place in Westport to work on *Twentieth Century*, I proceeded with the direction of *The Great Magoo*. It was my first contact with these eccentric extroverts. Hecht and MacArthur were known to the press as the Katzenjammer Kids, and they specialized in practical jokes, as did their friends Fowler, John Barrymore and other members of their group. It is no exaggeration to say that they spent fifty per-cent of their time thinking up ingenious pranks and another twenty-five percent regurgitating the details with childish joy. I confess that I was awed by Hecht and Fowler; yet at the same time I felt contemptuous of them. As workmen they seemed to me careless and inferior. I think that Billy Rose was impressed by them; the office conferences were full of jokes instead of hard labor. *The Great Magoo* was not a big success.

Then Dunning returned from Westport with a new story line. Hecht had sneered a little at the idea of our being able to lick the problem which had baffled him, but after reading the new draft he decided to go ahead with us. *Twentieth Century* was a hit, the first solid hit that I had been involved with in some time. Bill Frawley was funny in the supporting part, and Eugenie Leontovich was magnificent in the part of the actress.

Eugenie and I used to argue about the theatre—she defending the arty theatre, I defending the commercial one. One day at rehearsal she requested that her position on stage be changed. It seemed a good idea and I made the change; so that it would be perfectly clear that I was not playing favorites, I explained that the new position would be better for the leading man. Eugenie brooded over this and began to regret that she had spoken, for she had no interest in the leading man but merely the actress's usual preoccupation with herself. The following Sunday we went out for a ride and stopped off somewhere for a soda. Out of the blue she said, "You know, in that scene, I've changed my mind. I think now I would like to be back on other side of the stage." I blew my top. I railed. I told her what I thought of her phony pretensions on art, which didn't mean a thing when it came down to cases—she was just a selfish little ham trying to steal a scene from another actor. I got up and stormed out to the street. She followed. I slammed the car door and was waiting for the explosion. But instead of anger I heard a rather calm voice, "You know, it is quite interesting to see a man of your temperament get angry." No wonder we don't understand the Russians.

That winter I went off on another Palm Beach trip with the Artists and Writers. This time Neysa and Charlie Brackett came along, and the three of us became a unit for the duration of the trip. Neysa was invited everywhere, and we trailed along after her. When she and Charlie returned to New York I stayed on, took a little apartment there and served as an extra man for the rest of the winter.

The people in Palm Beach were very different from the Long Island set. They were more idle, a great many of them seemed to have married their money and most of them had pleasure as their objective. Unfortunately, pleasure is a very hard thing to achieve all by itself, so, in general, they were a rather bored group. The men who had married for money had accepted boredom as the price, and they displayed a slight hauteur to prove—mostly to themselves—that they were really very superior people. The women who had been married for their money were inclined to be hard and bitter because of what they knew in their hearts. Those who had inherited it were in a similar predicament; they had little meaning to their lives, for the spending of money isn't sufficient. Of course, there was another side of the coin. There was a good life there too. There was swimming and golf and tennis, beautiful parties, the balmy night air, beautiful people, beautiful clothes, and a sense of well-being. Once someone asked Somerset Maugham how he could waste his time visiting so many silly, empty society people, and he replied, "But they have such nice things."

While I wallowed in this luxury, my partner was worried; the banks were beginning to close. The *Twentieth Century* company had some sixty thousand dollars in the bank, and Phil decided to draw it out in gold. He carried it out to Westport for safety, and be advised that sixty thousand dollars in gold is a back-breaking burden. The next day the government ordered all gold returned to the banks and he had to take it back again.

There followed another summer at Sands Point. I wish I could find words to convey the idyllic nature of the life we lived. My childhood had been one of strain and stress; as a married man my life had been filled with love and togetherness, but also with struggle and scrimping and saving and planning. Now I was in a home dedicated to gaiety and fun. Perhaps the unconventional marriage of Jack and Neysa will be a model for the marriage of the future. I can only state the facts: whatever their early relationship had been, by the time I came to know them it had developed into companionship. There was no pretense of passion, they were only loving friends, but I do not believe there was ever a home in which there was more love, more consideration, more humor and more joy.

Perhaps the people who get along best in this world are those who are alike—and yet different. Jack and Neysa were very different. He was practical; she was vague. He never read anything but detective stories or history, and he hated music. Neysa, on the other hand, was an artist through her whole being; she loved music and literature passionately. But these differences in taste didn't matter, for they looked at life in the same way. They were both intelligent and forthright, they liked people and to them life was amusing.

Jack was a mining engineer, and when he graduated from Columbia he had done a nine-year stretch in South America. This had colored his life in many ways—one of them was that his vocabulary included much of the language of the mining camp. Jack's gaiety and good will were so patent that his friends were never shocked by his unique and ever-changing language. Most of us would find it unpleasant to be called a son-of-a-bitch, but somehow it was amusing to be called a retromingent son-of-a-bitch.

Neysa had come to New York from Quincy, Illinois, to be an actress. Though she had studied art in Chicago she had never worked in pastels until one day she saw some in the window of an art store. She was an incredible success in the new medium.

Neysa was proud of the aristocratic background of her Southern mother, but Mama had broken a hip while riding to hounds, leaving the young girl saddled with responsibility for a hopeless cripple. Until her mother died, Neysa did not marry. To some people this would have seemed gallant; to Neysa, it was just natural.

I know very little about the courtship of the handsome mining man back from South America and the glamorous artist who was the darling of the New York smart set. I do know that it had its highly unconventional aspects; the day after the wedding, Jack went West on a mining trip and Neysa went to Europe in the company of seven men. One day I asked Neysa about this. She explained matter-of-factly that it was the most logical thing in the world: after all, for some months she had planned her European trip, Jack had his business to attend to, and simply because they had decided to get married, there was no need to let that event overturn their whole lives.

When the Baragwanaths did finally share a residence together, they gradually evolved a pattern of life which suited them. Neysa went to the opera with Robert Benchley or someone else who could enjoy it, instead of inflicting it upon her husband. Jack liked pretty nitwit girls who bored Neysa, so sometimes she would arrange an attractive dinner for Jack and a girl friend while she attended some function which would not interest him. Home was always the center, but never the circumference of their lives.

Neysa was a strong character and yet she was loved by almost everyone. Objectivity was so much a part of her that two bitter enemies could each be her close friend. She had strong opinions of her own but was seldom drawn into petty quarrels or to taking sides in any of the feuds which were so frequent in her circle. She was a passionate nature-lover. I can still see her as a pensive woman with graceful hands walking around the yard holding a little posy and occasionally smelling it. On the Baragwanaths' place at Sands Point there were many trees—too many trees, really—but Neysa defended each as though it were the last of its kind. Inside the house everything was charming and haphazard. A rare Chinese lamp stood on a Grand Rapids table. Some furniture was good, some solid, some badly needing repair. It was quite old-fashioned, I suppose—I remember that there was a shawl on the piano. Most of their friends had better houses, but they didn't have better homes or better times.

The servants were Negroes. Three women ran the house and one man was a combination chauffeur and gardener. The women were pleasant and inefficient and had worked for the Baragwanaths for years and years. There was always a different man each summer. Neysa seldom lost her temper but I once heard her berating one of these temporary chauffeur-butlers in stinging tones, and no doubt in dramatic imitation of her revered mother, threatening to horsewhip him. The house servants reflected their employers and were kind and loving.

Neysa usually had breakfast in bed about eight o'clock, but Jack and I went down to the dining room. He wasn't very talkative at breakfast, although occasionally there would be some particularly amusing episode at the party the night before which he had to recount. After he had left for Port Washington to take the train I would take the morning paper out to the terrace, and presently Neysa would join me. We would play backgammon, talk and read. We talked about the theatre, books, music, life, manners, morals, motives, sex, love, bringing up children—and our experiences. I told her of my life; she told me of hers. Despite her objectivity on most things, Neysa had a few hates. She hated one woman who had tried to steal Jack from her early in their married life; she hated Ruth Hale (Heywood Broun's wife) for reasons I never could quite pin down. (It was of Ruth Hale that F.P.A. wrote when he described the Broun wedding as "the union of the sturdy vine and the clinging oak.")

Neysa also felt violently about certain causes. Her enthusiasm for the ASPCA was not just academic. In those days when there were many horses on the streets of New York, she was their defender, and she caused more than one driver to be hauled into court for cruelty to his animal. She had great courage; once, while walking with a woman friend in Central Park—then as now a favorite haunt of sexual perverts—she was suddenly confronted with an exhibitionist who exposed himself to them. Neysa picked up a rock and scored a bull's eye while her friend called a policeman; then they marched the fellow off to court to testify against him. Although she never went to church, Neysa was tolerant of all religions except Christian Science. She could get very excited and abusive about Mary Baker Eddy. It had something to do with a child which she felt had been neglected.

One of the facets in this woman's character which was baffling, fascinating and altogether charming, was her ability to face two directions at once with seeming sincerity. Though she professed to believe in neither heaven nor hell, she insisted that she believed in ghosts. In fact there were quite a few superstitions to which she gave lip service.

Neysa never complained, although she was buffeted a good deal by life. She was accident prone and in frequent physical distress of one kind or another, and she had many financial and emotional disappointments, but she never lost her serenity for any length of time. Once in talking about bringing up children, she said to me, "About all we can teach a child is to be able to take it."

Toward noon we'd go swimming and then again out on the terrace to have lunch. Neysa could make exciting events of the smallest things in life. We were both very fond of chocolate Mallomars, and she would remember that there was a box of them in the kitchen and have them brought out. As we devoured the whole box, it would seem like a trip to the Taj Mahal. In the afternoon we might go to one of the neighbors for croquet, and then get back in time for Jack's return from the city. He always arrived with a great complaint against the weather, the Long Island Railroad and life in general. Somehow this was very funny, and while he was describing the intense heat and suffering to which he had been subjected, we would rock with laughter. Jack was always sure that nature was singling him out unjustly; that some demonic force interfered with the true flight of his croquet ball or saw to it that he got worse cards than anyone else. He was not unaware of the fact that this was very entertaining.

In the first few moments after Jack arrived home from the city, there was always a time when I was shut out. The Baragwanaths would link arms and walk around the place enjoying the trees and talking over their private affairs. What they talked about, I don't know. Maybe their finances, their daughter Joan, their social plans, and perhaps indirectly a reaffirmation of the fact that although there was very little demonstration of it, they still loved each other.

I won't attempt a roster of the interesting and famous people who passed through that house, but one or two stand out in my memory. George Gershwin was a very conceited man—not about his music, oddly enough, but about his avocations. He was very vain about his painting, and when talking to a dinner partner, he would unblushingly compare himself to Leonardo da Vinci. Once in discussing him, a man asked, "Do you think Gershwin's music will be played one hundred years from now?" "It will," a wit replied, "if Gershwin is still alive." George was very happy at the piano and he presided there quite naturally. One weekend he was playing his melodies to us when Jack inquired, "Do you know 'Shuffle Off to Buffalo?'" Concealing his annoyance, George played it in a desultory fashion and then returned to his own music. Soon Jack asked again for "Shuffle Off to Buffalo," and the request was repeated several more times without George realizing that he was being ribbed. Neysa, a music-lover, gave Jack the cold eye, which put an end to that nonsense.

Bernard Baruch was also a good friend of the Baragwanaths. One evening when he dropped in the talk veered to Wall Street. He advised Jack to buy—to buy anything. Jack had no money with which to speculate, but I did, and I bought extensively. After a temporary rise my shares went down and kept going down; in fact one of them disappeared entirely. Now why was that? How could the great Baruch steer us wrong? I am sure that had Bernie known that his advice had been taken, he would have alerted us when the situation changed. But the fact was that the largest loss I ever had in the market came from information by one of its most successful operators. The moral is, don't take tips and don't eavesdrop.

Neysa had strong feelings about the rights and wrongs of social relationships. This seemingly vague and tolerant woman could sometimes act with extraordinary and exemplary decisiveness. She did not believe that people should be unduly imposed upon, and she considered that submission to such behavior was weakness, not generosity. For example, when the Baragwanaths decided to build a swimming pool, a casual acquaintance who happened to live nearby said, "I'm so delighted that you're putting in a pool. I love to swim." Neysa said, "When it is finished I'll invite you over." A couple of weeks later the neighbor received a note which said, "Do please come for a swim on Saturday, the 2nd, at eleven A.M." The neighbor got the idea and thereafter never presumed to drop in without being asked. Another time, at a rather large dinner party, a man showed up with two women who were obviously drunk. Neysa took them aside and said, "You can't come to the table in that condition, but I'd love to have something brought to you upstairs in my room." The women departed indignantly, but the next day when they sobered up both wrote letters of apology.

Herbert and Margaret Swope were among Neysa's most intimate friends, but they distressed her because they always arrived late. Not just late, *very* late. On one occasion, invited for eight o'clock, they came at ten; the meal was spoiled. As they were saying good night, Neysa said, "I'm very fond of you but my household can't cope with such delays, so I'm never going to ask you again!" And she never did.

Neysa also had a contempt for pretentious people and for phonies. There was a handsome woman in the local set who was almost a caricature of the Southern belle; her accent was full of magnolia blossoms, and she was kittenish and a great flatterer of men. Naturally she was not frowned upon by the men as much as by members of her own sex. It must have been a little sickening to the onlookers to hear her tell me that I was a Viking, but I rather liked it. Mrs. Southern Belle was an accomplished pianist but she always needed a lot of coaxing; she would bring her music to a party but it was only after much persuasion that she was finally inclined to sit down at the piano toward the end of the evening. Once there was a large party at Nelson Doubleday's, and the lady was asked to play. As usual, she demurred; Neysa, whose piano technique was that of a twelve-year-old, announced that she would love to play and proceeded to stumble gaily through some Victor Herbert numbers. Thus stimulated, Mrs. Southern Belle decided to oblige. Neysa, however, didn't wait for the concert but told her host good night and trooped out with all her house guests, who comprised about one quarter of the audience. Though she was seldom vindictive, Neysa really gloried in that night's work.

The most pleasant evenings were those when we stayed home for dinner. It was seldom, however, that we were not either going out or expecting guests. When we went out I always hoped that I would be sitting near Jack or Neysa. Jack was gay and witty and always gave a good time to the women who sat next to him. If he drew a very attractive woman he would complain about his misfortune in a loud voice and wonder why he was always getting stuck; if he sat next to an unattractive woman, he would flatter her and pretend to make a flirtatious pass. He would announce that his name was Handsome Jack, the Mining Man, and that he was highly emotional, so would she kindly refrain from putting her hand on his leg. Usually the woman would blush and choke on her soup and have the time of her life.

When the women left the men after dinner and a few raconteurs had said, "Stop me if you've heard this one," the talk would turn to business, politics, and a cross current of loud, seldom-changed opinions. Herbert Swope had developed a technique for holding the attention of the entire table while he spoke. He would start out with some such arresting statement as, "I was talking to the White House today." (He always referred to the President as the White House, and to Harry Hopkins as Mr. Sick.) He would then pause as the conversational level became hushed, and with great deliberation light a cigarette. After making his audience wait dramatically, he would continue in a quieter voice, never ending a paragraph or coming to a period where he could be interrupted, but always starting a new phrase before he made a pause. He loved to hold forth, and he did it very well. He was an interesting man, and he threw names, dates and facts at his listeners with remarkable facility. His audience was not sufficiently well-informed to judge their accuracy, but when Senator Brewster was my guest on one occasion he confided to me that in his opinion the dates were not as accurate as they were made to sound.

Sometimes there was a gathering of a more frivolous nature. Once a party was organized to which only men were invited and for which Harpo Marx, who was playing in a Broadway musical at the time, agreed to bring the women. The girls were all given the same name; each man found that his dinner partner was named Miss Benson. Jack reported later that he listened as Swope warmed up to his companion. Herbert was charming her with his profundity, and Jack heard some such mouthful as "fis-

cal integrity despite the fulminations of political demagoguery."
His little Miss Benson regarded the great man with awe, batted
her false eyelashes and exclaimed, "Hey, hey, Big Boy!"

Almost every evening ended with games, sometimes canasta
or backgammon or whatever game was in vogue at the time, and
sometimes parlor games. Whenever the party was at the Baragwanaths, Neysa would already have organized something. She was
the queen of party games, and this circle of enthusiastic players
invented many games which later were played throughout the
country. Once Jack returned from abroad with a game picked up
on shipboard in which you chose teams and drew pictures from
which your team was to guess a slogan or the title of a song.
Howard Dietz and Jack then invented a variation in which the
player acted out the syllables of the word, and thus was born
what we called The Game.

Neysa, Alexander Woollcott, Charlie MacArthur and a few
others had bought an island in Bomoseen, Vermont, where during the summer they repaired, allegedly for rest and change,
but actually to be together and have a good time. Woollcott was
the king, or, if you will, the queen of the island. In any case, he
was the Führer and only he decided when the other members
could come, what guest they could bring and when they should
depart. Neysa and I motored up there for a five-day visit.

The bizarreness of the next few days was symbolized for me
by the first man we met in Bomoseen. He was on the dock
and he had a trained fish; he rang a bell and the fish came and
was fed. After this demonstration we were rowed out to the
island where Woollcott, Harpo Marx and Alice Miller were waiting to greet us. At this time Woollcott was in his period of greatest influence. He had been not only an influential critic but also a
radio personality, and many books owed their popularity to his
vigorous support, *Goodbye, Mr. Chips* among them. I had been
one of his victims when he had printed an article depreciating
my contribution to *Coquette*. Why, he had asked, should I have
my name first on the program when I had made only a slight contribution as an author? I have no notion what prompted such an
unwarranted accusation—perhaps he thought his friend Jed had
written the play. At any rate, I started off not liking him very
much, and he started off not liking me at all.

Woollcott was a strange men. At the age of nineteen, he had caught a case of mumps which had rendered him impotent. He was not effeminate in the usual sense—quite the contrary, his thoughts toward women were those of a man—but his personality was waspish and old-maidish. He looked like a big owl but he had the tongue of a viper, and the stories of his rudeness were legion.

On the island there was boating, swimming, croquet, eating and conversation. The last, of course, was the most important. Woollcott presided at all meals and directed the conversation into whatever channels he chose. He was a wonderful talker and so were they all, but I never succeeded in getting into the spirit of the place. I was there on sufferance as the guest of their beloved Neysa, or Miss Beauty Queen, as she was known on the island.

Woollcott was in love with Neysa, as well as with Ruth Gordon. He was bitterly jealous of both of them, and never bothered to conceal his antipathy for any of their male friends. One day while four of us were playing croquet he began to ridicule me. With his feline instincts he was very clever at this; he would find your weak point and probe it mercilessly. He subtly poked fun at me as a small-town boy and a hick, and he kept forgetting my name—he pretended he thought it was Elmer. As a kind of personal, private revenge, while the game progressed I began to compose a limerick about him. It pleased me so much that I have never forgotten it. It went like this:

> A waggish old madcap named Alex
> Was only a weeny bit phallic.
> 'Tis true girls would groan
> When he got them alone
> But t'wasn't for matters italic.

I taught this to Ruth Fleischmann who repeated it to Woollcott. Instead of throwing me off the island, however, he seemed to develop some slight respect for me and I found myself treated with a little more caution thereafter.

The island was jealous of its privacy and No Trespassing signs were posted appropriately. Nevertheless there were intrusions; people from the mainland would row over hoping to look at the celebrities. On one occasion a group of picnickers had landed their boat, spread out their blankets and prepared to settle down for a day's fun when there was a growling noise in the bushes nearby. As they looked up a maniac emerged and advanced on them slowly—a naked man, red-headed, cross-eyed, swinging an axe. It was Harpo. The intruders fled in terror.

That fall Dunning and I produced two more plays, *Heat Lightning* and *The Drums Begin,* neither of which was a success. However, in *The Drums Begin* I got a chance to direct Judith Anderson. I liked her both as a person and as an actress, but I found it difficult to adjust myself to her method of preparing her part. Most important actresses speak out from the very first day of rehearsal. They may not give it the full treatment but they approximate the feeling, variety and natures of the character which they eventually will convey in full dimension. But Judith Anderson mutters so that she is inaudible, and the other actors have difficulty even in hearing their cues. I argued with her about this trait, but she gave me some abracadabra about having to let the character emerge gradually and professed great contempt for actors who jumped into the rehearsal with both feet. I suspect that her method was at least partly due to self-consciousness and that she probably rehearsed with plenty of volume when closeted alone. Certainly no one can quarrel with the emotional power she is able to give in a performance.

Judith had another habit which distressed me. She came late to rehearsals, and in trying to solve the problem I developed a technique which I have used ever since. A tardy star is always a dilemma. If you antagonize her unduly by laying down the law, it creates tension which makes a coöperative relationship difficult. On the other hand, if you permit it to continue you lose valuable time and are unfair to the hard-working actors who are there on the clock. I got a bright idea: I started my rehearsals punctually, but if the star was not on time, I put in the understudy. Now no star is afraid that the understudy will take her part away or show her up by being better; nevertheless, it is *her* part, she feels possessive about it, and it's not pleasant to come in and find some one-cylinder bit player saying your lines. It usu-

ally works, and it is a device which I recommend to all punctual
directors.

Next I was enthusiastic over a play about John Brown by
an English playwright named Ronald Gow. Dunning didn't like
it so I decided to produce it alone. I tried to get Lionel Barrymore
for the part, then Walter Huston, and when time was running out
I persuaded myself that I could play it. When we went into rehearsals I realized that things were not going well. Finally I
talked with Richard Maney, our press agent on the show, and he
said, "John Brown is a roarer. This part isn't written that way, but
that's what the public expects. You've got to be an Old Testament
prophet, a violent man." Well, my voice is penetrating but it isn't
big or deep or powerful. I was a failure, and the play was a failure. We closed it in three days, and I was about as tired as I have
ever been in my life, for I had produced, directed and played
the lead in it. I poured myself onto the train for Palm Beach with
the Artists and Writers, relieved to be out of the city.

How does a fellow feel when he has had a series of failures?
I don't remember being too depressed. I felt that it was obvious
that life was made up of both success and failure, of the smooth
and the rough, and I didn't think that I had lost my ability—
though I realized that if any of my associates were interested
enough to discuss the matter, they might be of the opinion that
I was slipping. I have always been a strong believer in Emerson's law of compensation. Out of every bad comes some good;
out of the mistakes we make, we profit thereby. Contrarily, from
success there is left a residue of conceit—a cockiness and an over-
confidence which handicaps our next effort. The course of a
man's achievement goes up and down like the graph of a stock
market: not regularly, not predictably, but inevitably.

I believed that the mistakes I had made were in choice of
subject matter and perhaps in writing, but not in direction. It
seemed to me that my direction of these failures was just as
conscientious and just as good as it had been with the big successes. I have always been very sure of myself as a director—
perhaps even conceited. I have felt that I have directed my
shows better than anyone else could have done; what's more,

and this is a very silly thing to admit, I have usually felt when seeing other people's direction I could improve on it.

Sometimes it is difficult to judge direction. It is hard to tell where writing and acting stop and where direction begins. Even when the style is unique you may be watching the author's conception rather than the director's treatment. If I were a drama critic and I found myself in this quandary I would note how well the minor parts were played. If they are well acted, it usually means that the director is in control. But if the butler is lousy, perhaps the director is lousy.

"The wages of sin is death," said the ancient preacher, doubtless hoping thereby to frighten his congregation into more orthodox conduct, and we have always accepted the edict without too much questioning. I think that most of us, at least the men, think of sin as sexual sin. They think the preacher warns that if you err with a forbidden woman, you are liable to contract a repulsive venereal disease. We make jokes to cover up our fears and say that a dose of clap is no worse than a bad cold. A prominent author once told me rather proudly, "I'm a three-time loser," and I believe that Casanova confessed to being a seven-time loser. This fear is one of the first things a young boy learns about sex, and the warning is apt to hang over him like a menace for most of his life. Or I should say might have hung over him, for with the discovery of sulfanilamide and penicillin, gonorrhea is indeed no worse than a bad cold. I once asked a doctor what class of people had venereal diseases, and he replied, "The promiscuous class." I think I was hoping that he would tell me that it was the lower classes, only dirty people, but that somehow or other, most clean, educated, high-minded, upright citizens were immune. I was not immune. I contracted gonorrhea, and not from a sordid woman but from a superior, intelligent woman who, like the poor creature in Boswell's memoirs, had thought that her infection had disappeared and that she might again lead a normal life. My guilts were overpowering. I sank into a deep well of self-condemnation. I felt that someone should walk in front of me calling out, "Unclean, unclean." As far as the woman was concerned, I behaved like a cad. Although I knew that there was not the slightest evil intent on her part, I emotionally held her responsible, and I didn't want to see her any more.

Should such a confession be included in this book? When my sister Polly read the paragraph, she pleaded with me to take it out. She said, "You don't know how that is going to look in print. It isn't necessary. It puts you in a wrong light. You'll regret saying such a thing!"

It certainly does not present me in the most favorable light, but after all, that is not my purpose. I could easily make myself a more attractive character by magnifying my good actions and minimizing my bad ones. But would I be that man? Montaigne, for whom I profess such admiration, said that he owed the whole truth about himself to his readers. I feel that I should follow him to the best of my ability. I cannot hope to be as wise, but at least I can be as honest.

There is a theory that those who are unlucky in love are lucky at cards, but I now found myself at the nadir in both my personal and my professional life. Then things took a turn for the better.

Courtney Burr was one of those producers who had never quite shed his amateur standing. When he had a big hit in *Sailor Beware*, his greatest pleasure seemed to derive from his ability to entertain friends at the bar he had installed in the theatre. He was happy to let someone else produce the shows if he could sun himself in the afterglow. He had charm, and people in the profession liked him, though many of them did not have a high opinion of his talents. Burr now offered me a very favorable percentage deal to produce two plays. I was to select the shows and to have a free hand in all so-called artistic matters. When I went to Phil and told him of the offer he agreed that I ought to take it.

The first play we produced under this arrangement was called *Small Miracle*, written by Norman Krasna, with Ilka Chase and Joseph Spurin Calleia in the cast. It was a success, though not a big one. The next, *Ladies' Money*, a melodrama, was a failure. One of the small roles in this show called for a red-headed gangster, and a boy who was a radio actor turned up who was just right for the part. He was so bright and so imaginative that I took to him immediately. At first I didn't know his name and simply called him Red, but about a year later I discovered that his hair wasn't red any more. It seems he had heard that there was an opening for a red-headed actor and he had borrowed money from Sam Levene to go out and have his hair dyed. His name was Garson Kanin, and he was to be my right-hand man for many years.

There is a tendency on the part of newspapers and the public to type-cast people, to put a label on them. "This is right up your street," they like to say. There had been plenty of comedy in the things that I had written and directed up to that time, but my successes had been mostly of a serious or a melodramatic nature. Without knowing it, I was now about to be typed in another direction: I was to become a producer of farces. Following that, although I little suspected it at this time, I was to be a producer of teen-age plays—the most loathsome label of all. Still later, people were to say to me, "You never do anything but musical comedies, do you?" So art is long and fame is fleeting, and lucky is the man who doesn't worry too much about what people say about him.

My start as a producer of farces began with an actor named Cecil Holm, who had written a show called *Hobby Horses* and had taken it to a press agent named Alex Yokel. Yokel had gone to Warner Brothers for backing, and they said they would back it if it was properly rewritten and directed. I believe that they suggested me for the job; at any rate, Yokel approached me and I read the script. It had good scenes and good characters but no organization and no last act. However, I could see very clearly what was needed. The notion that a little greeting-card writer could tell by intuition what horse would win a race had to be carried on to its extreme, to be blown up like a balloon; but at the same time it had to be logical enough for the audience to accept it. I thought of a way to do this and began work immediately.

We had a good cast. Sam Levene was the head gangster, Shirley Booth was a tough moll, and there was a comedy role for Lorenz Hart's younger brother Teddy. Edie Van Cleve, later a big wheel at MCA, was a lady reporter and Garson Kanin was a photographer. The assistant stage manager was a young boy named Bobby Griffith.

I thought of a good title, *Three Men on a Horse,* but the Warner Brothers front-office boys had an improvement. There had just been a successful picture called *Three on a Match,* and so naturally they wanted to change my title to *Three on a Horse.* I refused to give way, and though we had a few stormy sessions the title remained. The farce opened in Washington, created no stir, then received fine notices at the Playhouse in New York but did not sell out immediately. Somehow or other we couldn't dispose of the front rows of the mezzanine. Then Yokel put the price up and charged as much for the mezzanine as he did for the orchestra. Immediately it was a sellout.

But none of us knew at that time what a big hit *Three Men on a Horse* was to become. We sold the picture rights for a mere seventy-five thousand dollars. The popularity of the play grew and grew, and eventually there were three road companies and a London production.

People react to success in various ways. Sometimes, more often than not, it is good for them. People who have been too aggressive calm down when they really find that achievement has been realized. In the case of Alex Yokel, it had the reverse effect. He had started out as a meek little man eager to do anything he could to help; now all of a sudden he began to feel important, imperious, to give violent orders. My contract specifically stated that he was to have no authority whatever behind the curtain, but as soon as I was out of town, he would be backstage giving notes to the actors. He was a man with angles, as a good press agent should be, and he was good at making such deals as free meals at Lindy's because we used its name in the show. But some of his antics were truly ludicrous. When I got to Boston to see the company playing there, I was shocked to discover a red light on the bar in the second scene which flashed on and off advertising a roadhouse nearby. Not only did the blinking light have a rather distracting effect on the audience, but the roadhouse which it advertised was in Boston, whereas the action of the play was in New York. I quashed this, left my stage manager in charge of the various productions and went to Florida. The next thing I knew a friend sent me a program from the London production which

stated that Alex Yokel had directed the play. That was the end
of our relationship.

Alex Yokel's one hit was mostly a matter of luck, though one
has to give credit for persistence and ambition. However, had he
not found someone, in this case me, to write this show and direct
it he would have continued to be just a press agent. If he had
seen his success in proper perspective, he might have gone on to
other successes; instead, he got a swelled head and began to
carry on as though he were responsible for the success of *Three
Men on a Horse*. He later produced other plays, but they all
failed.

There is gold in them there Broadway hills, but those who
come to seek fame and fortune face hardships and danger. The
weak are trampled on ruthlessly and the foolish die by the way-
side. I don't mean to imply that only the good guys get there—
many devious and untrustworthy characters reach the goal. But
if the bad guy succeeds, he does it by keeping a level head and
knowing his own limitations; he does not forget that in this cruel
wilderness he is going to need someone else to guide him. The
unmarked graves and the whitened bones along Broadway belong to men who suffered delusions of grandeur, who thought
that they did it alone when they only watched it being done.

The records will show that there are quite a few producers
and playwrights who have had only one hit, and then nothing but
failures until they disappeared from the scene. Generally the records will also show that there was someone else connected with
the one hit show whose record was more consistent. George M.
Cohan is reported to have said to Sam Harris, apropos of an actor
who had displeased them, "We'll never use that son-of-a-bitch
again—unless we need him." That is a fine practical point of
view, and any Johnny-come-lately who is heard to call a show
"my hit" should pause and consider, because the bluffers and the
braggarts are apt to find themselves helpless, far from that there
gold, when they are on their own.

In that same year, 1935, Sam and Bella Spewack brought me
a comedy about Hollywood called *Boy Meets Girl*. Embittered
by my experiences with producers I got the bright idea of dis-
pensing with them—I would get a business manager to do the
job. I had to make all the decisions about casting, scenery and

so forth, anyhow, so why have a producer breathing down my neck and arguing with me? I went to Warner Brothers and got backing for the new show.

Now Richard Rodgers and Larry Hart wanted to know if I would like to work on a musical comedy with them. They had an idea for a musical about a hoofer who becomes a ballet dancer, with some satirical overtones about the Russians and Russian ballet, to be called *On Your Toes*. I was to work on the book and direct, and Balanchine was to do the dances. To acquaint myself with musical-comedy technique Rodgers and Hart thought that it might be a good idea for me to break in by doing another musical first, and they suggested *Jumbo*, for which they had done the songs and which Billy Rose was to produce. Hecht and MacArthur had written the book for this show about a circus, and it was to be produced at the Hippodrome. I went to see Billy Rose and it was agreed.

Jumbo was a beautiful spectacle, but in the vastness of the Hippodrome the book was almost lost. The circus part came off marvelously. I actually dreaded to watch some of the show because I didn't want to be present when those aerialists, hanging by their toenails from the top of the Hippodrome, came crashing down to the hard, hard ground. But though there were many other accidents, none of the circus performers had any big mishaps.

In the meantime, *On Your Toes* was being prepared more slowly than had been promised. Dwight D. Wiman, the producer, was another talented amateur who had money and taste but lacked the drive and know-how that comes from having to scratch your way to the top. He kept postponing. I grew impatient, asked them to get another director and took off for Palm Beach. They went into rehearsal in February, but when they had troubles on the road they began to bombard me with appeals to come to the rescue. Wiman wired me frantically, and then Dick Rodgers got on the phone and told me bluntly, "It's your show, and it's your obligation to come and protect it."

Arriving in Boston, where *On Your Toes* was playing its final week, I found things in better shape than I had expected. Ray Bolger was sensational in the lead, and "Slaughter on Tenth Avenue" remains in my memory as one of the best numbers I've ever seen in the theatre, both musically and choreographically. The book, however, was a mess; the story line had been destroyed by experimenting, and the actors were out of hand. I behaved ruthlessly to the cast to force them to play their parts instead of fighting for material, and I straightened the book out by the simple device of putting it back the way I had written it in the first place.

In this arbitrary and unpleasant fashion I brought things under control and achieved order and even smoothness by the New York opening. Let me say parenthetically that I do not believe sarcasm is a good weapon with actors, nor even a fair one, but that there are times when a company gets out of hand and disorganized; and when that happens, the director had better lay aside tact and assure the cast that he is in charge.

I had written a modern version of *Uncle Tom's Cabin* and in the fall of 1936, I produced it. I engaged Juanita Hall, later to score so beautifully as Bloody Mary in *South Pacific*, to take charge of the choral numbers, and I engaged Donald Oenslager to do the scenery. Donald and I agreed that the most important factor would be to have one scene meld into the other with no delay. For this reason, although there was already a turntable in the theatre, a new turntable forty-five feet in diameter was superimposed upon it. The production was beautiful, the singing was lovely, many scenes were tender and moving, but we had made one gross miscalculation. It takes sixty seconds for a forty-five-foot turntable to complete its revolution and so although the whole production was built on a premise of speed, it turned out to be a slow freight. There were ghastly waits, for one minute is an intolerable time to spend in the dark waiting for the next scene. The show did not succeed, but I loved it.

Brother Rat was a play about life in a military academy, written by Monks and Finklehoffe, who had attended VMI. It gave a first chance to Eddie Albert and another promising actor named José Ferrer. To help with the publicity, we hired a VMI boy named Frank McCarthy, who went on to become Assistant Secretary of State, and still later an important fellow in Hollywood.

Soon after, Gar Kanin urged me to take over *Room Service,* which Sam Harris had tried out in Philadelphia and abandoned. Gar insisted that the play was full of funny stuff and that if I got the story straightened out we would have a hit. He was right.

I worked on the script with the authors and then we produced it, using Phil Loeb from the original cast, plus a group of my old reliables. By this time I had quite a stock company of actors, many of whom had been developed in road companies of my shows, and they would be transferred or promoted whenever the occasion permitted. For *Room Service*, we brought Eddie Albert from *Brother Rat*, Sam Levene and Teddy Hart from *Three Men on a Horse*, Betty Field from another road company, added a few new actors here and there, then stirred thoroughly and served. It was a cast to delight one's heart. The actors had all the ability of stars, but they did not yet assume their prerogatives. I was working with experts, and yet I could control the production in each detail. I could give it a rhythm and a unity possible only when everyone is working coöperatively and enthusiastically.

After the opening night Neysa thought I would want to stay in the city until the reviews came out, but I told her that I was sure it was a success and that we might as well drive straight to the country, because we had an important croquet game in the morning. As I suspected, *Room Service* was a big hit. We had the usual road companies and a London production, and it was sold to RKO for the highest price ever paid for a picture property up to that time.

During this period of the 1930's, I had two or three shows running on Broadway all the time, and once as many as four. I was able to develop a great many new actors as well as stage managers, casting assistants and business managers. Ednah's nephew, Carl Fisher, who at first had thought he wanted to be an actor, had developed into a crack business manager, and Bobby Griffith had become a top-flight stage manager. Gar Kanin, Edie Van Cleve and Ezra Stone all helped me with casting, second-company productions, and maintaining the performances on Broadway.

To help keep the actors fresh and also to satisfy a curiosity I had had for a long time, I started rehearsing Shakespeare's plays with the actors in my companies two or three afternoons a week. I made abridged versions of *The Merchant of Venice, All's Well That Ends Well* and *King John*, assigned parts and started rehearsals. I had always felt that Shakespeare was a practical playwright

—that he wrote shows, not dramas, that he was trying to create excitement in the theatre with no thought of posterity, and that while he certainly hoped that his sonnets would bring him fame, he had never for a moment suspected that anyone would ever publish his plays.

I regret that I am not a scholar, and I do not have the gift for exhaustive research. I think that if I had, and if I could go through Shakespeare's plays seeking in them some hints of the man who wrote them, that possibly I might discover something worth while. I know of course that every line has been researched and re-searched, but what I mean is that a man who has written plays has a certain instinct and feeling about what of oneself goes into them. Not much of course, because the playwright is not writing about himself but about other people; still, certain things are self-evident. For instance, Shakespeare couldn't resist telling what he thought of actors and of acting, and his "Hold the mirror up to nature" speech is just as good advice for the stage now as it was then. It also contradicts all the hams who posture and rant when acting in his plays. Most of the actors of today who consider them-selves Shakespearean actors believe that the verse is most impor-tant. I cannot believe this. I am confident that Shakespeare wanted to move his audience—to carry them away, to make things real. To our modern ears his language is contrived and stylized, but so was all the language of that day. If you read the letters written in that era you will realize that their language, even on the level of greatest privacy, seems artificial to us. Actors should try to make Shakespeare's words sound like talk, not like pompous posturing.

When one becomes famous enough to have his name in the papers, people appear from his past—some pleasantly, some an-noyingly. Also, a great many people wish to borrow money, some only want fifty dollars to tide them over. Some five hundred dol-lars for singing lessons or one thousand dollars for an operation, and some five thousand dollars to be paid back out of certain revenues in the specific future. For the benefit of the young and inexperienced among my readers, let me tell you how this works. They *never* pay it back. Borrowers are not dishonest—they just suffer from a disease which ossifies the conscience. In their sub-conscious minds they are convinced that the world owes them a living; after all, why should they who need money make a sacrifice to pay back someone who has plenty and who will never miss it? There have been occasions when I was happy to be able to do something for individuals whom I had known in the past: for instance, a producer who was kind to me in my acting days. But there were other times that were simply comical.

One day a man came to the office who purported to be from Hamburg, New York, and indeed more than that, a member of the dear old football team of which I had been captain. Although his presence excited no faint spark of recognition, I accepted him as bona fide, and because of my habitual inability to remember people, I was doubly cordial. I furnished him with some theatre tickets, and then when just as he was leaving he discovered that he was financially embarrassed, I lent him some money. My secretary, Miss Linder, pointed a finger of suspicion in his direction and suggested to me that perhaps he was not the real article. When a couple of days later he telephoned that another financial crisis had arisen and he'd be over for more cash, I realized that she had been right about him, and we shut the door on this pal of yesteryear.

On a higher plane an incident took place which I thought enlightening inasmuch as it illustrated how the wheat and the chaff occasionally get mixed up. My cousin-in-law, Dorothy Thompson, had become in these years a very important person. Not only was her column widely read, but she herself had developed socially, had sought and been sought by a great many important people. I had not run across her in some time and only knew from the papers that she had married again, this time a Middle European playwright. When one day she called me, warmed my heart with her cordiality and invited me to a dinner at her place, I accepted. It was a very swank affair. There were some twenty or thirty politicians, writers, musicians and society folk. Could Hamburg have seen this and realized how important these people were, it would indeed have been impressed. After dinner, instead of the usual games or conversation, things reached an even higher plane: a string quartette arrived and we listened to Bach. Now my brow is not high enough to listen too long to chamber music—especially Bach. At the start, I am aware of its loveliness, then gradually my concentration fades. It all begins to sound the same.

I am always anxious to be in the presence of culture if I am absorbing some of it, but if I sit in its presence and nothing is happening to me, I feel that it is a waste of time. And since on this occasion, I knew that I had to get up and rehearse early in the morning, I felt that my duty was to go home and go to bed. As it was a large party I did not want to disrupt things by saying good night to the hostess, so with the intention to telephone her the next morning, I stole toward the front door. Before I could make my exit, Dorothy bore down upon me under full sail. Her husband had written a play, she said, and she was eager to know what I thought of it. I might want to produce it, and in any case she would appreciate a very frank appraisal of its merits.

It just happened to be right there on the table in the hall. I took the heavy script with me, my heart full of wonder and cynicism at the flaws sometimes exposed in superior people. I read the play and thought it a turgid and wordy affair, and since I had received such a good dinner and such superior music for my services as a playreader, I felt it only just to render as candid and factual an opinion as possible. Occasionally thereafter I saw Cousin Dorothy and we would nod politely, but it seemed that fate did not wish us to recapture our former intimacy and we never experienced another charming evening with Bach.

Through the years, Jack and I had become increasingly good friends. Gradually we had gravitated toward each other, finding mutual tastes and mutual humor, we had fun together. On many weekends I would have actresses out as my guests, and Jack and I would entertain them while Neysa entertained somebody like Cole Porter or Main Bocher. One night at dinner, a woman who was not familiar with our domestic situation referred to me as the house guest. Jack said, "House guest! The son-of-a-bitch has been here eight years. The first four years they thought he was Neysa's lover. Now they think he's mine."

What really cemented the friendship between Jack and me was Freedom Week. Jack's domestic freedom was actually in force for fifty-two weeks a year, but in his whimsical manner, he pretended that this one week when Neysa went to Vermont to visit Woollcott was the only moment he was unfettered by the marital yoke. He and Will Stewart, one of his oldest friends, invited me to join them in celebrating the great occasion. William Rhinelander Stewart was one of the most socially eligible and sought-after bachelors, and in addition to that, or should I say despite that, he was a great human being. His courtesy was not reserved solely for his important friends; it was given out freely to those who needed it: to the vulnerable, to the people who were uncomfortable at parties. Will was gay, debonair, good-natured and tactful, and though the three of us were different in character and outlook, we shared the same sense of humor and taste.

Jack's idea of celebrating Freedom Week was to entertain three different girls on each night. Moreover, the nights were to have categories: there was Models' Night, Actresses' Night, Neurotic Women's Night and so forth. Then on the weekend, we would either have girls we had known for a long time, or else pick out the guests we had enjoyed most during the week and ask them to return.

There was a certain treasured routine to Freedom Week. Will had a magnificent limousine and a dignified driver, who would collect the girls in the city and transport them to Sands Point. Sometimes the girls knew each other, sometimes they were absolute strangers, but generally by the time they had made the trip out they had become friends. Unless they knew us well, they arrived in some trepidation; they weren't quite sure what they had let themselves in for, and one could sense a certain guarded caution in their manner. When they reached their rooms, they found the rules for Freedom Week pinned on their doors. Some of the rules were practical ("everyone down for breakfast by ten A.M."), but most of them were silly (we must always precede them through a door, and they must never take their places at the table until we were seated). After cocktails and a swim the girls would begin to enjoy themselves. They would realize that they were not in a den of wolves, that we were "gentlemen," and that the occasion was one to be enjoyed, not to be feared.

We always dressed for dinner, but while the overtone was very formal, the evening was very informal. It was always a gay occasion. I suppose that we really used the girls as an audience, that what seemed so funny was our reactions to one another. Will was inclined to be the quiet one; Jack and I were the aggressors. We tore each other apart with exaggerated banter, and we all laughed a great deal.

Champagne adds to the gaiety of such an occasion. By this time I had relented to a slight degree in my lifelong hatred of liquor. This was quite conscious on my part; one day it occurred to me that most of the people whom I admired drank and that perhaps I was wrong in my feeling that it was an unmitigated evil. If these people were good, as I was sure they were, then it could not be quite so bad as I had felt. I certainly had no desire to become a whiskey drinker, but I decided in the name of tolerance to drink wine with dinner. I have found that a pleasant thing to do. Of course, drinking to escape is a horrible sickness, and drunkards bring misery to themselves and to their families, but bigotry is bad too, and perhaps moderation is more temperate than temperance.

Everyone arose from the table feeling the gay exhilaration which comes from strong, unadulterated fun, and then we played games. Jack had brought back from Cuba a variation of Chinese checkers called Kangaroo. It had the same board as the regular version but a more elaborate system of jumping, and we taught this to the girls. Later we played charades: not The Game, but real charades. We divided up in teams of two, and again there was much laughter, because in the charades we lampooned each other. On hot summer nights we would go swimming again. There were three hammocks on the place, one for each of us, and the great sport which went on year after year was for Jack to sneak up to Will's hammock and put a fire cracker under it. We never failed to think that this was hilarious. Sometimes if the occasion and the mood were right, we would play a game called corks. It was played with a saucepan, two dice and a cork for each player, and the loser of each round had to take off a piece of clothing. Does this sound evil? It wasn't; it was unconventional, but it wasn't sinister.

No doubt conventional people will consider these juvenile hijinks disgusting and undignified. Perhaps their contempt will be based partly on envy. At any rate, I don't believe that anyone's character was warped or his morals shattered by our various Freedom Weeks, and as I look back over my life it seems to me those days constituted the most fun I ever had. The girls were there, but it was the men that made the party.

Promptly at ten the next morning, in my role as major-domo and as the only one who hadn't been drinking too much, I would knock on all the doors and summon the group to breakfast. Then outdoor sports took over: badminton, croquet, bocce and, of course, swimming and more swimming. After lunch, Will's trusty chauffeur would appear. The girls would wave a fond farewell and be driven to town. We would go upstairs for a short rest before the next delegation arrived. By the end of the week, we were red-eyed.

Will and Jack differed from me so sharply about certain matters that we had many arguments—some jocular and some serious—about drinking, smoking and prostitution. They claimed that though abstinence from drinking and smoking may have made me a bit healthier, it deprived me of a great many of the pleasures of life. They also felt that my abhorrence for prostitutes was based upon ignorance, not upon sound judgment. To prove this, they once brought out a very good-looking call girl and introduced her to me as a Powers model. Somehow, even before I suspected that there was a joke involved, I didn't like this girl. She was pretty but spiritless. If they are successful, most models are either arrogant and demanding, or ambitious and eager. The energy that made them leave home and succeed in this competitive field shows forth as individuality. It may be a cold hauteur that is unattractive, but in any case it is not negative. The call-girl substitute was pleasant—she never argued about anything—but I thought her insipid. Jack's and Will's hope that I would be dazzled by this beautiful stranger and that I would become her suitor was never realized.

On one of our first Freedom Weeks, we had what we called Society Weekend, to which three women, all friends of ours, were invited. Among them was the beautiful Mrs. Janet Ryan. On a warm moonlight night when we were all in the pool, I noticed that Janet and Will weren't swimming as much as the rest of us but were off in a corner by themselves. Many years later, when Janet became Mrs. William Rhinelander Stewart, I was shown the date inside their engagement ring. It was the last night of that weekend.

When Will married Janet, he made only one stipulation; that their marriage was not to interfere with Freedom Week. Janet not only agreed to this; she even started to recruit for us. One summer a couple of weeks before the annual event was to take place, we met a new girl at a costume party—a dazzling, vivacious creature named Mrs. McFeeters. Janet suggested that I ask her for our Freedom Week, so I explained the idea to her and she accepted. On Friday night, just before the weekend guests were to arrive, Jack took me aside and said, "Good old Will has been so nice and let us have our pick of girls all week. Let's give him a break and let him have Mrs. McFeeters." It was agreed; but when Mrs. McFeeters arrived, Jack couldn't resist her charm. In the bathhouse, changing for a swim, he said to Will, "I'll give you five dollars if you'll let me have Mrs. McFeeters." Mrs. McFeeters, however, was a natural-born coquette who played the field—she favored Jack on Friday, Will on Saturday, and me on Sunday. A few years later she had quite a success in Hollywood under the name of Maria Montez.

Larry Hart had a strong protective feeling for his brother, and he got an idea to help Teddy, which he brought to Dick Rodgers and me: a musical comedy version of *The Comedy of Errors* with Teddy Hart and Jimmy Savo as the two Dromios. Originally the book was to be written by the three of us, but I got to work first and finished a rough draft. Larry and Dick thought that it was so right that they withdrew as collaborators. Jo Mielziner was engaged to do the scenery, Irene Sharaff the costumes, George Balanchine the choreography. I pulled Eddie Albert out of *Room Service* to play the romantic lead, and we had Marcy Wescott for the girl. I called the show *The Boys from Syracuse.*

Larry was drinking heavily, and would be absent for two or three days at a time during the preparation of the show. This didn't bother me because he was quick as lightning when he was there. If we needed a new verse, he'd pick up a pencil and paper, fidget himself into the next room for a few minutes and then come back with what we needed. I remember that this was how he wrote the verse for "Falling in Love with Love"; he scratched it on the back of an old piece of paper while Dick and I talked about something else.

Nevertheless, Dick was very concerned about Larry's growing addiction. For one thing, he saw his collaborator gradually deteriorating; secondly, he knew from experience that when a show got on the road, it needed a lyric writer ready for emergencies. Dick's fears were realized; when we went to Boston there was no Larry. But everything in the show fell into place so easily that we didn't need him. I don't recall changing the order of any numbers or adding any material once we began to perform the play. I do recall that at a benefit performance on the night before we opened in New York, the show died a terrible death, and we all were sunk in gloom; but on the following night, it was a success with the first-nighters and the reviews were as fine as you could wish. At this stage of my career musical comedy seemed very easy to me; I was as yet unaware of its trials and tribulations.

Twenty-five years later I was in Florida when an off-Broadway revival of *The Boys from Syracuse* was produced by Richard York. I was delighted to read of its outstanding success, and distressed that some of the reviewers referred to the old-fashioned jokes in the book. But I was puzzled when one of the reviewers cited one of these jokes, a corny pun: "Dozens of men are at my feet." "Yes, I know, chiropodists." This kind of humor is so alien to me that I knew I could never have written it; and when I got back to New York I found that the "old jokes" in the revival were new jokes inserted by Mr. York to "modernize" the script. I took out some of these gags, but because the production as a whole was so delightful, I couldn't get very angry.

Next I jumped to a very different kind of show. *What a Life* was a comedy about the problems of adolescence. It was a hit, but one of its by-products became even better known. The radio show, "Henry Aldrich," was started partly because we thought it would be good publicity for the legitimate show, but long after *What a Life* had been forgotten, "Henry Aldrich" carried on, and Ezra Stone typed himself forever with "Coming, Mother." He made a great deal of money out of it but it undoubtedly hurt his career. Had he devoted himself completely to the stage, he could have become a more versatile actor—and perhaps a more versatile director.

My daughter Judy was supposed to go to Vassar, but she came to me with an appeal—she wanted to go to the American Academy of Dramatic Arts instead. I recalled very vividly that when I was nineteen years old I knew exactly what I wanted to do, and I assumed—with logic I think, logic which a good many parents fail to apply—that she too knew what she wanted. I gave Judy a starvation allowance so that she would learn what life was like in a great city when you are on your own, and made sure that she had a suitable roommate. When she got out of the Academy, she was put in as one of the extras in *What a Life,* and later when it became a radio show, she played Agnes, Homer's girl friend, for several years.

Robert Buckner and Walter Hart had written an adaptation for the stage of the successful novel *February Hill,* but no one dared produce it for fear of lawsuits by the people who claimed it was based upon their lives. I decided to take the chance. We named the play *The Primrose Path* and took Betty Field out of *What a Life* for the ingénue. Helen Westley played the old lady; and there was a good, all-around cast. It was a shocking play. It opened up with the child, Marilyn Erskine, playing with a cat and the first line of the show came from the little innocent. She said, "Lay still, you son-of-a-bitch." It was, however, tragic and beautiful, and I think quite perfectly performed. I loved it. And when, as the years go by, people say to me, "You produce only farces, don't you?" or "You produce only musicals," I always have *The Primrose Path* and *Coquette* as my defense against those accusations.

A change had taken place at Sands Point. It had become impractical for the Baragwanaths to maintain both a place in New York and one in the country. Neysa's contract with *McCall's* magazine had not been renewed and Jack would have to be out of the country for some time, so they reluctantly decided to sell the house. To save this situation I bought the Sands Point property and we reversed our roles; for the next several years they were staying in my house, though I confess that it still seemed to be theirs.

Jack had taken a job as head of the Nicaro Nickel Company in Cuba, and in 1939 he invited this old lover of Cuba to come down for a month's visit. He had an attractive apartment opposite the Presidential Palace, and while he was at his office I could sit on the terrace and read, occasionally being interrupted by the clamor of Batista's entrances and exits—his motorcade throttling their engines wildly, creating that violent boastful challenge, that statement of virility, like roosters crowing, that seems so needed by some people.

In the late afternoon Jack would come home with his customary complaints against the weather and the cruel fates which had plotted against him that day. Then we would sally forth for the evening. Jack knew Havana—he knew the best people, he knew the worst. However, he was a failure in one department— he couldn't produce any good dancers. To my surprise the upper classes, the rich people, of Havana were not good dancers; in fact they showed very little interest in the native steps; their image of themselves was as members of the international set. They would have expert dancers to perform for them at parties, but with rare exceptions, they were unskilled themselves. Later, I realized that the same situation obtains throughout the world—Society is too engrossed with clothes and status to have enthusiasm left over for anything as demanding as good dancing.

Furthermore, even if I could have found superior dancers among them, tradition would not have permitted us going out. A few independent-minded divorcées were brave enough to appear unchaperoned, but generally speaking it was unthinkable. The picture I had formed of a gay dancing life in the tropics proved to be a mirage.

By diligent enquiry I solved the problem myself and located a joint called the Havana Sport, where one could dance with any number of partners at, as the song says, five cents a dance. When Jack had suggested prostitutes as a solution to my difficulty, I had expressed repugnance, so now he was amused because he said that not only were these girls prostitutes; they were unsuccessful prostitutes who couldn't get a job in a house and were forced into this inferior work. The Havana Sport had atmosphere. It was dark and crowded. The majority of the men there were short and swarthy but occasionally there would be a dignified gentleman who was obviously out for an evening of dancing and nothing more, and there were also a few superior-looking Orientals. The women were not handsome when looked at closely, but in this place of shadows and music they were, if not romantic, at least exotic. Nearly all of them wore evening dress, many of them had flowers in their hair. Two or three were obviously in an advanced stage of pregnancy. There was no gaiety, no laughter; the mood of the place was somber, almost sinister. The orchestra was on a platform to be reached only by a ladder, and an electric sign at one end of the hall told you what dance was coming up next. It would flash, *son* or *danson* or *tango* or once in a while just *fox*. The so-called *fox* was pretty sad, but the Latin rhythms were marvelous. At one side was a long bar whose bartender openly tossed a girl a chit if she brought you there for a drink. The place was well-policed; in fact, the police acted as unofficial doormen and expected to receive a tip for getting you a cab.

With good-natured condescension Jack would accompany me to this dive. He thought the girls were terrible and the music unpleasant, but he enjoyed watching me cavort and so he would sit at a table and buy drinks for the girls I brought over.

One night, becoming bored with the Havana Sport, Jack suggested that we take two of the girls to a nightclub. We learned that if the owner was paid one dollar and fifty cents per girl, the ones we had chosen could be excused for the rest of the evening. Outside in brighter light our ladies looked slightly sordid, but Jack didn't seem to mind and I regarded it as a romantic adventure. We went to a nightclub and I continued to dance. The girls kept going to the ladies' room. They had learned from experience that Americans usually gave them a quarter for the maid, and they went frequently. Finally Jack and his girl had had enough. He explained in Spanish to my partner that I was going to stay and dance, then he told me that she was to be taken to the bus when we finished and he advised me further that I should give her five dollars. Finally danced out, I paid the bill and escorted my partner outside and into a taxi where I assumed that she would tell the driver to take us to the bus. She spoke to him in Spanish, then the driver turned to me and said, "You want to go to small hotel anl spend de night?" "No," I said very firmly. "We want to go to the bus." We drove some more, until I no-

ticed that we had passed the same landmark twice. "Where the
hell do you think you're going?" I yelled at him. "I think maybe
you change your mind and go to small hotel and spend de night."
"No, damn it, I don't want any small hotel, I want to go to that
bus." We reached the bus stop shortly, and considerably ruffled, I
said good night and gave the girl five dollars. At this she registered such relief and joy that I realized I could have saved myself a long taxi ride had I given her the five dollars sooner.

The headwaiter at the Montmarte nightclub in Havana had
formerly worked at the Yumari in New York and was, so to speak,
a friend of mine. I asked if he couldn't introduce me to a good
dancer—not a tart, just a good dancer. He thought for a moment,
then told me to go for lunch at a certain restaurant and take a
booth, leave my name with the maitre d' and wait. I followed his
instructions, and soon there appeared a dark, heavy-set girl,
with rather bad skin, who spoke halting English. She was friendly,
but she seemed reluctant to go out dancing with me unchaperoned; she wanted me to join her and her "friend." The friend
turned out to be one of those square Cuban men with a big behind, very polite as nearly all Cubans are, who was happy to have
me dance with his girl. He was in the sugar business, and when I
didn't put sugar in my coffee he was very disappointed; he threw
a couple of spoonfuls on the tablecloth. "If you can't use it, waste
it," he said.

Of course, I was aware that this man was keeping my dancing friend. In fact, she intimated that if properly urged she was
willing to shift to a new management. I was, however, only ambitious to dance with her and not at all tempted to promote myself to a more personal category.

Next to sugar, prostitution seemed to be the leading Cuban
industry. One became aware of it first in its most blatant form:
poor hungry girls walking the streets soliciting passers-by. Next,
the pimps, mostly taxi drivers who wanted to steer you to an exhibition or a place where you could get a young *muchacha*. Then
there were the girls who worked in dance halls or nightclubs and
who were available for two dollars. Above these strata, prostitution was less obvious, but Jack explained the caste system to me.
At the top were the mistresses, the well-kept women who were, I
discovered, a good-looking, sexy, overblown set of Carmens. Cer-

tain places were *verboten* to them, but their men, the rich husbands of Havana, took them out openly to other places. By convention the Pan American Restaurant was the place to take your mistress, and no man was supposed to bring his wife there. Next in order of prestige came the very select bordellos which had a limited membership of twenty or thirty men who would operate the club exclusively for their own use. Further down came the carefully inspected call houses, then the better-class bordellos which were available to anyone and where the charge was eight dollars or ten dollars, and finally there were the cheap four-dollar and two-dollar places. When business got too brisk at the eight-dollar houses, they would send down to the two dollar houses and ask for a few replacements.

The whole Latin attitude toward women baffles me. No race of people loves little girls more than they do, but once the little girl attains puberty and becomes a woman, she is a hunted creature and every man is against her. Her father and her brothers may protect her, but more as a personal property than with tenderness. If a girl in Havana once slipped, once defied the conventions, was once caught out of bounds, she was on the blacklist and an outcast forever. If she was very rich, of course she would be sent away, but if not, she could only become a whore.

Back in New York that summer I had my appendix out. (I'm not going to tell you about all my operations, but this one has significance.) On doctor's orders, Neysa drove me over to Nassau Hospital in a great hurry. We were met at the door with a wheel chair, and though I did not feel all that sick, I was impressed and a little worried by their interest in my case. As soon as I was undressed, a nurse came in to find out such details as where to send the body after the operation, and whether I was a Catholic or a Protestant. For a moment I hesitated. I certainly was neither, but I didn't like the sound of that nasty word atheist; on the other hand, I didn't wish to be yellow on the brink of the grave and repudiate all my convictions. I couldn't explain to the nurse that I was a deist or a transcendentalist or a Confucianist or something like that. I couldn't take time to explain that a man could have an ethical code without subscribing to an established religion, so, it was with some trepidation that I said, "I'm an atheist." The nurse

blanched. She said, "Well, what should I put down?" I said, "Put
down I'm an atheist." She said, being a good Catholic girl, I suppose, "Well, should I put down Protestant?" I gave in. I said,
"Yes."

After the operation and during the recuperation period I had
a relapse and felt very, very ill. When I awoke the next morning,
the pain was gone, I was at peace. I found myself singing a hymn
—some hymn I had learned in my childhood. I thought, "Isn't it
funny. Some instinct in me makes me want to thank somebody or
something outside myself for my good fortune in getting well. I
am instinctively thanking God for my good fortune, when I should
be thanking these nurses and doctors who are taking care of me."
So I made up a little hymn of my own which went as follows:

"Holy, holy, holy,
Seaman and Newman,
McMonicle and Quist
And bacteriologist,
Blood test and urine,
Colonic irrigation,
All praise is due to
The Nassau Hospital."

I sang it to the nurses, Misses McMonicle and Quist, who
thought it was very funny, but I sang it to Dr. Seaman and he
didn't think it at all funny. I imagine he had visions of word
getting to the politicians of Nassau County that the hospital had
become a hotbed of atheistic propaganda.

In the early fall of 1939 I planned to do two shows. I was going to busy myself primarily with *Too Many Girls*, a musical with
a Rodgers-and-Hart score. I was particularly excited about it because it would have some Cuban atmosphere. Desi Arnaz and
Diosa Costello, who were from a local nightclub, were to be prominent members of the cast, as well as Eddie Bracken, who had
been taken from a *What a Life* road company. Bob Alton was in
charge of the dancing, and though the book was contrived and
artificial, the acting and songs were good. In rehearsal Larry Hart
disappeared again. He was really needed this time, for we had to

juggle things around during the tryout and to do quite a lot of patchwork. The second act opened with eleven girls singing about the woes of being deserted by their athlete lovers during football season. Rodgers thought it would be a good idea to have the first act open with eleven men singing about the fact that football season was the only time when they were important; during the rest of the year they were lifeguards, telegraph boys or camp counselors. Since Larry could not be found, Dick turned to and wrote the lyric himself, a very effective one. Therefore, when it was announced some twenty-three years later that he would write his own lyrics for *No Strings,* I was not one of the skeptical ones.

The other production for that fall was a slim farce called *See My Lawyer.* I entrusted the direction of this to Ezra Stone, and for the principal part we toyed with the idea of casting a new actor named Danny Kaye, who was making a hit at the Martinique nightclub. Then Milton Berle suddenly became available, and that settled it. Berle was superb. He is a fine legitimate actor when he wants to be, and he played the part straight, with no fooling around or ad libs of any kind.

I directed and produced four more shows that year. None of them was particularly good, and all are long since forgotten. During this flurry of work, my mother died. I didn't go to the funeral. My brother and sister went to Hamburg and took on all the responsibilities. Ostensibly I didn't go to the funeral because I was in rehearsal, but to be honest it was something I wished to avoid. My mother wouldn't have minded, I knew that. She always said, "If you want to give me any flowers, give them to me while I'm living." I had done just that; I had been able to make my mother's final years her happiest ones. These years of security were her best ones. She had worked relentlessly and fearlessly, and she had suffered uncomplainingly to achieve her great ambition: to bring her children to maturity to the best of her ability. Her story had a happy ending.

Dick Rodgers approached me with another idea, a very daring one: to make a musical out of John O'Hara's short story, *Pal Joey.* O'Hara had a script, but it was a disorganized set of scenes without a good story line and required work before we would be ready for rehearsal. Again Alton was engaged to do the dances, and Jo Mielziner was to design the sets. One of Rodgers' and Hart's favorite actresses, Vivienne Segal, was to be the married woman in the cast, and Gene Kelly, who had made a hit in Saroyan's *The Time Of Your Life,* was our choice for Pal Joey. June Havoc had a good part, and I promoted Van Johnson from the chorus of *Too Many Girls* to give him a small role.

We started rehearsals unsure of what the total effect was going to be. After a week Bob Alton thought the show was hopeless and wanted to quit, but Rodgers persuaded him to stick it out. Jo Mielziner made a major contribution to the production by suggesting that the curtain of Act One be a scene in which Joey envisions his future in the magnificent club which his new girl friend is going to buy him. It cost ten thousand dollars to build the set, a good deal of money in those days when a musical had a budget of one hundred thousand dollars, but I accepted the suggestion unhesitatingly. This is a perfect illustration of how many collaborators there really are in a musical comedy.

John O'Hara came to rehearsals very little. When I needed rewriting I would do it on the set, and later he would drop into the theatre, look over what I had done, go to an empty dressing room, rewrite the new material and depart. I am sure that *Pal Joey* must have been important to him; but I can never remember his demonstrating any approbation or enthusiasm—nor, on the other hand, any criticism. He seemed disinterested, but I am sure that this was just his manner.

When the show opened in New York, it had a mixed reception. Some hailed it as the best show they had ever seen in their lives; others hated it. Brooks Atkinson, certainly one of our best critics, was shocked by it. But here is an example of the fallibility of criticism: ten years later when *Pal Joey* was revived, Atkinson thought it was perfectly charming—it didn't shock him at all. Did he see it on an off night the first time, or did he just grow up to it in ten years?

John O'Hara was drama critic on the old *Life Magazine,* and in that capacity he dropped into the theatre after the play had run for a long time and there had been many cast changes, and gave us a bad notice.

·   ·   ·

People are always asking, "What do you think of the critics?" Well, I think the critics are people like the rest of us—with the same anxieties, loyalties, prejudices, headaches and ambitions. Disappointed playwrights, some people call them. Is that bad? I don't think so. It only means that a love for the theatre has been turned into another channel. The critics have great power, it is true, and they can destroy a play. But in my opinion the plays they destroy usually deserve it; in fact, I believe that there is more justice in accusing them of being soft than in accusing them of being destructive. In certain respects they seem to me very vulnerable. Critics feel that stars should be treated kindly, and they will invariably ignore the miscasting of a star. A fifty-year-old woman can play a nineteen-year-old girl and not draw one adverse comment. Also, it seems to me that they are too prone to give a helping hand to anything that seems "worthy." If a play has a smell of Art about it, the critics seem to feel that it needs their special protection and that they must cajole the public into attending it, whether it rates very high as entertainment or not. But in general, critics are honest men doing their very best, sitting through a dozen tedious plays to see one exciting one; trying to inform you about what is good and what they think its value is. Since, like all of us, they desire to excel at their job, they try to be right. It is true that sometimes they try to be cute at our expense, but that's part of the game; in fact, unless the barb is directed against us personally, we rather enjoy it.

I would hate to be a critic. I would despair of being able to leave the theatre, put my thoughts in order and write a well-organized critique within the next hour. It is extraordinarily difficult to be objective. The audience sees a play through the medium of its feelings, and a show doesn't look as good to a man with business worries or an upset stomach as it does to a happy fellow who has just made a lot of money or fallen in love. The critic must be able to ignore such superficial influences. There is one type of critic, however, who should be eliminated: the drunk. It seems as though we always have one with us, and it is not fair to us in the theatre to be judged by a man who is only half there.

We sold *Too Many Girls* to RKO and they engaged me to write and direct the screen play. I wanted to use our cast *in toto*,

but RKO thought some picture names were necessary, so Lucille
Ball and Ann Miller were hired. I took Desi Arnaz and Eddie
Bracken from our company and about six of the important girl
dancers, as well as Van Johnson. After the day's shooting we used
to go down to El Zarapi, have dinner and dance. One night I invited Lucille Ball to join us, and I asked Desi to bring her. When
I arrived at the club, they were already there; I expected them to
join us, but I could see that they did not intend to. The next day
Desi apologized. He said Lucille had suggested that they stay
by themselves. Well, that was the beginning of staying by themselves. They kept at it for quite a long time.

In the summer of 1942 my father died. He had re-established
himself as an honored member of the community, and various
fraternal organizations mourned him in a manner which would
have gladdened his heart. I stayed away. I was in rehearsal, and
again I stayed away while my brother and sister again took over
the responsibilities of the funeral. I eased my conscience about
the burden on them by alloting them my share of the inheritance,
but from a moral point of view I had no qualms of conscience.
Funerals have never seemed important to me—and this pertains
to my own as well as to others. I have seen to it that no one must
come and be sad when I die. My body is to be cremated, and my
eyes will be given to the Eye Bank. Later on, if some of my
friends should talk about me or remember something funny or interesting that has happened to us, that will be all the obsequies I
desire. As I write this, both Neysa McMein and Bobby Griffith
are dead, but if either of them could hear how frequently their
friends speak of them and with what warm affection they are remembered, they would be very pleased indeed.

Much of my father's life was sad, but certainly his death was
not. He had faced the adversary and he had won. When I confess that the death of my parents gave me no great sense of loss, I
suppose that I will be considered a monster by most people. Is
this because they really feel differently, or because they think
they ought to feel differently? Is my own lack of sentiment in the
matter objectivity, maturity, indifference or coldness? I don't
know the answer, but since I am trying to write an honest docu-
ment, I must try to report accurately. It seems to me natural that

old people die. Indeed, sometimes it seems a shame that they
don't die sooner. By this I mean only that senescence and second-
childhood is an unattractive age and that it would be better if all
of us could be spared. My parents had not reached that stage. I
believe that they were happier than they had ever been, and I
had helped them to achieve that happiness. There was nothing
further I could do. Going to the funeral would be an empty gesture, a knuckling under to convention, and I didn't go.

My theatrical batting average during the 1940's was not too
good. It wasn't exactly bad—I had hits. I always had at least one
play running—in fact, from 1935 to this time I have, with the exception of a week or two, always had at least one play running on
Broadway. But during this period I had some dandy failures and
the worst of these was *Beat the Band*. It was the poorest job of
producing and directing that I ever did; I was guilty of mistake
after mistake. The first mistake was in thinking that it was any
good; the second was in the casting; and the third and biggest
was in not abandoning it when it obviously was a failure. I didn't
realize what a disaster it was in New Haven, and when the press
agent said, "We can send back the photographers without paying
them if you want to," I hotly rejected any such notion. After a bad
opening in Boston, I telephoned Dick Rodgers and asked him if he
would come up and give me a hand. He came, found the mess
too deep-seated to be able to offer any constructive suggestions,
but he did stay around and keep us company. Even after *Beat the
Band* opened in New York, I continued to work on it and was
able to make small improvements. But its basic flaws were impossible to correct and eventually it died, teaching me some valuable
lessons.

One day my secretary came in to my office and said, "There's
an awfully cute girl outside whose picture was on the cover of
Life last week. I think you ought to see her." Her name was Joan
Caulfield, and because I thought she had what it takes I gave her
a small part in *Beat the Band* just to let her get some stage experience. Then along came a script, that I knew was good, requiring a
teen-age girl for the lead. *Kiss and Tell* was a hit and so was Joan
Caulfield. Richard Widmark, an actor from radio who had been
recommended by Arlene Francis, played opposite her. Later,

when I took him out of the cast to promote him to a leading part in another show, his role was taken by Kirk Douglas. Thus I continued to furnish fodder for the Hollywood hopper.

Some plays need work, but once in a while one comes along that is, as they say, a natural. *Kiss and Tell* was one of these; there was scarcely anything to do except to polish it.

William Saroyan had written a play called *Get Away, Old Man.* It had very obvious faults, but my admiration for the author was so great that I decided to produce it, faults and all. With all his great gift for words, Saroyan is not very good at construction. It did not hold together as a story and failed.

Next came *On the Town.* A new choreographer named Jerome Robbins had joined up with a young composer and conductor named Leonard Bernstein to create the ballet "Fancy Free," a fresh and original conception. It concerned three sailors and their shore leave in New York City. Robbins had a notion that the ballet could be the basis of a musical comedy, and he induced Betty Comden and Adolph Green, who had written a great deal of nightclub material, to join him and Bernstein in the enterprise. Oliver Smith and Paul Feigay were going to produce it, but they knew that it had loose ends, and they wanted a more experienced hand to settle their battles and to give the enterprise some unity. I was approached, and I met with them and listened to the material. They were a very engaging crew, the kind of people I like to work with—eager, emotional, enthusiastic. Oliver Smith, who had already had considerable success as a scene designer, expressed himself dryly and with a quiet smile; he was an elegant young man who looked as though he could play a leading part in an English drawing-room comedy at a moment's notice. His partner, Paul Feigay, was the contact man, the go-getter, the fellow who was supposed to raise the money, and he had the qualifications necessary for that—he made you feel good. Leonard Bernstein looked just the way Chopin and Lord Byron should have looked; he had wavy hair, a classic profile and the assurance of genius. Adolph Green was ostensibly the clown, but he turned out to be a most erudite fellow. He probably knows more about music, and certainly can quote more lyrics, than any man in the world. He and Betty Comden were a wonderful team. Reposed, where Adolph was exuberant, she was a dark, quiet girl possess-

ing more than her share of handsome sex appeal. She was, however, devotedly in love with Steve Kyle, her husband.

I liked *On the Town* but I thought some things were wrong,
and it seemed best to say so early in the game. For instance, there
were many long and involved interruptions of the main plot by
a judge and an old lady, two characters I thought unnecessary.
They argued with me until finally I said, "You'll have to take your
choice between me and the old lady." They chose me, and we
used the old lady simply as a crossover.

The inexperienced managers had allowed only two weeks for
the tryout in Boston. This was much too brief by all normal standards, and the problem was further aggravated by the snowstorm
which delayed the scenery's arrival. In actual fact, we were to
have but ten days in which to get the show ready for Broadway.
At the first performance in Boston I had to come before the audience to tell them our problems and ask them to be patient with
the delays in changing scenery which had not yet been properly
hung. They were tolerant as audiences always are when there is
an emergency in the theatre; it seems as though participating in
these crises adds a zest to the evening which more than com-
pensates for any awkwardness.

During those ten days we cut out a musical number and two
songs, threw away one of our best-looking sets, added a new song
and changed stage managers. When we returned to New York,
we had two more performances in which to polish the show before opening with the changes made in just the nick of time. *On
the Town* was a big hit. Nancy Walker, Comden and Green, Alice
Pearce and Chris Alexander were all marvelous, and as always,
Robbins' dances were perfection.

We all worked together on this show in the way that I love to
work: each putting forth his opinion, yet remaining objective,
and subordinating everything to the main end; working with
happy excitement, with passionate enthusiasm, with a wonderful
feeling of warmth and togetherness. During these rehearsals I
had an emotional reaction which I have often felt since. I felt as
though I were Jewish. Except for Oliver Smith, all my associates
in this venture were Jews, and I felt myself to be one of them. I
do not mean to imply that all the warm, enthusiastic people in the
theatre are Jews, nor that I am the only lucky Anglo-Saxon who

has this inner heat. In general, however, it is true that both in their work and in their social life Jewish people are warm, have deep feelings and seem to give more of themselves.

There is no anti-Semitism in the theatre. There are good actors and bad; there are inspired directors and hacks, honest producers and crooks, successful writers and mediocrities. Everyone is rated by his ability, not by his race. Of course, there are exceptions. One can always find people who feel so inferior that they must try to feel superior in another way. One of the easier ways is to feel superior to a whole class of people—a race for instance.

Races do have characteristics, I admit. Once I saw a graphic demonstration of this at Madison Square Garden. An opera was being sung by a Negro cast, and the audience which was assembling was also mostly Negro. I was there early, and I watched the slow, relaxed couples taking their places, their low quiet voices almost like music. Against this peaceful sound was a sharp penetrating one, the high imperious cries of the Jewish vendors—a tense race contrasted to a relaxed one.

Jews haven't all got good manners. Who has? It takes time, training and the right environment to learn these things. If a race has had the guts to survive through two thousand years of persecution, it is bound to have some assertive impulses. And manners are mostly by example. The American of Jewish extraction has the same manners as any of us, perhaps better. The second generation of any race improves, culturally at least, over its predecessor. Surroundings also make a difference. People in New York City have worse manners than people in Los Angeles. It isn't due to race; it is because of environment. The Irish are supposed to be an amiable people, but I don't think the New York police can be awarded any blue ribbon. To me Latin Americans seem inherently polite, and I believe that the best-mannered taxi drivers in New York are the Puerto Ricans.

At any rate, I have always felt *simpatico* with my Jewish coworkers. If I am ever present when someone makes a denigrating remark against Jews, I feel as though he were insulting me, and I generally get into the argument.

Life is so full in New York City that every time you make a new friend it seems that you have to lose an old one. Or perhaps "friend" is too strong a word. Friends last whether you see them or not, but there are only seven days in the week and if you suddenly meet a person who takes up four or five of those days, something else has to give. This sounds ruthless, but actually it is a very healthy thing. We don't want a static and petrified existence. If acquaintances are changing with you, they are also changing with others.

One of the ways to meet a lot of new people is to go to cocktail parties. Being a non-drinker and a very bad small-talker, I usually find them boring. But like a lot of other people who damn them, I sometimes go to them. Sherman Fairchild gives unique cocktail parties. To start with, he lives in a unique house. There are no stairs in it; you proceed by ramps from one level to another. Sherman is an engineer, and so his parties are handled very systematically. He knows what you are interested in and he tries to introduce you to those who have similar tastes. There are always a great number of beautiful women present—models, actresses, career girls. There are also a great many smartly dressed men. Sherman takes the wolves over to the beautiful models and in a very short time you will see notebooks come out and telephone numbers being jotted down. Sherman loves music and there will always be music lovers at his parties who presently gather around the piano and listen to Hoagy Carmichael do his inimitable songs. Businessmen are there too, and there will be an aura of high finance to add dignity to the proceedings. As you walk across the room you will hear not only, "Where have you been all my life, baby?" but, "He could have got the stock ten points down, but he didn't have the guts." Throughout all this, Sherman maintains a vague, far-off manner, as though his body was there but his mind was upstairs solving some engineering problem. As he talks to you, he looks vaguely in your direction but he is likely to stop in the middle of a sentence and walk off somewhere else. The interests I shared with Sherman were tennis and dancing; on this fatal afternoon in the midst of my rehearsals for *On the Town*, he led me past the tennis group and introduced me to Vici Raaf who was, he said, a beautiful rumba dancer. I went dancing with Vici two or three times and on each occasion she reminded me that I had promised to interview a friend of hers who wanted to be an actress. It was a girl named Mary Sinclair, who was working for the Conover Model Agency, and I told Vici to have her come to the office, but it proved to be impossible because she worked during office hours. Finally, I made an appointment to meet Miss Sinclair at five o'clock at the St. Regis, where I lived at the time.

Nobody has ever been able to explain what we call "chemistry" between two people. It is a strange, sudden physical excitement that comes just from another's presence, as if some sixth sense were operating. Of course, I know that it isn't really chemistry, that it really isn't just the presence of the two bodies, for it is all too familiar an experience when we have let time do its work to find that the two bodies can be present without any attraction whatsoever. But when Mary Sinclair entered my apartment at the St. Regis, I felt that strange elation and excitement. She was a white-faced, black-haired girl, at that time quite full of figure— not fat, not heavy exactly, but full, like a figure in a Goya painting. I didn't think her beautiful but I was powerfully drawn to her. She seemed shy, almost wild. It seemed that she had come to New York to go on the stage, and had been encouraged by Marlene Dietrich and some others who were interested in a small West Coast theatre in which she had been acting. She had earned a living as a model; and when she couldn't get a job in the theatre, she returned to her trade. Mary told me that she had entered a modeling contest and won three hundred dollars, but she didn't bother to explain that at the time she had been twenty pounds lighter, so I was a little puzzled at this. After that she went to work in Harry Conover's as an office manager.

I would have liked very much to have told this girl something that would have pleased her. She had excited me; I felt as though ghosts were walking through my insides. But despite rumors to the contrary, integrity in the legitimate theatre is a very strong thing. I don't think we intentionally give much false advice just to please people; I don't think I have ever told a girl that I thought she had a future in the theatre unless I firmly believed it. Consequently I was honest with Mary Sinclair. I told her that she was neither a leading woman, nor an ingénue, nor a character woman; that the parts for which she was suitable were few and far between. Recently I had produced *A Highland Fling*, which had a barmaid in it, and I mentioned it as a possible role for her. Furthermore, she had another drawback: although she had the body of a woman, she had the voice of a young girl. Altogether, I did not hold out too much hope to Mary, but she accepted my bad reaction graciously and left.

The train took *On the Town* and me to Boston the next morning, where a thousand problems kept me from thinking much about my love life. However, I did write Mary two or three bantering letters without receiving any answer. On the day before we were to return to New York, I called her and asked if she would have dinner with me on the following night. She said yes. Our reunion was a success and so, of course, was *On the Town*. The world seemed a very exhilarating place. Every moment with Mary was a joy. True, sometimes she became distressed by something I could not understand, but it was only a passing cloud over that dear face, and I thought of her as one of the most serene and placid individuals I had ever known.

Business comes first with men—that is, if they like their business, and it may be taken as axiomatic that everyone who is at all successful in the theatre likes his business. Now business called me, and so in the midst of this delightful, sentimental euphoria, I had to take the plane for the sentimental capital of the world, out where they sell sentiment by the foot—Hollywood— to make a picture of *Kiss and Tell*.

Harry Cohn, who for many years was the power at Columbia Pictures, was the last of the great tycoons of Hollywood. He ran the studio as his own personal property and no one dared interfere with him. Hollywood admired Harry Cohn because of his ability; it feared him because of his power and the tyrannical way in which he enforced it. Those who worked for Columbia Pictures were ever at his mercy. There were no flaws in his armor; no qualms of conscience or petty sympathies ever stood in his way. Like an ancient warrior in his chariot, he rode ruthlessly over his subordinates without compunction; no ancient friendships, no promises, ever complicated his decisions. The only armor against Harry Cohn was a contract; the only thing that gave him pause was a lawyer. In our contract for the production of *Kiss and Tell*, Hugh Herbert and I had seen to it that we would have a free hand. Neither in the casting, writing, nor direction could

Cohn overrule us. Entering the enemy camp with such power, one became almost equal—or at least a respected subordinate. I found myself admiring Cohn's vigorous efficiency. He had no education and no manners; he spoke like a thug, but he had magnetism, force and vigor, and like all dynamic men, he had charm when he wanted to use it. I was flattered at any interest he took in me; in fact, I liked him.

Though I had been in Hollywood before, this was my first contact with a typical studio—the kind of organization that had been developed by L. B. Mayer at Metro, by the Warner brothers, by Laemmle at Universal, and by Harry Cohn at Columbia. These men all shared certain traits and so did their studios; as is generally the case, the subordinates, aping the masters, also fitted into the pattern.

Arriving in Hollywood to do a picture, one is given the warmest of welcomes. When you report for work, the austere gateman at the studio knows all about you and is terribly glad to see you. You are shown to an office where there is a wonderful secretary, an awful lot of pencils, and big yellow pads and big white pads. They teach you how to work the complicated telephone system, and they tell you that Mr. Big is on the long distance phone but that he wants to see you just as soon as he can get free. You open the window and let in the beautiful California sunshine, then lie back on your especially soft sofa and wait for Mr. Big. Word comes that Mr. Big is going to be tied up with some men from the New York office until three o'clock, but that you are invited to have lunch in the executive dining room—that is, if you are a producer or a director you are so invited. If you happen to be an actor you are not, and if you should be someone as low as a writer, you have no chance at all.

You go out and wander around the studio until you find the executive dining room. There someone recognizes you and introduces you, telling what you have done in New York to give you a little standing. Everyone is very polite, but underneath the cordiality there is a certain antagonism. It takes a long time for a Broadway personality to be accepted in Hollywood; there exists an unspoken rivalry. They are suspicious of you, and perhaps defensively you look down your nose at them. People from the legitimate theatre often regard Hollywood as a sort of rich old party who deserves to be swindled. They go out there on fat contracts, stall around for months doing some hack writing that they could easily have finished in weeks and regard the whole thing as a perfectly legitimate way to make some easy money, like cheating a corporation. Hollywood, on the other hand, regards the people from Broadway as outsiders, as transients whose brains are to be picked, and who are then to be discarded without further ceremony, to be cast out as so much used-up material. Hollywood is jealous of Broadway because it is better, and Broadway is jealous of Hollywood because it is richer.

In the executive dining room, the talk in your honor may turn politely to the legitimate theatre of New York City, but it soon veers back to the one topic of common interest to them all: pictures, past and present. Sometimes baseball or prizefights creep into the conversation, or motor cars, or stock prices—and, of course, broads. After a while, Mr. Big comes in, flanked by two or three assistants. He takes his place at the head of the table and presides after his own fashion. He may be the type of man who has whispered conferences, but he is more likely to relax and direct the conversation at will. If he tells a story, everyone listens; if he makes a joke, everyone laughs. Just to keep a veneer of democracy, a reckless fellow will argue with him, or even make a joke at his expense. But Mr. Big is clearly the king and everyone at the table automatically becomes a yes-man.

At three o'clock, you go for your interview. There are two secretaries in the outer office, and there are other people there waiting for an audience. Silent doors open; people hurry out with papers. You are sent in ahead of the others, given a hearty welcome and a comfortable chair. Mr. Big is relaxed and friendly. He wants to know if you are happily situated in Hollywood, if everyone has treated you well here on the lot. Once in a while the little box on his desk buzzes and he talks through the squawker to somebody, impressing you by the ease with which he spends the company's money. He flips a lever and leans back in his chair.

Mr. Big: "Yeah."

The box: "Squawk, squawk."

Mr. Big: "Listen, Charlie, I told you I wanted that title."

Box: "Squawk, squawk, squawk."

Mr. Big: "Never mind all that crap, you just get on your horse and get busy. *Baby, Oh, Baby* has got appeal, and I want it for our picture. And I'll tell you something else, Charlie, just between you and I, it might be a title I'll use not only for the song, but for the picture too. No, no—you quit worrying about the price."

Box: "Squawk, squawk, squawk."

Mr. Big: "Twenty thousand? Goddamn robber. Okay, we'll take it."

Throughout Hollywood the caste system prevails. At the top, you find the producers, then the directors, then the important actors. Next come the writers and technicians, and finally there are the bit actors and stage hands, and last of all the serfs—the extras. The producers are about evenly divided between talented men and parasites. Nepotism exists in every studio in its most flagrant form: people inherit or marry their jobs. An executive producer at the head of a studio has to have brains and a sense of organization, but a producer of a single picture can be a complete washout. In most cases, the director is the one who puts his stamp upon a picture. He is the one who does the actual work; the producer is more or less a figurehead. Still, the producer is theoretically the head man, and his office is bigger and his secretary gets a higher salary. Directors have to be capable, because nobody can hold the bag for them. A cutter may help, a good assistant may help, but in the long run the director makes the decisions—and the decisions show.

A successful picture director must have great physical vitality to stand up under the strain, and he must have infinite patience. Sometimes a director will take years to make his product. He must prepare his picture over long weeks of dull tests and other details that seem tiresome. He must be vain enough, ambitious enough and subjective enough to keep trying for perfection; he must be able to endure boring repetitions of shots until he gets what he wants—in fact, until he has half a dozen choices of what he wants. Then he must have that most important ingredient, a dramatic flair, and a technical skill with the tools at his disposal.

Actors don't rate very high in the studio echelon until they become important; then they rate *very* high. Often the actor carries a deep grievance dating from the early stages of his career, a resentment that his talents were not appreciated, a hurt pride because of past humiliations. Now when he suddenly finds that he is the one who can draw the public, he slaps a hammerlock on his old tormentors and pins them to the mat. Once the actor knows that he is needed, he can—and often does—make ridiculous demands and behave outrageously. He can be late; he can be indifferent and rebellious during the shooting; he can dawdle on the set and then unpredictably decide that he doesn't feel well or that he wants to play golf. What can a producer do? The company will make money on the picture, so the management shuts its eyes to the injustice of it all, lets the minions on the set bear the emotional pangs of the turmoil and ends up with a product which shows a profit. On the other hand, though a supporting actor is well paid—even extravagantly paid by the standards of the legitimate stage—he may not work for many weeks out of the year, and in the studio he has no standing.

The technical people—the cameramen, grips, electricians and so forth—are well organized, well paid and efficient. To see a first-class head grip and his coördinated crew at work is a delight. Each man knows his function: one places the ladder; another is up like a streak; another passes the hammer. They are like a well-trained football team with the head man calling the signals. If someone has forgotten that a Leaning Tower of Pisa is needed on the set, they will build one in fifteen minutes.

At the bottom of the scale—and well deserving their position—are the studio extras, who are dedicated to doing as little as possible. Probably this lackluster indifference to the welfare of the picture is their only defense against the tyranny of their bosses. At one time or another most of them have been ambitious to get ahead, but now they seem defeated. Seldom do you see an extra who is eager or energetic. When they are taken in buses to the set, they disembark and disappear; they simply fade away into the scenery. When the time for shooting comes, the director's assistant tries to herd them on the stage. He screams; he yells. Moving slowly with impassive faces, the extras drift toward the set stopping to chat together, apparently paying no attention to the commands. Some never appear, spending the whole day in some secluded spot to come out only in time to ride back and pick up their checks. They are paid a salary that varies according to what type of wardrobe they furnish, and they are well protected by many restrictions and rules laid down by their union. One is not allowed to swear at them—which is a pity, because they're awfully goddamn lazy.

Everything went smoothly in the filming of *Kiss and Tell,* and I enjoyed this stretch in Hollywood. As just a producer, not a director, it was fun to find myself in a leisurely mood during the shooting, to be able to go out to the beach or play tennis instead of being anchored to the camera with tension, tension, tension. Things went so well with the picture that Harry Cohn entered into a contract with me to produce *Snafu,* giving me the same authority over the production. The authors of *Snafu,* Louis Solomon and Harold Buchman, were educated, well-read fellows, and, in my snobbish mind that made them smarter than Harry Cohn, who had never heard of Fowler's *English Usage.* Thus it was that I committed a terrible error; I appointed a director they recommended who was vigorously protested by Mr. Cohn. Then I returned to New York, where I was to produce the musical comedy *Billion Dollar Baby* with my friends Comden and Green and with music by Morton Gould and choreography by Jerome Robbins. *Billion Dollar Baby* was not up to *On the Town.* The principal ballet was too long, making the second act drag; Joan McCracken, though a fine actress, was not right for her part. The show had enough merit, however, to be a passable success. In the midst of rehearsals Harry Cohn called me to tell me that the picture was being absolutely ruined and urging me to do something about it. I am ashamed to say that I took a very cavalier attitude. I said, "Well, it's only money," or some such flippancy, and refused to let my thoughts be distracted from Broadway. It turned out eventually that I had made a complete fool of myself. The picture was a mess, Cohn had been right, and I had behaved inexcusably.

In the meantime my personal life had changed. Since my wife's death I had never been a one-woman man. Also, I had been a little smug about my friendships with people of various worlds and tastes. Now for the first time I found myself neglecting my dancing friends, my theatre friends, my social friends, my funny friends, my pretty friends and even some of my old friends in order to spend more and more time with Mary Sinclair. When summer came she was frequently my guest at Sands

Point, and I think Neysa, with a woman's intuition, sensed that this new girl was different, a menace to our little domestic paradise which had endured all these years.

I remember that there was one crisis which surprised me. In the country one Sunday I realized that I had not seen Mary for an hour or so, and upon investigating I found her crying in her room. She said she had to go home. These were my friends, and she didn't want to disrupt my life in any way, but it was obvious that Neysa didn't like her. It turned out that she had been rebuked for calling Neysa by her first name. This seemed to me strange since I knew that Neysa encouraged everybody she knew to so address her. I smoothed the situation over and forgot it. On the surface everything seemed placid.

My fondness for Mary continued and then a terrible thing happened. A sinister word kept poking out of my subconscious and flashing through my brain, and though I suppressed it and pushed it into the background it would come bubbling up again. Did you ever take a hearing test? You sit in a little room with giant earphones muffling out the world, and you are told to press a button when you hear any sound. Listening hard, you seem to hear what is like a spark, a tiny light at the end of a long tunnel. This grows into the buzz of an insect and then gradually louder. Well, this terrible four-syllable word, even before I could hear it, seemed to be there in the distance. Matrimony. Marriage I thought was the last thing in the world that I wanted. My life seemed complete as it was. I had enjoyed as happy a marriage as I could hope to achieve; besides, by disposition I was a person who liked to be alone and untrammeled. Nevertheless, this insidious word kept coming back. It was a word which Mary Sinclair had never uttered, but I knew that she was unhappy with our present relationship, and she let me know in a sweet way that eventually it would have to cease. There was no future for her. Should I lose this jewel among women? Should I allow this priceless creature to escape from me because of my selfish desire for bachelorhood? Ought I not perhaps drop my unconventional life and take up a worthwhile pattern of existence—home every night with the same loving woman, my affection centered conventionally on this serene beautiful soul?

Finally I broached the matter to Mary tentatively. Wouldn't

it be ridiculous, I said, for a man so much older to contemplate marrying her? She said that she didn't know whether I wanted to get married, but if I did certainly age was no barrier. I would never be old, she assured me. I was young in spirit; I was a young person essentially, I was even young biologically. I seemed younger, she told me, than her first husband, who was her own age, thirty years my junior. Oh, no, she could never think of me as old. But suppose we should do such a crazy thing. What about the routine of my life; what about the house in Sands Point, what would we do about all that? We would leave it just as it was, she assured me; of course. What about the Baragwanaths? They would live with me just as they always had; she wouldn't think for a moment of disrupting my life in any way.

I let a couple of intimate friends know that I was thinking of getting married. Intimate friends have learned that generally an inquiry about marriage is followed by the act, no matter what advice they give, and that if they voice an adverse opinion they only gain the animosity of the new bride and lose the friendship of the couple. I received guarded answers. I consulted my doctor. He seemed amused that I was finally thinking of taking the step, and he could think of no physiological objections.

When I broke the news to the Baragwanaths there was a stony silence. A day later they informed me that Bill Paley had graciously offered them a cottage on his place in Manhasset and that this would be their future summer home. Thanks just as much, they would move out. It was difficult for me to close that chapter, but a man's life must go on. The die had been cast.

Part Five

A PLAYWRIGHT KNOWS the form of what he is going to write before he puts down a single word. The construction, the manner in which one scene leads into another, what the characters say and what they think as the action progresses, is usually all in his head before he begins. But when I started on this effort at self-revelation, I had no form in mind. As I proceeded with the writing, I discovered that I was separating it into periods which pertained to my personal life, rather than to my work. This section, it seems, is to be about my second marriage. And so, dear Mary Sinclair, who was good and sweet and kind in all her intentions, who loved me very dearly, and who nearly turned me inside out with her imaginary grievances, her insecurity and her tempers, will have to forgive me if I write about us as impersonally as though we were two imaginary characters in a story.

We decided to be married at my sister's house in Upper Montclair. To me, whatever marriage ceremony we would have to go through with was just a disagreeable formality, but Mary

considered it an event and outfitted herself with a new hat and
suit for the occasion. Gradually, without my having realized it,
she had lost weight, and as I looked at her on our wedding day, I
suddenly saw that I was marrying a very beautiful woman. I got
little joy from it. I was embarrassed by most of the formalities;
I thought that the clerk who issued the license must think I was
an old goat carrying off a charming creature much too young for
me. My sister found a second assistant Presbyterian minister from
the neighborhood and he performed the ceremony. Judy, my
daughter, was there, and everyone was all smiles.

On the way back to New York, Mary was strangely silent. I
talked to her, but I could not penetrate this ominous reserve
which made me feel that I had done something wrong—I didn't
know what. We drove to Sands Point, where we had already
taken residence and where the servants had planned a special
wedding dinner. That evening we had a quarrel, and the next
afternoon, while we were outdoors working in the garden, Mary
grew angry at me about something and began to scold me. The
scolding grew, and in a moment she was shrieking at me.

I couldn't make any sense of what was happening. It was as
though a train were being wrecked and I was in it; there was
nothing to do but sit there and let it get wrecked. In all my life I
had never experienced anything like this. My family had gone
through many crises, but they were always controlled. In the
Baragwanath household there were never any angry voices. I
thought this sort of thing belonged to another world, yet here I
was standing in my garden with the servants listening at the windows and my beautiful bride railing at me, looking more like a
witch with her disheveled hair and her blazing eyes and her
screaming voice than the sweet and gentle Mary whom I had married.

The day after such scenes she would become my sweet and
gentle Mary, the most loving, most exciting, imaginative, gay and
charming female that a man could hope to find. There were
idyllic days in which she filled my cup of happiness to overflow-
ing with her charm and warmth; then incomprehensibly there
would come these violent scenes with which I could not cope.
When she was good, she was very, very good, but when she was
bad, she was horrid.

When people don't get along, you nearly always find yourself on the side of the person who's telling the story. When a divorced woman tells me how she extracted a good settlement from her husband, it all seems fairly rational because I am given the impression that the husband was a good deal of a bastard. But there is always another side to the story, and of course there is to this one too. Mary's entrance into my life was very difficult for her. She had to accept my house, my servants, my friends and my money. Later I learned how to spend money on both my house and my wife, but at the time I was inexperienced in these matters. As a result I was to sit in a lawyer's office five years later and listen to a smartly dressed, incredibly beautiful woman tell of such domestic injustices as my refusing to buy a new garbage pail.

I have often been accused of being tight—and I am. Once I was having an argument with someone about whether or not there was an after life, and my opponent said, "You mean to tell me that you think Hitler is having the same reward as, for instance, a man like Thomas A. Edison?" I answered, "Hitler was a wicked man to us, but to himself he was not. He justified everything he did in his own mind, as we all do. He considered that he suffered, worked and died gloriously for a great cause."

No criminal thinks himself a criminal. He thinks that the world is unfair and has abused him, and he is fighting back with the only weapons he has. And we tightwads also justify ourselves. The group to which I belong might be called frugal. We hate waste. We eat everything put before us because we cannot stand to see food wasted; we turn out lights in hotels as conscientiously as we do in our own houses; we buy the very best things because they last longer. We are not stingy in good deeds, but we refuse to give money just for the appearance of being generous. We wish to be sure that our money is well spent. We are not stingy in our tips, but we refuse to be blackmailed by waiters or others. We refuse to buy favors; we wish to be liked for ourselves, not for our money. Usually we spend more by using charge accounts and checks than we do with cash in our pockets; the cash represents a compulsive emotion which became ingrained when we were young and which is difficult to eradicate, whereas the check is only a piece of paper. The idea of spending is not repugnant to us—but the mechanics are. The kind of tightwad whom I describe so knowingly does not want something for nothing; nor does he want anyone to do him any favors. He always wants to pay his share; indeed, sometimes he wants to pay more than his share in order to help some other up-and-coming tightwad. But he is stubbornly determined not to spend money foolishly or for show.

There is another type of tightwad, of course, and this one I do not understand quite as well. I refer to the man who dodges his obligations. These fellows are usually big spenders. They invite a group to dine, but just as the check is due they have to go to the telephone. What is their psychology? How do they justify themselves? I imagine that they think they are being clever in not being stuck with the check. They feel it is astute to let other people pay for them.

In any case, I did not understand all the things that a man ought to do for his wife, and I had to learn about them the hard way. I had to learn that a man ought to be proud of his wife, and want her to have expensive clothes. I had to learn that the Sands Point house, which I had always considered ideal, was really an old-fashioned Victorian mess and should be done over from top to bottom. All of this was a gradual process and a fascinating subject to me, but I doubt whether my readers would care for all the details. So let me pass over them lightly and simply say that eventually the house was done over, that Mary became very well dressed indeed, and that eventually we even got a new garbage pail.

It is always easier to describe hell than heaven. There was a good side to our life; there was gay companionship, and there was the great love which Mary showered upon me. I was proud of her because she was so beautiful, and it is very pleasant to have a beautiful woman jumping into your lap all day long and telling you how wonderful you are while smothering you with caresses. But I was completely undone by the other side of Mary's character. I didn't know how to deal with unreasonable anger, accusations of injustice and jealousy. Mary would ridicule Neysa and Jack, my daughter, my dead wife, and all the girls she ever thought I had been fond of. If I went to their defense, I was in for a row that would last a couple of days. I didn't know how to act when she flew into a rage in the middle of dinner and went upstairs to weep while I, feeling embarrassed before the servants, finished out my lonely meal. Then I would go into the living room and read, and at about ten o'clock she would come downstairs full of repentance, crawl into my lap, and again we would be friends.

It was a crazy existence, but it had its funny sides too. At first, I planned to entrust Mary with the housekeeping, but I found that this role was not for her. She had head-on collisions with the servants, and I was constantly being forced into the role of peacemaker. Also, a checkbook was something of a mystery to Mary. When, on one occasion, she couldn't straighten her accounts, she settled the whole matter by burning the checkbooks.

One summer day we had a luncheon for several neighbors. Jack and Neysa were there, and during the luncheon Mary talked gaily about the possibility of knocking out one wall to make a wider entrance to the terrace. Now Jack had designed this house with loving care, and he and Neysa cherished it as though it were a part of themselves. To them, Mary's talk was a little like proposing to cut their dog's legs off because you wanted a shorter dog. They finished lunch in silence and then swept grimly and grandly out and into their car and away. I was very distressed.

In general, my good friends rallied around and were very good to Mary. Mrs. Emerson was particularly thoughtful and kind, so were Harry and Alicia Guggenheim, and we spent a great deal of time with Alfred Vanderbilt and his wife, Jeanne Murray. At parties, Mary was nearly always a success. She was a good player of games and was ready to respond enthusiastically to anything that was going on, once she got there. But getting there was quite a problem, for just as it was time to leave, she went through a period of thinking that she wasn't wanted. This would be followed by an interval of feeling that she wasn't wearing the right dress, or that her hair was all wrong. Our gay evenings would frequently start with me sitting in the car honking the horn and yelling to her that we were already an hour late.

Mary was candid and honest, and we would often talk over our problems and try to marriage-counsel ourselves into a better relationship. When I asked her why she had never shown jealousy of me before we were married, she replied, "I didn't have any rights." Women will undoubtedly understand this comment, but it only puzzled me. She was immediately attracted to any helpless person. With insecure people she gained security. One night we were walking along Sixth Avenue (what a silly thing to try and change it to Avenue of the Americas and how satisfying it is that New Yorkers won't have any part of it, that the only people who call it by its new and fancy title are out-of-towners) when a woman's voice was heard saying, "Somebody ought to help this man." The woman stood by the curb and down in the street was a dirty old man slumped over. In her bright, clean dress, Mary was down in the gutter beside him like a flash. She put her arms around him. "It's all right," she said. "You'll be all right." Soon a crowd gathered and a policeman arrived and took over, but the emotion which that impulsive gesture of hers had stirred in me lingered on and made me love her very dearly.

Once again I was hired as a play doctor. The trouble with fixing plays is that so much damage has already been done, so many wrong commitments made, that one is always in the position of trying to patch the sail with shoddy materials. I think I could have made a hit show out of *A Beggar's Holiday* had I been able to have the proper changes of cast. But having extravagantly squandered hundreds of thousands of dollars, the management now suddenly became penurious and was unwilling to squander a little more to salvage what they had already wasted. As a result, they lost it all, though Oliver Smith's sets for the show were breathtaking.

I kept working. *It Takes Two* was a failure. *Barefoot Boy with Cheek* was a middling success.

My marriage, meantime, was going through its usual alternate spasms of sunshine and storm. It seemed that one possible solution to our problem would be to give Mary more to do. She had a dress shop called The Mannequin, which I was now financing and which made very good clothes indeed, but which did not make money. But now she confessed that her real love was still the theatre. In fact, she resented deeply my having discouraged her in her pursuit of her career as an actress; she said that it was my discouraging comments that had turned her from her goal. I decided to make amends by financing a stock company in Ogunquit, Maine, where, as the boss's wife, she could be guaranteed some good parts. Mary had a great deal to do with the planning of this company, and it turned out to be first-rate. For a producer we had a highly recommended new boy by the name of Bob Fryer, and Alex Segal was the director.

Mary was anxious for me to go to Ogunquit and help, but I had visions of a rather peaceful summer in Sands Point, and I adhered resolutely to my decision. As the time came for Mary to leave for Maine, our quarrels became more and more frequent. She wanted to go, but she also wanted to stay. On the day of her departure we had a violent quarrel, but finally I took her to Grand Central and put her on the overnight train for Maine, which would leave an hour later, then I returned home and went to bed. At four o'clock in the morning, Mary appeared in my room. She had gotten undressed and into her berth, then had lain there worrying about me and thinking that she couldn't possibly go away with that last quarrel between us, so she had disembarked before the train left and taken a taxi back to Sands Point. Startled at this apparition, I screamed at her, "What the hell are you doing here?" Mary fled in tears and on foot began walking back to New York. I gathered myself together, caught up with her and succeeded in placating her. The next day we had to devise a very complicated airplane schedule so that she could get to Ogunquit for the first rehearsal, but of course she was late.

In July, I went up to Maine to see a performance of *The Little Foxes*. Both Mary and the production were good, but the atmosphere about the whole place was tense. Everybody seemed to be fighting with everybody else, and I was glad to leave.

Summer evenings in New York are often gentle; the streets are comparatively empty and there is a nostalgic tinge to the world. On such an evening I had left my office and was strolling to my car when I saw another lone figure. It was Will Stewart: a faded Will, a thin version of Will. I knew that he had been ill, but I was shocked to find him so obviously fragile. We were glad to see each other. He asked me to change my plans and to have dinner with him at the Brook Club. It was good for his purposes he said, because of its elevator; he was supposed to avoid walking upstairs.

I shall never forget that evening. Will knew that he was dying, but he talked with incredible grace and charm about life and of the things he loved in it. We talked about the things we had done together—the gay things—about the mysteries of conduct and human relations, and about his love for Janet and his wish that it was possible for her to comprehend and share all his most intimate thoughts. After dinner we parted. A few weeks later I went to his funeral. I was invited to be an usher, but when I got to the church his friends—the friends of the other part of his life— were in charge. I felt almost an interloper, and I sat in the last pew. It was an Episcopal service—a beautiful one, I suppose, but I wasn't listening. About halfway through, I stole unobserved out into the street, where children were playing and taxis were honking and all the city was going about its business in the usual desperate fashion. I walked downtown thinking about my friend. Dear Will—everybody loved him.

Mary would soon be back from Ogunquit, and I felt a need to be busy. A few weeks earlier, a show called *High Button Shoes* had been offered to me to direct. I liked the music by Jule Styne and Sammy Cahn, but the book had seemed to me impossible. Now, rather than be idle, I asked if the job was still open, and when I learned that it was I accepted it. Phil Silvers and Nanette Fabray had the leads, and Jerome Robbins was to do the dances. When I was sent the final script on the day before rehearsals started, I realized that I had let myself in for something difficult. The book, by Stephen Longstreet, wasn't really finished. During rehearsals I had to rewrite the show with the help of Phil Silvers, who had a great many funny things to suggest. The producers, Joe Kipness and Monty Proser, with the Shuberts in the background, paid me author's royalties, which was a generous thing to do, since there was nothing in my contract requiring it and since Longstreet had refused to take any cut. Later, in the middle of an argument with Longstreet, Phil Silvers is said to have told him, "You'd better be careful—some night we might play your original version."

Robbins was growing more sure of himself each year and he did a wonderful job with *High Button Shoes*. Anyone who saw it is bound to remember the Mack Sennett ballet. The cast was nearly perfect and the whole show delightful.

Rehearsals are quite a refuge from the cares of the world. The need for concentration upon your problem is so intense and so insistent that you are forced to push aside what seem to be the small and petty cares besetting you. The director sits in his chair or walks about the stage, his mind entirely upon what he is doing and what ought to be done. Sometimes when people come to me in the middle of rehearsals to give me a message, it takes me a second or two to bring myself back to the factual world and realize what they are talking about. My mind is so preoccupied that I cannot adjust to the real world. I cannot quite comprehend what is being said; names which should be perfectly familiar seem foreign. This sort of projection into limbo is exhausting in its own way, but in another way it is also a peaceful little heaven. No telephone message is important; no letter needs to be answered; no social obligation must be acknowledged. You make few engagements because you're not sure that you can keep them. Even outside the theatre you're not free from the rehearsal demon which sits on your back. There are always problems: problems of rewriting; sometimes emotional problems in which the conflict between your loyalty and affection for some actor and your loyalty to the play are at loggerheads. But the play always wins— you have to be ruthless.

There are several stages in the course of the play's progress, and though they repeat themselves time after time one never gets used to them, is never insulated against the shocks. First, there is the optimism of early rehearsals and the excitement over the actors, who you always feel are going to be marvelous in their parts. Then there is an added excitement when you perform the play on the bare stage for invited actors from other shows who, knowing that it is in a formative stage, overlook its defects and with their imaginations working in your behalf often give it a quality that it never achieves later with scenery and costumes. Next, there is the dress rehearsal, which is always a frightful letdown, and then there is the first performance before an audience which never, never, never comes out exactly as you expected it to. And finally there is that last, terrible drain upon your nervous system: the opening night in New York. After which, no matter whether it is a success or a failure, the show is an old shoe, a cast-off lover, and you don't care if you ever see it again.

Now Jerry Robbins had a new project. He had conceived the idea of a musical based upon the trials and tribulations of a touring ballet company. He had enlisted the services of two new playwrights named Lawrence and Lee to write the book, and Hugh Martin to do the music. *Look, Ma, I'm Dancin'!* was the title, and it had a good part for Nancy Walker. I was excited about it and we all went to work. Jerry started his dance rehearsals two weeks earlier than the rest of us in order to perfect a rather spectacular ballet he had planned. I kept away from these because I know from my own experience that it is no fun to have someone peering over your shoulder critically when you are in the formative stages of your work. But I kept getting word from my stage manager that progress seemed to be slow. One Sunday I was out in the country when a message came that Jerry wanted to see me immediately. I rushed into town, and he asked me to look at what he had done. It was not good; he knew it and he wanted to have it verified. We immediately jettisoned the whole ballet, and he started on a new one. His two weeks' work later became a little fragment used as atmosphere in another scene. The best dance which Jerry did for this show was conceived and executed in two days while we were on the road. It was the "Sleepwalker's Ballet," and it required a lot of unusual techniques from the dancers because they had to stand erect on each other's shoulders and be carried around as though in a trance.

We had some trouble with the costumes for *Look, Ma, I'm Dancin'!*, but Mary and The Mannequin came to our assistance nobly. It was almost a great show—but not quite. I don't think I can remember a funnier entrance than Nancy Walker coming down the New York Central platform with a gigantic wolfhound as tall as she was. My combination gardener and chauffeur, Lawrence Larry, had a chance to go on the stage as a redcap, and he was put in charge of the dog. One night, out of kindness, one of the stagehands brought the wolfhound a bone. When the time came for his entrance, the wolfhound didn't want to leave his bone; he became ferocious, and for a time it looked as though the dog would lose his entrance and the redcap would lose an arm. But Larry had a great way with animals, and he was able to drag the beast onstage just at the last minute, though the audience may have wondered why the dog was looking so longingly off-stage right.

Unfortunately Nancy kept losing her voice, and sometimes she was out for weeks at a time. And Nancy is a unique personality, difficult to replace. Her sister was the understudy, and she looked something like Nancy, but she was not Nancy. We suffered just at a time when things were beginning to roll well; and night after night we would have to disappoint our audience. Had it not been for this unfortunate illness, I think that the play would have been a big hit.

At this time Mary invited a couple of visitors from the West to come and live with us. One was a fierce collie named Val, known to all my friends as Fangs. He was a remarkable beast and a great individualist. He arrived in Sands Point groggy after five or six days in a baggage car. The family next door had two aggressive and disagreeable Doberman pinschers and a boxer. These dogs intruded upon our property frequently, snarling at us and making themselves generally unpleasant. Now, sensing that there was a newcomer on the premises, they came over to investigate. They found Val in the garage recuperating from his ride, but when they threatened him he rose on groggy feet and offered to give battle. We came to his rescue. The next day, however, we had to leave Val, for we were going on a trip for ten days. We gave the servants instructions to protect him as best they could and took off for the Adirondacks.

As our car came up the drive on return, a wild beast charged out snapping and barking as though he were going to tear the machine to pieces. Val had recovered. He became a cringing, affectionate, wonderful warm dog the minute he recognized Mary, but though he accepted me he would have nothing to do with me. From the servants we learned that Val had grown strong enough a day or two after our departure to take on the neighboring dogs singly and collectively until he had become master of the field.

One day we were all out on the terrace, and the dog was being patted as he went from one guest to another; as he passed by me I too gave him an affectionate tap, whereupon he turned and bit me in the face. Mary telephoned her mother in California to find if the dog had had rabies shots; there seemed to be a great deal of uncertainty, so to be safe Abbott had to have shots for a couple of weeks. But Val was contrite about his attack on me and became docile and friendly. When winter came we couldn't take him to the city and had to put him in a kennel. We went out to visit him a couple of times, but he always put on such a scene that it was more than we could bear. He was a rugged individual; he never gave in; he barked all winter long and never accepted the prison to which we had sentenced him. By spring, he had almost lost his voice, and he had certainly lost his health. I grew to like him better than any dog I ever knew, and when he died that summer I felt that I had brought this about by an unjust sentence. He was a terror to everybody but his friends, but he was loyal to them. The next year we got another collie, but he was a poor substitute. He was too aristocratic; he seemed a tepid dog after fierce old Val. He was very handsome, however, and somebody stole him.

Our other visitor from the West was a good-looking friend of Mary's named Julia Trissell, who had once been a model with Mary at Magnin's in Hollywood. Julia had come East for a change of scene after a divorce. She lived with us all summer and was a great addition to the place, for she was a passionate gardener and an interesting though ungrammatical conversationalist. She went to work at The Mannequin as Mary's partner, and while the institution continued to lose money, it lost it in a much more distinguished fashion from there on.

One of the leading theatrical lawyers in New York is Howard Reinheimer, of whom Oscar Hammerstein once said, "The trouble with Howard is that he won't take yes for an answer." In the fall of 1947 he called to ask if I would see two new producers of whom he thought very highly. Their names were Cy Feuer and Ernest Martin, and they had a property that they thought would interest me. It did indeed; they had acquired the rights to *Charley's Aunt* and they had hired Frank Loesser to write the songs and Ray Bolger to play the leading part. They wanted me to make the adaptation and direct it. I took fire immediately. Frank Loesser's songs had already made him well known, although he had never composed anything for the stage. At a party two years before this, I had heard Frank and his wife sing "Baby, It's Cold Outside" with great success. I had called him the next day and tried unsuccessfully to induce him to do a musical with me, so of course, now I welcomed the chance to work with this man. I went out to the Coast for a conference and there we got started. Later Frank pointed out to me that in this show, which we called *Where's Charley?* (not a very good title), all the songs were kept in the production exactly as we planned them. Usually there is a great shifting around of numbers, but in this case the only changes were at the end of Act One, which was, I regret to say, a dream ballet, a number that was already beginning to be passé. For the most part we all worked harmoniously on the show, though I do remember one evening in Philadelphia when there was a violent altercation. Loesser and I had assigned some solo parts to members of the chorus, and Feuer and Martin thought the voices were not good enough. At the height of the debate, Martin said, "We haven't won an argument with you two yet and we're going to win this one." This seemed a rather poor reason for making a decision, but it also seemed a trivial matter for such a clash of wills and so they won this argument.

During our married life, Mary had been hurt and angry at me from time to time because I was so remiss in the matter of anniversaries, birthdays and other occasions which should be remembered by any considerate husband. I had been free from such responsibilities for so many years that I was almost unaware of how one should act. The next summer, reminded by Florence, my trusty housekeeper, that Mrs. Abbott's birthday was imminent, I decided to make amends by having a big surprise party. I invited all the most attractive neighbors and felt that for once I was going to rise to the occasion. The natal day dawned and as it progressed, bright and sunny, with many events that had nothing to do with birthdays, Mary became more and more tense. She thought I had forgotten, and finally she launched a full-scale attack upon my callous negligence. In defense I had to scream back that indeed I had known about it and that I had even planned a party. Reconciliation, apology and love followed. We decided that at least we should put on a good show for those who were supposed to surprise her, so that evening when the guests, according to time-honored routine, were hidden in the library, I descended the stairs with Mary, and for their benefit we engaged in a fine domestic argument which I am sure deceived everyone. After the cries of "Surprise, surprise" issued forth, we were all bright and merry.

My old friend, Joe Kipness, who had been one of the producers of *High Button Shoes,* recommended that I see a clever revue which was being performed at Catholic University. Walter Kerr, who was teaching at the college, and his wife Jean were the authors, and it had pleasant music by a professional, Jay Gorney. I journeyed down to Washington and found it well worth the trip. We decided to bring it in to Broadway under the title of *Touch and Go,* with Walter Kerr directing. Two of the amateur actors had seemed pretty good in their production, and the Kerrs wished to use them for the professional production. This proved to be disastrous and probably kept the review from being a much bigger hit. It did fairly well, however, and was a success later in London. One of my worst judgments about a theatrical effect took place in this show. The Kerrs had written a sketch about Cinderella in which the sound of a flushing toilet was the climax. To me this seemed vulgar, but they insisted on using it, and it got one of the biggest laughs I have ever heard in the theatre.

Every time Mary and I had a row, I was thrown into a turmoil about a solution to our dilemma. On occasion I had suggested that we have separate domiciles to be used as cyclone cellars to which we could escape from each other when things were not going well. Mary would have none of this. Each time we had a quarrel she was sure that it would never happen again; also, with what we men like to call feminine logic, she rather justified quarreling. She said it was healthy, that people who didn't quarrel were just vegetables. Well, this vegetable reached the point where he knew that he couldn't be happy in an atmosphere of such emotional violence and in a low Machiavellian way he began to plan to do something about it.

Mary had an opportunity to go to Sun Valley for two weeks to do some publicity pictures, and I urged her to accept. Shortly after she arrived there I sent her a letter saying that I loved her very much, but that to protect this love I must be able to escape from the contentions which seemed to be an ineradicable part of it. Therefore, from now on I was now going to have a separate residence; when we were living in amity we would be together, but if there was a quarrel, I would move out. Though it may seem cowardly of me to have taken this step behind Mary's back, I knew that the only way I could make my ultimatum stick was to make it impossible for her to confront me in person and dissuade me. From that time on, I had an apartment at the Hampshire House and Mary had an apartment on Park Avenue, and this arrangement solved many of our problems. Knowing of this situation, my lawyer—or counselor, as those fellows like to be called these days—advised me to make a definite financial arrangement which would be on record in case we later got a divorce. I told him that there was not the slightest thought of divorce; that furthermore, if by some incredible chance there should be a divorce, Mary was too proud to take anything from me; that whenever we had a quarrel, the first thing she did was to leave all the jewelry I had ever given her on my dresser. Like doctors, lawyers look at life with cynical and, I'm afraid, realistic eyes. Mine didn't argue with me; he was tolerant of my confidence in the great love that existed between Mary and me, but he insisted that some definite, specific, and—in the eyes of the law—ample sum be paid to her monthly. It was so done.

Mary's energies and imagination fastened on the idea of forming a company to produce television shows. I lent the organization my name and put up the money to implement it. They started out well, being, I think, the first ones to use game-playing as a television device. But quarreling set in, and the outfit fell apart. One of the members of this group was a bright young fellow named Hal Prince, who had recently been graduated from the University of Pennsylvania. I thought that he was somebody who ought to be developed and I hired him as assistant stage manager on the next show I worked on.

That summer Leland Hayward asked me to direct *Call Me Madam*. Ethel Merman was the star, Paul Lukas was to be the leading man, the composer was Irving Berlin, and Lindsay and

Crouse were the authors. In other words there were a lot of big guns involved in this one. I remembered Lindsay as the quiet young man who had directed the road company of *Dulcy* so skillfully. Crouse I had known for many years, both socially and as one of the authors of *Gentlemen of the Press*.

As was customary, Jerome Robbins started work first with his dances. He had conceived a big number about the wild men from the mountains coming down and dancing in the village. Eventually this number had to be jettisoned. Time and time again the ambitious dance effort will fail, whereas something conceived for practical purposes and on the spur of the moment will be a success. This is equally true of songs.

One morning during rehearsals, there being no authors around, I had to write a few words into the show. Before I had the time to explain the reason for this to Lindsay and Crouse, they walked into rehearsal. Lindsay listened to the new lines and then said in front of the cast, "Well, I hope we still have the same title." It was an uncomfortable moment. I dismissed the company and asked the authors to come out into the lobby with me. Alone with them I explained that I was working for the good of the show, that to do this I had to have a free hand, and that there must be no contention in front of the cast. They agreed, and henceforth rehearsals proceeded without incident.

I have always found that in the theatre it is best to face and solve personality clashes without delay. Sometimes it can't be done, but with men of good will it should be easy. A misunderstanding is just what the word implies, and if the reason for it can be brought to light, the adjustment should not be difficult. In the above case, both parties were wrong. I must confess that one of my major defects as a director is an incurable impatience. I should have waited until I could consult with the authors about any new lines. On the other hand, Howard should not have sounded off before the cast.

During the tryout of *Call Me Madam* we discovered that we needed a new song to fill a certain spot in Act Two. I had been very much taken with one old song of Berlin's called "Sing Something Simple," which was done in counterpoint and which had a revival of popularity at this time. When I urged him to contrive something along those lines for this spot, Irving went back to the hotel and disappeared for the day. Crouse had a room directly over Berlin's and he, therefore, would give us reports from time to time about the music which floated up to him. Two mornings later he hurried into the theatre with a big grin and said gleefully, "I think he's got something. I keep hearing the same tune over and over." Indeed he had got something: that wonderful counterpoint melody called "You're Not Sick, You're Just in Love," with which Ethel Merman and Russell Nype stopped the show every night.

One day up in Boston I told Irving Berlin that I admired a melody he had used in the release (the middle part) of a certain song. "Oh, yes," he said, "I've used that a lot of times." When I asked him what he meant, he answered in that high voice of his, "Every composer's only got five or six tunes." I don't quite understand this because it seems to me—and to most music lovers— that Irving Berlin has a thousand tunes, but he obviously meant what he said.

Ethel Merman gave a beautiful performance on opening night and the show was a tremendous hit. Later on in the run, she got angry at Paul Lukas and wouldn't look at him. Night after night I would have to go backstage and give her notes telling her that she ought to look at the leading man during love scenes. She would agree blandly and would look at him for a couple of performances, but when I returned the next week I'd find her standing there talking to the audience and leaving Lukas out on a limb all by himself. The audience didn't seem to mind, however; only the theatre-wise knew the difference.

Mary had remained great friends with Bob Fryer since the Ogunquit season, and now she told me that he had a property that she thought I ought to look into. Bob had acquired the musical comedy rights to *A Tree Grows in Brooklyn,* and because he wanted to get started as a producer he was willing to accept a minor role in a partnership on this show. I took it over and agreed to work on the book with Betty Smith, the author of the original novel. We engaged Arthur Schwartz and Dorothy Fields to do the songs, and Leland Hayward took a large financial interest in the production and gave us some valuable advice.

New Year's Day, 1950, Mary and I were supposed to go to a big party given by Billy Rose on the Ziegfeld Roof. But at the last moment, Mary became upset with me about something and refused to come, so I went alone in a very sulky mood. Later I went on to another party given by Lila King, who had worked for me as a singer in *On the Town*. When I asked her casually what she was planning to do next, she told me that she was going to sing on a Moore-McCormack cruise ship going to South America. I gathered that the boat took a couple of dancers to give lessons, and a couple of singers, and these entertainers furnished a shipboard show. On the spur of the moment, and as a refuge from domestic contention, I decided to take that cruise. I had a lot of work to do on the book of *A Tree Grows in Brooklyn*. Mary too, when I consulted her about it, approved of my taking this vacation.

From experience I knew that a great peace always settles on my soul whenever I am on a ship at sea. There are an awful lot of porpoises between New York and Brazil, and I never grew tired of watching them leaping out of the water as we cut through the blue Caribbean. We arrived in Rio at carnival time and stayed there for three days. The harbor is just as dramatic as its pictures, the Copacabana is as attractive as you have been led to expect, and always high above stands the gigantic statue of the Christus, looking more like some ancient pagan deity than like the author of the Sermon on the Mount.

Night and day the streets were filled with marching, singing people in costumes. At first I thought that Brazil was loaded with homosexuals, because so many of the men wore women's clothes, but it was explained to me that most people were too poor to buy cloth for original costumes, and so the only way that they could dress up was to borrow clothes from the women of their families. Few were drunk on liquor, but everybody was drunk on the music and gaiety and on the little cans of ether which they squirted at each other. I wangled an invitation to the Municipal Ball, which was quite a swank affair. One thing that makes Brazilian parties attractive—or at least this particular party—is the singing. When we North Americans have a dance, our steps do not encourage the dancers to burst into song. But in Brazil they march rather than dance. They do a little jiggly step, very elusive and impossible for a clumsy Yanqui to capture at first try. They march around the room counter-clockwise, arms around each other, four, eight or even sixteen abreast, all singing. Sometimes a woman jumps up on a pedestal and leads the others with arms outstretched. Everyone is in almost hysterically high spirits, even though there is nothing to drink except a very sweet champagne and soda pop. (Apparently the upper classes don't squirt ether at each other—they leave that for the hoi polloi.) I have never seen a more spontaneous outburst of good spirits, nor such an exuberant manifestation of the sheer joy of living.

Brazil has frightfully poor people and frightfully rich people, and it is dirty, disorderly and gay. I had paid very little attention to the itinerary of the cruise, but when I came on deck on the following morning, I knew that we had entered an entirely different kind of land. Here was no happy disorder; here was a clean dock, ropes coiled, everything orderly and shipshape. No disorganized people were yelling at each other; everything was calm and businesslike. No one can be in Uruguay for long without finding it a very superior country—a country which I learned had had a practicing socialism for some fifty years, a country with a large middle class. Though they do not demonstrate fun in the hysterical way of the Latins, the Uruguayans have a very gay time, stay up late and balance work and play in a most practical fashion.

In Buenos Aires, Argentina, I stayed with Ambassador Stanton Griffis for four days. Stanton liked politics, but he hated tourists. Or rather he didn't hate them, they just bored the hell out of him—as indeed they would bore any intelligent person. He had perfected a technique to protect himself against the invading hordes. When he was forced to give cocktail parties for friends of Senator Stupenagle, he would appear, shake hands with everybody and be charming. Suddenly an attaché would hurry in importantly and tell the Ambassador that he was wanted on the telephone. Stanton would disappear, leaving the attaché to carry on, and somehow he never was able to get back to the party. While the squares from Tallahassee were drinking his liquor and enjoying the thrill of contact with the American Embassy, the attaché's wife, Stanton and I would be upstairs playing canasta.

On the voyage home I worked hard and stayed in my cabin half of each day until I had finished my draft of Act Two of *A Tree Grows in Brooklyn*.

. . . .

Along about this time I did a television show. Offers had come to me to work in this medium before, but such opportunities were always accompanied by options which would continue for years. I thought it would be a good idea to get some experience in this field but I wanted to be free to return to the theatre whenever I wished. Now came the chance to be the master of ceremonies and director of a half-hour program to be known as the U. S. Rubber Showcase. There were no options attached, and I accepted. It was a variety show, and though some programs turned out well, most of them were mediocre. I didn't learn as much as I had hoped to, but I had some interesting experiences.

The position of the advertising agencies in the television world is an astounding one. How can they be entrusted with such power when they know so little? Their business is dealing with words, and yet in many cases they seem only half educated. I do not quibble with their split infinitives or the use of "like" for "as"; perhaps "grammarwise" they are ahead of the times and usage will prove them correct. But why doesn't somebody in one of these giant organizations refer to a dictionary sometime? My favorite hate in vulgar pronunciation is saying egg for x—lugzury, eggcluzive.

One of the most interesting personalities to perform on this program was Ezio Pinza. We had three other fine singers on the program with him, and then a quartet by Mozart. For a lighter moment I devised a scene portraying the kind of church social I remembered in Hamburg. Pinza sang "Asleep in the Deep," and then the mixed quartet rendered a hymn such as I had heard at my grandfather's funeral.

Now Pinza was celebrated not only as a great basso, but as a great lover. In general, men who pinch women are frustrated males who have to steal favors because so few women offer them any. This was not the case with Ezio; many women were mad for him, but despite this he continued his relentless search. The girls in *South Pacific* had many a humorous episode to relate and there were continual rumors of his unrelenting—and unsuccessful—pursuit of Mary Martin.

I had looked forward to meeting Pinza, and I found him to be a man of great charm and warmth—and also that the rumors about him were true. In the mixed-quartet number, the alto was a woman of about two hundred and fifty pounds who had a very pretty face. One afternoon during rehearsal the quartet was seated on a bench when the fat lady let out a piercing scream and jumped to her feet. A roar of comprehending laughter went up from the rest of us, while Pinza sat there looking smug and not at all embarrassed. I said, "I always heard that about you. Now I know."

"We're old friends," said the contralto.

That fall of 1952 Bob Fryer came to me and said, "At last I have a chance to become a producer on my own. I have a great property and a great star and all I need is you to direct it."

"What is it?"

"A musical version of *My Sister Eileen*. And Rosalind says . . ."

"I read it two years ago. I didn't like it."

"The authors are willing to rewrite."

"They weren't two years ago."

"They are now and want you to work with them."

"Can Rosalind Russell sing?"

"Sure, she used to be in musicals before she went to Hollywood."

"And she'll really do it?"

"She will if you will."

Joseph Fields and Jerome Chodorov proved to be both amicable and inventive, and by the end of summer they had what seemed to me a very good musical-comedy book. In the meantime, however, the men who had been engaged to do the songs did not seem to have made the same progress. At the last minute with the rehearsal date approaching, we—and by this time "we" included Rosalind Russell—felt it absolutely essential to secure a new composer and a new lyricist. In this dilemma I turned to my old friends, Betty Comden and Adolph Green. They read the book and liked it, and they suggested getting Leonard Bernstein to write the music. It seemed that he had just finished a symphony tour and was in the mood for some creative labor. The three of them started working at a furious pace. Nearly every day they had something new to show me. We went ahead with our casting and hired a newcomer named Edie Adams for Eileen, and that talented photographer-actor, Chris Alexander, for the part of Frank Lippencott. It was a good cast.

But now the nature of our play began to change. Bernstein, Comden and Green were sophisticated writers whose emphasis was inescapably on satire rather than on sentiment. Fields and Chodorov were distressed at the turn the show was taking. Such dissonances as "The Wrong-Note Rag" were most distasteful to them, far from the mood which they had envisioned for their musical. They clung tenaciously to the old theatre they knew. There was more hysterical debate, more acrimony, more tension and more screaming connected with this play than with any other show I was ever involved with.

All authors are neurotic. I'll go even further: everybody in the creative side of the theatre is neurotic. The reason is obvious. A child who has a happy, carefree, extroverted childhood does not turn his thoughts inward, does not stimulate his imagination with another world in order to escape from this one. It is the boy or girl with troubles who is thrown back upon himself, who lives in a fantasy world, who develops an ability and talent for the make-believe. Generally, however, the neuroses are under control and a certain objectivity is in command until the production is launched.

But in this show emotions dominated almost from the first day. The climax came at the dress rehearsal, always the most devastating moment in the production of a play. It is the moment when you see everything up there in cold reality; when you have to face what the show is—and face it without the response of an audience—instead of seeing what you would like to have it be. Although I know that this ordeal is coming and although I make a great effort to steel myself against it, I always suffer a frightful depression from the anticlimax. In this case, on the night before we were to open in New Haven, Fields and Chodorov had the worst case of dress-rehearsalitis that I ever saw in my life. In their panic they turned upon the rest of us and reviled the play and what had been done to it. The whole show was lousy and it was doomed to terrible failure. Things must be changed. Not later! Right now! Numbers should be changed before tomorrow night! We sat in that cold, empty theatre after that rehearsal, our quarrels out in the open, our voices penetrating to the deepest basement dressing room, shouting, arguing, name-calling. Obscenities filled the air.

As the director I could not have made changes at this point even if I had approved of them. Any such decision would have thrown the cast into such confusion that our opening night would have inevitably become a shambles. I finally concluded the debate by walking out on it.

We opened, we were a hit, and we sold out in New Haven even though Rosalind Russell was ill and the understudy had to play for three performances. Later on in Boston, Jerry Robbins came to the rescue once again and helped to complete some of the numbers. By the time *Wonderful Town* reached New York it was a very slick show indeed, and it deserved the big success which awaited it. However, amity was never completely restored among all of us. Sometimes a success will make all problems disappear, all differences evaporate, but in this case the antagonism between the writers of the book and all the rest of us continued. They were in the enemy camp and they never fraternized with us.

After this show Mary and I took a cruise to Venezuela, around the Carribbean and back. The ship was filled with seasick honeymooners, and there weren't any porpoises to be seen on this run, but we had a very pleasant voyage. On the first day out, we played a game of chess, a game which I had taught Mary reluctantly because I didn't believe that women could comprehend the intricacies of its logic. Now she said to me, "You know, I can really beat you at chess." When I laughed it off she proposed a wager, and so we decided to play the best out of fifteen games. When I won only two out of fifteen I was surprised and very shocked; I thought that I either ought to give up chess or get a divorce.

But our divorce came in a very different fashion. We had a most amicable winter; my retreat over at the Hampshire House had hardly been used at all. Then, since I was deep in rehearsals of a new play, Mary thought that she would like to go to Paris. She had made several trips, usually with Julia Trissell, and she always returned with a lot of new clothes and one charming young unhousebroken French poodle, which in due time would be given away. Sometimes other matters were secretly accomplished, such as an operation on a perfectly cute nose, or a trial at dyeing her hair red, but she was always glad to be back and gay and happy over her adventures.

This particular trip was made with three women who were dress buyers. I stayed in the apartment on Park Avenue, rehearsed the show all day and usually had a girl for dinner at night. When at last Mary returned from Paris, she was not as gay and enthusiastic as usual. In fact she seemed to me to be mysterious. Indeed, my intuition had not deceived me; there was mystery. Mary had had me watched while she was away. It had never occurred to me that a man whose wife was in Paris going to parties and having a fine time was supposed to be in an isolation booth at home. In fact, although I had really considered myself a free agent since our semi-separation two years previously, there had been nothing during this interval that I would have made an effort to hide. We argued the point. This time Mary was different—there was no anger; she was almost sweetly tolerant of me. I felt that she had been influenced by someone, and as the discussion developed, I became convinced that the three women with whom she had been traveling had talked to her about her rights and instructed her about "handling" the situation. Mary told me that while she was greatly distressed at my conduct, she was willing to forgive all if I would agree to certain new conditions in our domestic arrangement. I must agree to sell my house in the country and get a new one of her choosing; she was to have her own car; she was to be in charge of the servants. I replied that if she could show me a better house, I would be willing to change; that she could have her own car as soon as she got a driver's license; but that as far as the servants are concerned, I would not give her control over them. She would fire them, and then get another set of servants, and then she would fire them, and it would go on indefinitely. She had proven that she could not get along with the servants; these people were my trusted friends, had worked for me for years and I could not throw them out. Very well, then she would not forgive me. She rushed upstairs to make her report to Julie Trissell, who lived in the apartment on the floor above.

Our play was ready to go out of town and I left for New

Haven a day later. On the afternoon of the first matinée, Mary and some companions appeared, and as soon as the show was over she asked to see me. After telling me that the show was no good, she wanted to know if I had decided to accept her ultimatum. I said no. A beautiful woman was seen leaving the Shubert Theatre a little glassy-eyed, bumping into a few people. She went straight to California, and on her return a month later, she announced over the telephone that she wanted a divorce.

My wife, who had always been so hypersensitive about taking anything in the past, returned no jewelry on this occasion. A change had taken place. Like so many American women good and true, it seemed that she had decided to make this a profitable operation. When I talked to her and attempted to point out that some adjustment could be made in our mutual way of living which would not involve the messiness of a divorce, she said calmly, "Let the lawyers handle that, dear, let the lawyers handle it." It turned out that she had indeed already put her affairs into the hands of one of the big divorce specialists, Louis Nizer.

One pleasant summer day Edward E. Colton, my attorney-at-law, phoned me in the country to report some bad news. Eddie is a cheerful fellow who sometimes gives the impression that he thinks bad news is good clean fun which causes him no particular pain to dish out, and that if you're half a man, you should be able to take it—and furthermore, that even if it hurts, it is good for you. He told me that Nizer had called to say that his client was willing to settle out of court for one hundred and fifty thousand dollars cash, forty thousand dollars a year, suitable payments if she married again, and so on and so forth. Eddie went on to say that these were just asking terms and that he felt hopeful that we could do better, but that he wanted to apprise me of the situation.

Abbott was depressed.

There was another cause for depression at that time. When we made a picture of *Kiss and Tell*, we did so on a capital-gains setup. The government was now contesting that arrangement, claiming that we should pay the tax as income, not as capital gains. If Uncle Sam won, this would give me a personal assessment of several hundred thousand dollars; moreover, I would feel responsible for moneys to be collected from various backers, especially some of my relatives, who I knew had long ago spent the money and who would be hard put to meet such assessments. Our hero didn't face these impending financial calamities with all the urbanity that one might desire. In fact, he went about complaining to the world and giving his side of the story to anyone who would listen, until finally Bill Paley said, "What are you worrying about? It's only that green stuff you take out of a box."

I felt as though I had committed some criminal negligence. Here I was, a man who had always tried to be cautious and fore-sighted, a man well aware of the pitfalls inherent in both the theatre and matrimony, who was caught off guard by both institutions. I could blame my advisers for the *Kiss and Tell* mess, but whom could I blame for my domestic situation?

By nature I am optimistic, and in a day or so I began to feel that life wasn't so bad after all; that, as my mother always used to say when she was comforting me, "Ten years from now you won't know the difference;" that a great many worse things had happened to me—being sick, for instance. I began to regard my dilemmas as interesting antagonists and to think about solutions to them.

The *Kiss and Tell* case was going into the courts in California. There was nothing I could do except trust the lawyers. The divorce, on the other hand, began to be rather an interesting business, subject to much plotting and many conferences with Eddie Colton. Naïvely, I had thought that as soon as I calmed down, I would be able to reach some amicable adjustment with Mary. Usually, she recovered from any disagreement in two days; this, however, had become a matter of weeks and weeks. When we met I used all the persuasion at my command. But it didn't work; some influence stronger than mine was at work upon her and she was firmly decided upon this course of action.

Colton's instructions were melodramatic. Change the locks on all my doors, he told me; be careful of my conduct—I was probably being trailed. He gave me a long briefing on the techniques of getting a divorce in the legally backward State of New York—and on the possibilities of successful defense, the chances of a settlement, the chance of a trial and the consequent embarrassment, what constituted adultery in the eyes of the law, what constituted condoning of the same. What idiots law-makers have been! How preoccupied with copulation, how little interested in kindness.

I began to take an interest in the contest. "Let the lawyers settle it," Mary had said. So be it. It became a kind of game with me. I was living at the Hampshire House, and I would walk through the Essex Hotel next door which has a long lobby extending from Fifty-ninth to Fifty-eighth Street through which it would almost be impossible for a man to follow without being observed. My other device was to go to the Imperial Theatre where *Call Me Madam* was playing and to enter the stage door on Forty-sixth Street. Knowing that no detective could get by the doorman, I would walk through the theatre and out the lobby entrance on Forty-fifth Street feeling very much like a character in a paperback novel.

Finally there came the afternoon for man and wife, backed by their respective legal advisers—or perhaps I should say, led by them—to meet. Colton and I went down to Nizer's office. It was a very elegant place—rich, but in good taste, as befits so successful a man. Nizer is a small man, and like so many of his stature, he apparently craved large surroundings. The little man sat behind a very large desk, looking to me much like a confident spider waiting for his prey. Now I don't know how Louis Nizer looks to those whom he is defending—say John Henry Faulk or Quentin Reynolds—probably like a steel spring of righteousness, but I saw him from a different angle.

Nizer had kinky black hair, bright eyes and a face that I thought crafty. He had personality and, when he wanted to exercise it, a great deal of charm. He would turn on the charm for a minute and then turn tough; he alternated the winning manner with the menacing one, and I felt that I was being given notice that I had two choices: I could lose pleasantly, or I could lose unpleasantly.

After a bit, we were led down a corridor to another office—deeper into the web, as it were. There another lawyer appeared with Mary, who looked like a cover of *Vogue*—chic and elegant. She was calm, almost regal. The talk proceeded pleasantly—everyone was trying to sound very reasonable—though I do recall that at one point Mary became agitated as she produced her version of L'Affaire Garbage Pail.

In kindly tones, Mr. Nizer pointed out to me that I was an old man about to die, and that I might just as well give this beautiful and deserving creature a good chunk of money. Mr. Colton then replied in his own smiling, rational way with a lot of double talk. He pointed out that under the Provision W, Subdivision X, of the Supreme Court Decision of Y, the defendant had already established income which had been agreed upon previously in pursuant of District Court Decision Z, and that he would continue to give her the income which had been *ipso facto* established. The deciding issues in this debate were not spoken at any time. I won't bore my readers with the sordid financial details, but both the innocent young San Diego maiden and the lecherous old theatrical character came out of the affair without too much damage.

I would not want to relive the five stormy years of my second marriage, but on the other hand I do not regret them. I'm glad it happened; in fact, I think it was inevitable. I was in a mood to change my life; had I not married Mary, I would probably have married someone else—perhaps someone less emotional, but also perhaps a lot less interesting. For though our emotions and moods were multifarious and violent, one thing to be said about our relationship was that it was never, never boring.

A little later the government lost its case against *Kiss and Tell*, and promptly went about changing the laws in order to prevent others from producing pictures under the same tax setup. But I was saved.

So it seems Mother was right. Ten years from then it *didn't* make any difference. Perhaps statistics would show that most calamities never happen.

Part Six

I HAD ENTERED MARRIAGE seeking a peaceful haven, and now I re-entered bachelorhood for the same reason. And I found it. Today my life is very pleasant indeed.

Each of us has different needs. One of mine is to live simply. I like to be alone occasionally, and I dread complications and involvements. Now I had none. I awoke in the morning and breathed deeply of freedom. I had not sought it, but since it had happened to me I found it good. I discovered that I had no hangover of bitterness toward Mary; in fact, after the divorce I took her out occasionally. I remember that we went to the Tennis Ball at Forest Hills, but our being together produced so many sly comments from the bystanders and the columnists that I found myself embarrassed and self-conscious. Gradually we saw less and less of each other.

In the meantime, I was fortunately busy with a number of things. One day I received a call from Dick Rodgers inquiring about my political convictions and hoping that I was a Democrat.

I was, as a matter of fact, much less interested in politics than my friends told me I should be, but whatever political prejudices I did have (and I think politics is seventy percent prejudice and thirty percent opinion) were for the Republicans. In my youth I had heard over and over that the Grand Old Party was the life blood of the nation. The superior people were Republicans; the inferior ones were Democrats. Moreover, I felt admiration and a warm loyalty for Eisenhower. I had seen Ike in person only once; he made a speech at the Dutch Treat Club and his transparent goodness and sincerity came across so strongly that I would gladly have taken a banner and followed him at that moment.

As the 1952 campaign progressed, however, Eisenhower did not seem to fulfill the picture I had formed. His point of view seemed to become dimmed; he seemed to be speaking what the politicians wrote for him, rather than his own thoughts. He indulged in all the broad, meaningless generalities characteristic of political utterances, and for me he became a pawn being pushed around by the professionals. At the same time Stevenson was electrifying the liberals of the country with his fresh, inspiring, eloquent and forthright words.

Rodgers asked me to take charge of the Stevenson rally at Madison Square Garden which was to be a climax of his campaign. I accepted—and my subsequent contact with some of the local Tammany politicians was enough to turn me back to the Republican Party forever. I might add that my associates, most of whom were violently emotional Democrats, grew to despise their local co-workers as much as I did. Why did we despise them? Because they didn't give a damn about Stevenson, or principles, or anything beyond their petty power on a local level. Our conflicting attitudes had a head-on collision on the night of the big rally. We had planned that two hours of entertainment and speeches were to be broadcast locally prior to the entrance of Governor Stevenson at ten P.M., at which time we went on a national hookup. The speakers had been allocated five minutes each, but in common with most people who love to appear in public, they were under the ever so false impression that the longer they stayed on stage the better they were. Thus, they drooled along with their seemingly endless, repetitive platitudes, each of them taking seven or eight minutes instead of five. We were going to be way overtime, and so we sent panicky instructions to speed up. Mrs. Roosevelt and Averell Harriman shortened their prepared talks, but none of the others complied.

To be present when Mrs. Roosevelt made her entrance at a large political gathering was a great experience. The crowd had been huzzahing, applauding and being its noisy self, when suddenly there was a different sound—a warm, deep sound. It grew. It grew to a joyous roar as the knowledge that she was entering spread through the auditorium. Now it was sincere—it was from deep inside. The People loved her. Then while this roar of admiration, respect and affection swelled around her, this large, plain, fearless woman walked slowly, almost gently to her seat, the image of goodness and security to them. It warmed the heart.

But to get back to the bad guys. The last speech before Adlai went on the air was delivered by John Cashmore, President of the Borough of Brooklyn. We sent word that he would have to wind up by ten o'clock. Then a red-faced politician with thin lips and a pale blue eye stuck his head over the platform to say a few trenchant words to our little committee, which was gathered around the instrument panel below the platform level. Alan Lerner, Joe Mankiewicz, Herman Wouk and I were I think on duty at the time. He delivered a tight-lipped threat that we better not cut off his man and departed. Several messages went back and forth, and in the meantime Cashmore ground on and on, showing not the slightest sign of speeding up or of coöperating in any way. Again we sent word that we would have to turn off the mike at the appointed hour; again Redface appeared and summoned me with a menacing crook of his finger. When I didn't move he came down the ladder and asked us in more placating tones to be reasonable. We explained that the object of the rally was to get Stevenson's speech before the nation, and that we intended to do so. He retired grimly to confer with a row of political figures sitting on the platform. Ten o'clock arrived. Cashmore was carrying on louder than ever and showing no sign of concluding his harangue. We turned off the spotlight and we turned off the microphone. Cashmore raised his voice, he screamed, he ranted, but he had become only a vague, gesticulating figure indulging in frantic pantomine, for the crowd was now buzzing with wonder at these strange goings on—and with anticipation of the entrance

of the candidate himself. Cashmore rushed down to Stevenson's
dressing room, grabbed him by the arm as he was about to make
his entrance and made his complaints. As a result, before he went
into his prepared address, the Governor made a humorous
apology because we had cut this man off the air. Politics seem so
debasing. Even the statesmen have to be infected with its compromises if they are to play the game.

That same winter, Dick Rogers called me again. He asked if
I would read a new script which he and Oscar Hammerstein were
going to produce with a view, if I liked it, of my becoming its director. Of course, I was eager to do so.

Since my last business dealings with Dick, he and Oscar had
become almost an institution. They had written and produced
one long-run musical after another. I had never worked with Oscar, but I had become acquainted with him by serving on those
inevitable committees, and I had admired his seeming objectivity
toward life and his calm, poised way. His sense of humor about
himself appealed to me; once, in taking one of those large ads in
Variety which becomes the obligation of people in the theatre, he
listed his failures instead of all his successes, and had printed in
bold type at the bottom, "We've done it before and we can do it
again." I also liked the story Leland Hayward once told me about
him. It seems that Oscar was trying out a new show in New
Haven. About halfway through the first performance he realized
that he was involved in a sure failure, so he went out to the
nearby park and started working on a new play.

The script of *Me and Juliet* arrived. It was melodramatic and
sentimental, and I didn't like it. I had picked it up with high hopes
but what I read seemed shoddy. Still, these were smart fellows,
and I could be wrong. Also, there was an unknown factor in the
script: this was a backstage play and some of the action was to be
done in dance, portraying the play within the play which was
supposedly taking place on the stage, and in which the characters
were involved as actors. This play within the play was hardly
described at all, but remembering Rodgers' "Slaughter on Tenth
Avenue" I had visions of magic moments. On the other hand, they
had engaged a routine, old-fashioned choreographer, Bob Alton,
to do this work, not George Balanchine. Still, despite all my

doubts, I did not feel I could afford to turn down an opportunity to work with these men. The three of us met and discussed the cast and the script. Oscar said, "Take it home, cut it, make notes, treat it as ruthlessly as though it were your own." I did and in the main my cuts were accepted.

We began auditions. For the actor this is an agonizing ordeal. If he is a performer of experience, it is humiliating to be forced to sell himself again; if he is inexperienced, he feels that his whole future hangs on those few precious moments there on that badly lighted stage with no audience save a few cold-faced men slumping in their seats.

And while we're on this subject I would like to give some advice to young actors and actresses who are auditioning for a job in the theatre. Don't think if you sing a long song, you are going to be more effective than with a short song. Don't think that when you're asked to sing one chorus if you slip in a lot of special material you're making a good impression. You are not. The director can tell in a very few moments whether or not you are possible for the purposes he has in mind. But if you drag out your audition interminably, you may create such a boring impression that none of those listening will ever want to see you again. Do what you are asked to do and do it as well as you can, and give others the credit for having intelligence enough to appreciate your merits.

Clarence Day once wrote a little book speculating upon the nature of the human race had it evolved from some other species such as cats or pachyderms, instead of the chattering monkeys. Our similarity to the latter is remarkable. We talk aimlessly just for the pleasure of talking and we talk too much. We substitute quantity for quality and we feel important if we have talked a great deal, without giving any thought to the worth of what we have said. This instinct is not confined to a group of gabby women endlessly repeating their own experiences, interrupting each other, with scarcely even a pretext of listening to what another says; the same symptoms are to be found in the judge, or the lawyer or the writer, and those raconteurs—the men who tell you stories, each one drawn out a little longer before it gets to the point. Is it any wonder, when senators and generals and civic leaders are so fascinated by the sound of themselves, that actors, our emotional citizens, stay on the stage too long? It seems as though a nightclub performer never knows enough to get off while he is still exciting to his audience. He can't be objective enough to realize that the applause has now become polite and has ceased to be enthusiastic. Actors are well aware of this weakness and they often speak of a rival as being "on too long," but they seldom have the objectivity to see the same flaw in their own techniques.

At auditions I am always scrupulously polite to the actor, no matter how bad he is, as long as he stays within the prescribed bounds, but if he cheats and goes on and on, I interrupt him. Of course there are times when you want to hear more. Sometimes the actor will show talent but be suited for an entirely different part than the one for which he is auditioning. Then you must give him a different type of thing to do in order to find out. Sometimes, too, the actor will be so marvelous that you can't believe your good fortune and you have him do more just to reassure yourself and your associates.

At any rate, I think that Dick made up his mind at auditions as quickly as I did, but he was much more paternalistic in his attitude toward the performer. He would often talk to an actor or an actress in a warm, personal way, and would advise or reassure them. He had a bedside manner. He showed a sympathetic interest in the case as he eased them on their way. I was perhaps inclined to be an IBM machine, while he was the family doctor.

Oscar maintained an Olympian aloofness and calm throughout the proceedings. He had very definite and fixed opinions, but he took his time about asserting them. Only once did I see any crack in his placidity. Walking into rehearsal one day, he heard the leading lady singing the wrong words to one of his lyrics. He reproved her in no uncertain terms; for a few moments lightning flashed and there was ominous thunder from Mount Olympus.

At that time Rodgers and Hammerstein seemed to me, and I think to everyone, to be at the height of their careers, and I think they seemed that way to themselves. Sure. Unassailable. Everything they had done since *Oklahoma,* with the exception of *Allegro,* had been a success; but unforseen by any of us, they were in fact about to have troubles. That cycle in the affairs of all men and women, from the high to the low, was beginning to operate. *Me and Juliet* was to be a failure, and it was to be followed by another. Sometimes when the same thing has happened to me, I have thought in retrospect that I had grown too sure of myself. Were they? I don't know.

This team had one weakness: they craved publicity. I had always been aware that they gave themselves prominent billing in large type, but this was justified on practical grounds—their names sold tickets. But working with them every day I became aware of how important they felt it was to keep their names before the public. They employed not only the usual press agent for each production but another man whose sole task was to secure publicity for them personally on a country-wide basis.

Dick and Oscar worked together with perfect understanding. Each respected the other not only as a person but as a workman, and I think that each made a very conscious effort not to jeopardize the relationship. Each had a town house and a country place, and each had a beautiful, elegantly dressed wife named Dorothy. They exchanged gifts, went to the same parties, and at work were congenial and tactful with each other. They also shared the same political views and espoused the same causes in various degrees, though Dick did not lend his name to causes with anything like the prolificacy of his partner. Oscar seemed to have a passion for being on committees, and his name was associated with almost every money-raising venture that came along. My admiration of him led me into brief endorsements of such causes as the World Federalists; but after a while causes seemed to me words rather than accomplishments, my fervor evaporated and I joined the boys on the fence.

Dick, who later proved that he could work with other lyric writers, or could function successfully alone, had in those days quite a feeling of dependence on his collaborators. I knew he had been inordinately tolerant of Larry Hart's irresponsibility— partly because he was fond of him, but also because he felt that he needed him. Now, having achieved even greater success with Oscar, he cherished him. One day he said to me, "I never want to have another collaborator as long as I live."

Each collaborator had affected Rodgers' work. Oddly enough, the shy, insecure, maladjusted Hart was a much more sophisticated writer than the mature, assured, poised Hammerstein. Hart saw everything fancifully. His tongue was in his cheek, his poetry was light and airy. He saw love dancing on the ceiling. Oscar saw it across a crowded room. Dick's music took on a more solid, earthy character when he began to work with Hammerstein. The hits Rodgers wrote with Hammerstein were much bigger than those with Hart, and the financial reward was also much bigger. The solid meat is more popular than the soufflé. To be sure, there was another factor: the shows done with Hart were produced in the depression era, when a musical that ran a full season was a big hit, while those done with Hammerstein occurred in a boom period when many musicals ran for two years or more.

The songs that the great team had written for *Me and Juliet* were not their best. They were too talented to write a bad score, but it was not top-drawer Rodgers and Hammerstein. Some of Dick's music was lovely—it has to be if he writes it. He brought that beautiful tango from "Victory at Sea" into the score, but I felt that its title, "No Other Love Have I," was pretentious.

What fatally handicapped the play, however, was the nebulous play within a play. No one had thought it out; Oscar, who wrote the book, was almost sphinxlike about it. He probably hoped that the choreographer would invent something, but Alton, completely at a loss, just devised some Altonesque dances. The audience was baffled and indifferent at these interpolations; the story was lost during them and could not continue effectively thereafter.

Me and Juliet did not fail violently—its advance sale was too large for that—it just died gently. While it was still running, I suggested to Rodgers that we revive *On Your Toes*. At first Dick reacted with caution, but he finally agreed. It did not have a long run, however, so my reunion with Rodgers was not as fruitful a one as I would have wished.

Even as this association was fizzling out, a great new series of hits and a pleasant working relationship were awaiting me. Bobby Griffith, who was now stage manager of *Wonderful Town*, wanted to become a producer. I must confess that I had not been aware of this; I, who had helped to forward the career of so many actors, had supposed that my stage manager was content to be just what he was. But now he came to me with an idea. He had read a book by Richard Bissell called *7½ Cents,* which he thought would make a musical comedy. He had talked the idea over with Hal Prince, who was acting as his assistant, and Hal shared his enthusiasm. Together they consulted Rosalind Russell, and she told them that her husband, Frederick Brisson, would be willing to raise half the money if they took him in as their partner. They agreed.

At first I was not optimistic. I was not against the project, but I was not for it either, and since I was at the moment involved in something else, I did not feel that I wanted to do the adaptation. However, I did wish to help, and I began to have interviews with several authors in the hope that some good writer would accept the assignment. Others seemed to be even more shy of the material than I was; they felt that a garment factory and a strike was too serious and controversial a subject for a jolly musical. It was after a luncheon with Abe Burrows at the Harvard Club, where I had again failed to enlist an author, that as a result of my argument to Abe I began to see a new plot development.

There are playwrights I know who, given a set of characters and an idea, will start writing without knowing exactly where their plot is going, but my whole training and experience makes me place construction, or story line, first, and words second. A playwright seems to me like an architect—he must know what the whole building is like before he begins, and he must put up the iron girders first and then after the unadorned frame is standing begin to add the things that show. A novelist can afford to wander, but just let the playwright bring in a new set of unrelated characters in the middle of Act Two and see what happens to him.

Many good plays are diffuse plays, but the big hits have unity. The difference between the passable success and the smash hit is that the latter never lets down—that in it each scene leads to the next with interest, so that when it is over there is a feeling of wanting more, a feeling that no matter how long the show is it has been a short evening.

Walking up Fifth Avenue that day I thought of the title, *The Pajama Game,* almost in the same moment that I thought of the subplot, and I hurried back to the office and told Bobby and Hal that if they would get Bissell to come on from the West, I would collaborate with him in writing the book.

Bissell is a Harvard man and one of the smartest fellows you ever saw, but for reasons best known to himself he likes to play the part of a hick and a Midwestern eccentric. He arrived at our office wearing a checkered vest, dirty white buckskin shoes and speaking in a high nasal Western voice. We all took to him immediately. He was great fun; what is more, he turned out to be a good playwright.

We approached several established composers about writing the music, but they were all afraid of it and felt that either it would be pedestrian because it was about a pajama factory and a strike, or that it would be so controversial that it would get them into trouble. Frank Loesser turned us down, but he liked the property and he suggested two protegés of his named Adler and Ross. They agreed to write five songs on speculation. They did and we signed a contract.

We tried to get Jerome Robbins to do the choreography but he couldn't; he did, however, recommend a newcomer named Bob Fosse. When rehearsals started Fosse did excellent work on many of the numbers, but later he needed help and Robbins was called in.

A new career began for Fosse as it did for Adler and Ross, for Brisson, Griffith and Prince, for Bissell and for various members of the cast. The established actors like John Raitt, Eddie Foy, Jr., and Janis Paige benefited, but not in the same proportion as a newcomer like Carol Haney, not to mention the one now known best of all, Shirley MacLaine. Carol came from the Coast to be our principal dancer, but she showed such comic ability that Bissell and I wrote her a new part during the rehearsal period. Then just to make the story-book situation complete, Shirley MacLaine, who was her understudy, went on in her place on the night that a Hollywood producer happened to be in the audience.

I had been rehearsing with Carol Haney for two weeks before Robbins joined our group. I felt that I was on easy terms with her and that I knew her fairly well, but I could not help observing that within an hour or so after Jerry began to work, she was more relaxed with him than with me. It made me conscious again of something I had often observed: the clannishness of dancers. They

live in their own world. They talk to the rest of us, they sometimes marry us, but at the same time they shut us out. We can
never learn to speak their language unless we become one of
them. We call them the gypsies—and they call themselves that.
They are homeless, wandering people for the most part, defying
all the conventions. They dress as they please—sloppy slacks and
beat-up old sweaters seem to be the most popular street garments.
As soon as they arrive at the theatre, they change into rehearsal
clothes of an unglamorous nature. The contrast between the
lovely air-borne creatures who will appear in music and light and
color upon the stage, and these drab lackluster girls in their
brown, black and gray union suits known as leotards, is always incredible.

Male dancers in the theatre today are mostly homosexual,
though there are always a few married men among them. The females are a dedicated lot. Some are married, some have a boy-
friend, many are shy and maladjusted to normal, social life, but
most of them live only for their art. They have turned to the
dance because of a need to express themselves. Though the males
follow an unorthodox sexual pattern, the females are seldom lesbi-
ans.

The gypsies spend their lives in great camaraderie; they
eat together, go to parties in each other's rooms and stay in little
groups even on the stage. They massage each others' necks to ease
tension, lend each other money and listen to each others' troubles. Their diet is haphazard and atrocious. Once in a while they
gather around a table in some favorite off-beat restaurant and
have a legitimate meal, but in general they seem to feed out of
paper cartons. They arrive for rehearsal in the morning with a
carton of coffee. At every break during the day one of them will
sally forth to return with assorted sandwiches and coffee. Nearly
all of them smoke, which, I shall have to admit, does not seem to
affect their wind. Their life is an unending struggle against the
body. Forcing the human organism into the postures of the modern dance puts a great strain on it—even a very young body stiff-
ens up after such exercise—and it is necessary to warm up before
each rehearsal or performance. The lazy dancer who neglects to
do so gets injured.

Brisson, Griffith and Prince had had a terrible time raising the money for this show. There were no big stars to sell, and with the exception of myself, there was no one connected with the production who was at all well known. No large ticket sale awaited us when we opened in New York, but Broadway is a magic and wonderful place when you hit the jackpot. The big lines soon formed at the ticket windows.

The Pajama Game had one hundred and thirty-four investors. Griffith and Prince were always grateful to the original investors and never dropped them from their lists when, as time went by, there was a great demand to invest in their subsequent shows. There was an amusing incident concerning one of them, a wardrobe lady who had put up five hundred dollars. After the show was a hit, she received a check every month which she deposited in her local bank in the suburbs. One day the president of the bank asked to speak to her, and when she went to his office in some trepidation he asked her about *The Pajama Game* check which she kept depositing. She told him that it was from an investment in a play. The weeks went by and when she went in the next time, the president asked to speak to her again. He said, "I have talked it over with my wife and we've decided that we would like to invest in this *Pajama Game*."

This play became a success despite incredible difficulties. Or was it because of them? The very presence of problems in the theatre sometimes causes an extra effort that makes for perfection. And in this connection one cannot help but look with a certain amount of skepticism upon plans to improve the theatre by subsidizing it. I have seen so many men and women do better work in the days of struggle than in the days of complacency that I fear a government dole would not increase their skill but on the other hand would go for handsome offices and a large, arty looking prospectus instead of hard competitive work. Furthermore, I do not see how writers are going to produce better output under such a stimulus. The reward for a successful play is already present. Right now those who produce successes are well paid by the theatre. If someone gave us a lot of money we might produce more plays, but would they be any better? Do we want to ask Uncle Sam to finance failures? Who's going to sit through them? I don't want to.

Richard Bissell made a novel out of his experiences with *The*

Pajama Game and called it *Say Darling*. Later he and his wife and Abe Burrows made a play out of that. It almost looked as though he had discovered perpetual motion.

Meantime back in New York, an agent brought me a novel called *The Year the Yankees Lost the Pennant*, by Douglass Wallop. Brisson, Griffith and Prince entered into the proposition with me, and it was agreed that I write the book with Wallop and direct the musical. Again we secured the services of Adler and Ross. I named it *Damn Yankees*. It was a hit, comparable to *Pajama Game*.

Freedom Week made a futile attempt to revive itself. Jack and I tried it as a twosome, but it was no good without Will. It was a failure, and by mutual unspoken accord we never attempted to resume it.

About this time, largely because people made comment about it, I became aware of this Mister Abbott business. My associates, my friends of many years, addressed me that way, and even my granddaughter Amy was heard to tell someone who was looking for me, "Mr. Abbott has gone swimming." When Stanley Prager and Georgeann Johnson got married, they announced that they decided to name their baby after me—Mister Abbott Prager. I made some protests to my friends, Bobby and Hal, over this formality, and indeed, when we were off duty I succeeded in becoming George but would find myself being Mistered again when we got back to the office.

I don't feel either formal or formidable, but I guess I must be. I can understand it in the theatre, although I think by any other name I would still be in charge, but I don't quite comprehend why it persists so stubbornly in my more intimate life.

Cuba continued to beckon even after Castro took over. In fact in those early days of the revolution, I, like many other optimistic people, hoped that great things would come from it. Hal and I took rooms at The Nacional, partly to see and partly from the habit of going there each winter. We stayed a week at The Nacional. In many ways the country was improved; there were no beggars, no street-walkers, no taxi drivers whispering their offers to find you young girls, and the people at that time seemed content with the new regime. But the frequent entry into nightclubs and casinos by soldiers who had come to collect the government's take—a belligerent group of small men with large guns, beards and sloppy uniforms—was disquieting.

The following year a group of us went to Puerto Rico. It provided an interesting contrast with Cuba, which reflected to the glory and praise of that much abused character, good old Uncle Sam. This country, which started with a handicap much greater than any which Cuba ever endured, is cleaner, happier and more efficient in every way. One sees good roads, polite people, neat little children on their way to school and a bustling atmosphere of prosperity on every side. My only complaint was that it was too American—I couldn't find any native music. At a cocktail party at the Governor's house, I complained to Luis Muñoz Marin about this, and he said the atmosphere was there if one knew where to look and instructed one of his aides to give me some advice. We went to a place about four miles out of town called The Three Palms, where the admission was forty cents and the dancing was authentic and the music was great.

We also visited the rain forest. After ascending two thousand feet on a winding road we found ourselves needing sweaters. Suddenly we could hear sweet singing, and when we asked what those wonderful little birds were, we were told that they were tree toads. Occasionally we saw a mongoose. There are no snakes in Puerto Rico; they imported the mongoose to clean out the snakes, and now the only problem is the snakes are gone and the mongooses want to clean out the chickens too.

Contacts are very important in the theatre. By this I don't mean pull—that can do one very little good in the long run—but happening to know someone who provides an opportunity. My next production came about in such a roundabout way.

While shooting *Pajama Game* in Hollywood, Doris Day told me that she admired some songs which Bob Merrill had written for a picture version of O'Neill's *Anna Christie*, which MGM had planned and then abandoned. Since Merrill was now in New York, I phoned Griffith and Prince to investigate his songs and his availability, and when I returned East my first appointment was to hear the score. I was enthusiastic, so we went to MGM and made a deal with them to do the stage version. The book was to be by me, the score by Merrill, Fosse was engaged to do the dances and Gwen Verdon was to play Anna.

Fosse worked in preparation for this show with Gwen, who would dance the leading part. The number which they held dearest was a dream ballet showing life in a house of prostitution as Anna visualized it. I made no protest against this number, nor did my associates, until we saw it before an audience. Then the cold, shocked reaction of the viewers made us realize that the sequence was just plain dirty. We wanted to take it out, but Gwen and Fosse fought for it like tigers. We argued that the dream ballet was a device already worn threadbare by its frequent use on Broadway; that in any case the ballet was false because it pictured the bordello in glamorous, exciting terms, whereas Anna Christie had nothing but loathing for her past; and finally, that the audience hated it. They replied that it was high art, that they didn't care what the audience liked, and that people had thrown fruit at Stravinsky. We tried to point out that the act of throwing fruit at a project was not in the strictest logic an absolute proof of its high art, but our argument was not able to pierce the emotional armor with which they had invested their creation.

We hated to have to lock horns and come to a head-on clash of wills about this ballet, but there seemed to be no alternative. We made the decision, and the number was deleted. Then Fosse asked if he could at least have the privilege of creating another dance to take the place of the dream ballet. We agreed, but though the new dance started off differently it somehow seemed to end up as the same old peep show. That ballet was like a disease—I couldn't eradicate it. I would give Fosse orders to work on the waltz number, but if I happened to drop into his rehearsals I would find him flogging away at that same damn ballet. He didn't call it the same one but it turned out to have the same old steps in it, and what was worse, the same old postures. It was a very depressing experience, both in its effect on us and its effect on the audience.

New Girl in Town was never right as a result of this and other things. Gwen Verdon, who is a really magnificent actress as well as a beautiful dancer, played the part to perfection, but her singing voice is not strong and she was not really able to do jus-

tice to the songs allotted to Anna. Then there was another problem that hampered us. Originally we had planned to have very
little dancing in the show, for in the story Anna obviously had few
moments of elation. But the public disagreed; they wanted to
see Gwen dance. During the tryout you could literally feel the
audience's disappointment when a scene did not lead into a
dance for her. As a result, we had to keep adding dance numbers, to go against the nature of the play to satisfy the expecta-
tions aroused by our casting of it.

Each spring the theatrical folk of Broadway gather to applaud each other and hand out the Antoinette Perry awards.
They are, I suppose, a sort of poor man's Oscar. At least it seems to
imitate that great Hollywood fandango, and the recipients vary
their performance in about the same fashion. The majority use the
moment to thank everyone connected with the project, others indulge in an emotional orgy of ludicrous proportions and a few
lighten the evening with humor.

After the awards there is dancing—and, of course, griping
about the decisions. In April of 1955 *Damn Yankees* won a whole
flock of awards in various categories, so, of course, I wasn't griping. I was dancing contentedly with my daughter when Charlie
MacArthur stopped us and asked me if I would go to Paris and
play the lead in *The Skin of Our Teeth* with Mary Martin and
Helen Hayes. At first I thought this was one of his practical jokes,
but as the evening wore on and I talked to Helen, I realized that
the offer was on the level. I was flattered that these two great
ladies of the theatre wanted me for their leading man. In addition
to these two distinguished women, Florence Reed was to play the
part of the fortune teller. I went to see Robert Whitehead, the
producer, and Alan Schneider, the director, and told them that I
didn't know whether I should attempt the role or not, that I
thought it would be fun to go on this trip to Paris for one week,
but that I wasn't sure that I could play the part and that I ought
to audition for them. After all, it was twenty-five or thirty years
since I had acted. It is true that as a director I had been acting
for actors all this time, but only in short bursts; it would be quite
a different matter to get up on a stage and sustain a part for the
whole evening.

I had always admired *The Skin of Our Teeth.* Now I got a copy and read it. Then I read some of it aloud. I thought that I sounded all right, so it was agreed.

Alan Schneider's method of direction was very personal. He made notes and then took each actor aside and talked to him privately. My method has always been to give all instruction in front of the entire cast or whoever happens to be on stage. I think there's a certain virtue in this. If there should happen to be such a thing as a selfish actor who might wish to call attention to himself at the expense of his fellows, it is well to say before the others, "Please don't make that move because it hurts So-and-so's effect." In case he transgresses he then has not only the eyes of the director upon him but the eyes of the entire cast. If you talk to him privately, he may want to weasel out of a situation with a lot of double talk; but if you simply say it's good for the show to do it in such and such a way, he has very little comeback. Also, it's a good thing to make direction as impersonal as possible. It's a business. Everyone is there for the same reason: to try to get the show in as perfect condition as possible. And the endeavor shouldn't involve emotions or personalities or pettinesses. Anyhow, there was no pettiness in our organization; everybody took direction as well as he could. One actor who had been educated by the Actors Studio delayed us a bit with double talk about the underlying meanings. Florence Reed asked a few querulous questions once in a while just for the sheer fun of it, but there was no major trouble. As far as I was concerned, I never thought for a moment of arguing with the director. I was now an actor, and I put myself in his hands to the best of my ability. I was in for one great shock: when we had our dress rehearsal in Paris, Alan came back and told me that they couldn't hear me. I had always assumed that while my voice was not deep or beautiful, it was strong and penetrating and this therefore was a terrible blow to my whole conception of myself. I did not however for a moment question his ability to tell me the truth about the matter. I did not, as so many actors often do, say "Why, I have always been heard everywhere." But I tried to talk louder and clearer. I guess the truth was, my vocal equipment had grown a little rusty through twenty-five years of disuse.

One day Gertrude Macy, who did the publicity for the show, asked me if I wanted to go to a big dance given by the Rothschilds. She said, "I think the convention in this matter is that I sit with the old ladies and that you dance." This seemed like a fine idea. On arrival we found a beautiful house, beautiful gardens and a so-so orchestra. The women looked surprisingly unchic. I had thought that the French women at such an affair would outdo Americans, but I suspect that the war had made some of them so poor that they were wearing finery out of a trunk. After we met the hostess and her family, I danced with Gertrude. Nobody introduced us to anyone. Finally, I dragged my hostess around the room for a while hoping that she might broaden my horizons, but she only made general conversation and did not offer to introduce me to others. I began to wonder if I was going to be able to circulate among some of the more attractive women there. Eventually I bumped into an Englishman I had met on Long Island and I asked him if cutting in was permitted. He said, "Oh, my God, no. My fiancée is out there dancing and I wouldn't dare cut in on her." So Miss Macy and I were stuck with each other. We danced and we sat and watched and had a pleasant but puzzling evening.

The Egyptian trip was the only time that I had been to Europe on a vacation. I had been to London because work had taken me there, but never to Paris. Like everyone else, I thought Paris the most beautiful city in the world, though I missed the politeness one finds in public places in England. It was nice to have breathing space and beauty instead of narrow, claustrophobic streets. I loved everything about Paris, but I must confess that after about a month the rich food palled and I began to long for some ham and eggs and a cup of American coffee.

I got the American coffee soon enough, but I got no rest from *The Skin of Our Teeth*. It was decided to continue the run and to play for two weeks in both Washington and Chicago, before coming to New York for our last stand. If I dropped out, I would ruin the project, so I made a really great sacrifice; instead of being beside my beloved swimming pool that summer, I was flogging around mercilessly hot cities, sweating on stage each night in my coonskin coat—not for art, not for money, but just to be a good fellow. At the end of our run, we performed the play for television, and I rather enjoyed that. But, boy oh boy, it was good to be through with acting. Sometimes I have been a little arrogant with actors and have told them that acting wasn't work. Directing is work, writing is work, I would say—they require concentration and unrelenting effort—but not acting. Now I had to eat my words. After the age of thirty, acting *is* work.

At about this time an interesting collaboration started which never bore fruit: I was going to write a musical comedy with William Saroyan. He had submitted a scenario that was inept by professional standards, being simply the story of a soldier who had fallen in love at first sight on the eve of being shipped to Korea. The rest of the action took place when he returned home and began his search for the girl. This took him to all parts of San Francisco and provided opportunities for dances in Chinatown, scenes on Nob Hill and so on.

While this was a skimpy idea, it occurred to me that an elaboration of it might be possible. Griffith and Prince and I thought that a fanciful plot might give scope to the kind of magic words which Saroyan can write, and we hoped that with my construction and his flair we could produce something special. When we brought Saroyan in from the Coast he approved of the idea. Perhaps he did not approve of it enthusiastically, but at least he accepted it. He did emphasize his doubts about his ability to collaborate with me or anyone else; he had never done it before and it was difficult for him to think of working in tandem. But he needed the money—like so many geniuses of song and story, Saroyan always seemed to need money—and so we signed a contract.

A few days later we sat down together to discuss the characters and the story line. I wrote out a very explicit scenario for the first few scenes, and Bill returned to his hotel to begin work on the rough draft. The next morning he came in with ten pages, much of it delightful. He had created a charming Saroyanesque character—a bawdy old lady, an ex-mistress of the Lieutenant Governor of Louisiana, who ran a gambling joint and was interested in higher education. Duly applauded, Bill departed to turn out the next day's work. Again he appeared punctually, but this time his pages deviated from the story line; he had introduced irrelevant material and new characters who seemed to the rest of us to have nothing to do with our story.

We argued. I tried to impress on him the need to keep to our plan, and again he returned to his hotel. The next day he was late, and when we phoned he wasn't there. He came in two hours later with no new material. He had decided that we were going about this collaboration the wrong way; he should be the one to lay out the story line, and I should do the rough draft. I tried to persuade him that our talents lay in opposite directions, that indeed the thing that had kept him from being as successful as his talent deserved was his inability to construct a play. But when I talked about the need for a beginning, a middle and an end, he replied that in his opinion the best construction had no beginning or middle or end.

He seemed sincere but William Saroyan is a difficult man to comprehend. Within that tough-looking man with the brusque manner and the big voice is hidden a tender, quixotic soul. A stranger meeting him might think he bossed a gang on the waterfront but would never believe that he wrote *The Beautiful People*.

Anyhow, reposing in a file somewhere in our office are several pages of delightful never-to-be-used Saroyan dialogue.

Lucky is the man who has friends. What an inclusive word. How many things it can mean. There are men you lunch with at your club, of whose lives you know little, who share with you only a congenial outlook; there are closer friends whom you must visit and who visit you; there are the friends you dine with and dance with; the friends with whom you produce plays; the friends with whom you fall in love. Some friends are people who work for you and know you not at all socially, but know you better than almost all the others.

What a warm, comforting thing it is to trust people—and to be trusted by them. And how pleasant indeed is just plain honesty. I have friends varying from a cook to a newspaper editor who would answer any question I might ask with candor and forthrightness. And though I feel that I am lucky because this is so, I am partly responsible too. It is not all luck; these friends know that I welcome and value honesty.

One of the people whom I trust completely is a woman named Celia Linder. She is a woman now, but she was a girl when she first became my secretary twenty-five years ago. I know little of Celia's life, but she knows all about mine; I have no secrets from her.

Florence Larry, my housekeeper, is a more recent friend— she has been with me only twenty years. She is a Negro, originally from the West Indies. She is incorruptibly honest. Our housekeeping is operated on a cash basis. There is no accounting. I give her a few hundred dollars at a time, and she lets me know when it is gone. Florence is very religious, but she seems to exempt me from any censure because of my agnostic and amoral conduct. She is also afraid of airplanes, and when we go to California or Florida she takes the train. Occasionally I ridicule this fear, but to no avail. One day while we were talking about heaven, a subject which sometimes comes up, I said, "But Florence, you're going to be in trouble when it comes time to go to heaven—you're afraid to fly. You'll be afraid to take your wings."

"Oh no," she said, "I'll take my wings—that's different. And you'll be up there too."

"I don't know, Florence, I may not make it."

"Oh, I'd die if you didn't," she said in anguish. "Don't you see, Mr. Abbott, it's going to be just like here, only all together."

White and black living in amity and without prejudice, that is my Florence's idea of heaven. Well, I hope so. Perhaps in that far-off land, everything will be reversed and poetic justice shall be done: Florence will write plays and I'll cook.

I also have some relatives who are friends. I don't feel that there is anything obligatory about such a relationship, but if a relative can also be an intimate, it is indeed frosting on the cake. For many, many years, my sister Polly and I seldom saw each other, but this did not affect our congenial relationship. Polly and her family—a husband, four children and a lot of grandchildren, the whole matriarchy—spent their summers in Merriewold, the club in the Catskills which Ednah and I had loved so much. Now, in my new state of bachelorhood, I began to think about that retreat from the tensions of the city. Perhaps something in me craved closer family ties, or perhaps I just remembered the relaxation and health of that cool altitude, with its fragrance of pine needles on a sunny day and the feeling of remoteness and strength which seemed to emanate from the acres and acres of great trees. I told Polly that if she could find a fairly secluded place I would buy it and spend a month up there every summer. In short order she found a point of land jutting out into the lake and built me a charming Japanese house. It proved to be a great addition to my life, and as time has gone by I have spent more and more time there.

Probably my best friend is my daughter Judy. We are not close in the way many relatives are: we are very independent. My mother always taught that when the bird leaves the nest it is ready to use its own wings, and I always behaved that way toward Judy; we have never been demonstrative. Our way with each other has been easy, natural and mature. Our individuality is not impaired by our congeniality. Judy is gregarious, loves company, loves to sit talking and laughing with theatre people until four A.M. I am too impatient and find myself bored by such groups. Judy smokes, I loathe smoking; she is a cocktail and highball drinker, I am abstemious. But Judy is interested in my welfare and I am interested in hers. She decided that my life would be more comfortable if I made certain changes. The nomadic hotel life which had been mine during the winter months was not good enough; I should be so organized that I could have Florence look after me all the time. She began to high-pressure me to sell the big house in Sands Point and to take an apartment in New York. I resisted; I grumbled that it would be too much of a nuisance. "No nuisance at all," said Judy. She would find me an apartment and get me moved while I was out of town.

Logic was on her side. Sands Point was changing its nature. Ranch houses were springing up, the suburbs were taking over and most of my friends had moved elsewhere. Finally I succumbed, we sold the house, and Judy found me an attractive coöperative overlooking Central Park.

Although I had pictured spending my old age in that Sands Point house—I had moved bushes, planted a whole grove of dogwoods, had had the house done over to my taste—when I did leave, it dropped from my consciousness almost at once. I shed that house as easily as a snake sheds its skin.

We Americans are rootless creatures. We seldom become attached to the land in the way that our European forebears did. We need change; we need growth, not petrification. The move brought new comforts and pleasures to me and made my life richer.

One of the next shows I directed grew, survived and lived to a respectable old age under the most unfavorable conditions. In the summer of 1958 there was a tryout of a little fantasy called "The Princess and the Pea," which was based, as you might guess, on that charming and satirical fable. Jean and Bill Eckart decided to expand it and produce it at the Phoenix Theatre, and they asked me to direct it. I heard the songs by Mary Rodgers and Marshall Barer and was enthusiastic, but the book seemed to me confused and naïve—though often very funny. I made suggestions for a rewrite; the authors and the Eckarts retired for a couple of weeks, and when they reappeared with a much improved version I said yes.

One day in the office we were discussing possible titles for the show when Bobby Griffith said, "Call it 'Once Upon a Mattress.'" We all laughed at his joke, but Jean Eckart said, "Why not?" She clung to this title so tenaciously that, despite some violent objections, she triumphed—and so did the show. In her first try at the legitimate theatre, Carol Burnett was a tremendous success. Eventually *Once Upon a Mattress* had no theatre to play in because of other bookings, but it went up to Broadway and lasted for another year despite being pushed from house to house. Later it boasted two road companies as well as a London company.

I had never won a Pulitzer Prize but I was about to do so. It all came about by the usual indirect circumstances. Griffith and Prince had bought the rights to do a musical based on the life of Fiorello La Guardia and they had engaged Jerome Weidman to write the book. When it seemed that progress was not going well, Arthur Penn, the director, wanted to be released to work on something else and they asked me if I would collaborate on the book and direct it. I had just abandoned a script on which I had been working and was ready for a new task.

Their attempt to do the story had, up to this time, been cen-

tered upon La Guardia and Thea, Fiorello's first wife. Shortly after
I began work, I became convinced that the second wife, Marie,
was the principal woman character, and that the love story
should center around her life-long devotion to the Little Flower.
I was lying in bed one morning thinking about this when I
began to visualize the dialogue which would occur when Fiorello
finally proposed to Marie after some fifteen or twenty years of a
platonic relationship. I got up and wrote this out so that I wouldn't
forget it. We had our first meeting in my office that noon. Bock
and Harnick, the composers, were there as well as Griffith, Prince
and Jerome Weidman. I passed over to Jerry Weidman the scenario of the story as I had thought it should run and also the new
scene. He looked a little baffled. The following morning I was
again lying in bed thinking about the characters when more dialogue came into my thoughts. Again I got up and wrote it down
and took it to the daily conference. Again no comment from
Weidman. I mentioned this to Griffith and Prince, and with a gasp
of remorse these two usually meticulous fellows admitted that
they had forgotten to tell Jerry that I was going to collaborate on
the show. May I say, however, that he welcomed me and that we
got along just fine.

Many changes were made during the tryout period but all of
them were accomplished without friction among us. The actors
turned out to be a troupe of very skillful and flexible people. *Fiorello* came close to my picture of what it should be, and when it
won all the awards in sight, I felt that it deserved them.

My associates got a great deal more pleasure out of these
awards than I did. I heard some of them making plans for photo-
stating the Pulitzer award and hanging it in their homes for the
visitors to see. I have long since stopped being overly elated at
such honors. Perhaps it's a defense; if you don't get too emotional when they like you, you will be less likely to get too emotional when they don't like you. Anyhow, the object of working in
the theatre is not to have somebody applaud you; it is the pleasure of doing the work and feeling that you've done it well.

"Exactly what is the Abbott touch?" an interviewer asked me
the other day. "I make them say their final syllables," I answered.
A joke, but with much sense to it. One of the major faults of too

many productions is that the actors have sloppy diction. It requires great persistence to get a play clearly spoken, and the actor who swallows his words is cheating. Generally he doesn't know he is not distinct; he is striving for a certain quality and since he knows his words he presumes you do. The method actor is a frequent culprit—he has worked so hard for inner feeling that he forgets to bring it out into the light where we can get a look at it. He has struggled successfully at such difficult tasks as pretending that he is a tree in full bloom, but he has never learned to say a final *t*. When actresses come into an audition and take off their shoes before beginning to read, or go one side to commune with their inner selves while we all wait, I suspect them of being phonies; I fear that they will be fakers who have thought a lot about feeling and little about technique.

If I were to give a serious answer to the question about my method, I would say that the quality which I impart to a show that may make it seem different is taste. By taste I mean artistic judgment—the decision as to just how much to do or not to do, at what point to leave one scene and get into another, and for the actor, how much to express and how much to imply. Some reader who has seen *Never Too Late* may be saying, "How can a man who gets comedy out of bringing bathroom fixtures onto the stage claim he has taste?" But that is the point: it can be vulgar or it can be hilarious—it depends upon how it's done. And finally, the one thing a play should not have, is just simple uncontrolled speed. The director who thinks that pace is just hurry makes a tragic mistake and produces a noisy, violent hodgepodge devoid of any illusion.

The director must always function to some extent as a collaborator. Sometimes he is one, of course; and in many cases he is one in fact even though he receives no program credit for his work. But outside of these instances in which he collaborates in the actual writing, he is always an influence upon the shape of the play. He influences what is put in and what is taken out. The director cannot keep up interest in the play no matter how skillful he is if a scene becomes so protracted that the audience loses interest. An audience wants to give itself to the show. That's why it came—it hopes to be taken up by the action and carried out of this world. However, if the show lets him down, if the man who has come to be entertained once drifts away from the story and back to outside matters, it is not easy to reclaim him.

An actor is never a slacker. He wants to be as good as he can. If he has an effective pause, he is quite likely to think a longer pause will be still more effective. The director who can see things from the front and judge the overall picture must control such matters. The great actor knows that if the scene is good he is good and he does not have to be urged to pick up his cues, but there are other actors under the impression that the more time they can consume the better they will be—and so over and over they must be told to pick up the cue. Not only told—shown —because their ears cheat for them and they leave just a little unwanted space between those precious words.

The fine actor seldom has to be admonished to think. He is likely instinctively to identify himself with the words his character is saying and to give them a ring of reality. But there are other actors who become involved with the sound of their voices or a thought they feel is housed in the lines and they sound utterly false. Actors often worry about readings instead of thought—they will accent one word out of proportion instead of speaking the sentence in a natural fashion as the author intended.

Anticipation is another menace to illusion on the stage. The actor begins to hear what is to be said to him before it has been uttered. The spectator usually has no idea what makes the scene so lackluster, but he knows it is. The actor has reacted before he has listened—he fights back before he is insulted. It is empty.

Curtain calls are one of my pet hates. They are an anachronism—a part of another kind of theatre which we still cling to. When I first went into the theatre there were calls, lots of them, after each act, then Arthur Hopkins boldly postponed calls until the end of the show, and the rest of us followed. If they are not too long-drawn-out then I admit that they may be a pleasant way for the actors and the audience to say goodbye to each other, but usually they go on beyond the wishes of the audience. People are polite and they will applaud if the cast appears before them, but you can't fool the public into thinking it has had a fine time just by taking ten curtain calls—quite the contrary. And what is more ridiculous than those calls which are forced upon the public at the opera and at the ballet!

. . .

I like rich people, especially when they are flexible and intelligent. A great deal has been written about two-car families; well, Mr. and Mrs. Harry Guggenheim were a two-plantation family. Harry had his place in South Carolina, Cain Hoy, known to all the racing world because he runs his horses under its banner; whereas Mrs. Guggenheim—Alicia Patterson in professional life, the editor and publisher of *Newsday*—had her place in Kingsland, Georgia. Alicia and I had both been friends of Neysa's and of each other for years, and I visited her in Kingsland nearly every winter. I was unequipped for the main recreation at her plantation, because I had neither the will nor the skill to shoot quail. But there were other attractions—horses to ride, a tennis court, a river to swim in, canoes, motor boats, wonderfully mysterious bayous to explore, violent, catastrophic games of scrabble, and argument. We argued about everything. The plantation was Alicia's retreat from the tensions of her violent and energetic life, the place where she recharged her batteries. Every hard-working executive should have one.

Alfred and Jean Vanderbilt spend the winters at Cape Haze on the west coast of Florida, where he has a housing development, and where they are close enough to Hialeah so that a man with a private plane can get there and back in an afternoon without trouble. In the Spring of 1960, while I was visiting them, my life underwent another change—and I mean a real change: a change that caused me to buy a new house, change my working conditions and the places I lived. The Vanderbilts were golfers, and one day I decided to walk around the last nine holes of the course with them. It was a lovely day. The game looked easy and I wondered why I had made no progress in my efforts with it many years before. I borrowed a club and knocked off a daisy's head. Quite a lot of fun after all. I decided to try to play. I scored a neat 150 or thereabouts, but I enjoyed it and each day thereafter I improved. I was hooked.

As soon as I returned to New York I started taking golf lessons. It had been my habit to play an hour of tennis at the River Club on the way to the office nearly every morning, but now I gave this up because I wanted to save my energies for the golf lesson. When you take up a game at the age of seventy-two you have no time to fool around—you've got to keep at it. There is a small pitch and putt course at Merriewold, and I was out there every day when summer came. About twenty minutes from Merriewold is the famous Grossinger Hotel, which has a fine golf course that I was invited to use. I inquired about the best place to play in the winter and ended up buying a house in Miami Beach, with the Atlantic Ocean in my front yard and Indian Creek Country Club five minutes away. In New York, Bobby Griffith, who had formerly been quite a good player, resumed his interest in the game. Tommy Valando, the music publisher, was our most frequent companion, and through him, I joined the Westchester Country Club. Making good golf shots took first place among my fantasies.

Everyone liked Bobby and everyone wished him well for he had qualities of simple goodness that could be appreciated by all. Once at dinner I seated him next to Alicia. I didn't know how he would get along with this erudite woman, and later I was a little surprised when she spoke warmly about him.

"Why?" I asked.

"Because he's so unphony."

Take Her, She's Mine was a challenge because most of the characters were of college age. The actors had to be "discovered," and I like the satisfaction of not knowing a single thing about the performer except what I see up there on the stage where he is auditioning.

In the theatre I can judge an actor as soon as I hear him read, and it is always a source of amazement to me that there should be such vacillation on the part of others in either accepting or rejecting a candidate. To me it seems very simple: either they ring the bell or they don't. Occasionally they don't ring *the* bell, but *a* bell; that is, you sense a talent, but not for the part which the actor is auditioning. In this particular production June Harding came to audition for Molly, the lead; she wasn't right, but there was a quality there which I didn't want to lose. I asked her to read for the younger sister. My associates were worried about my sanity, for she was dressed for the older part, but my instinct—my hunch if you will, but really my judgment based on experience— was justified by her performance. When people read the names of those who appeared in *Take Her, She's Mine* fifteen years from now, they will be astounded by the number of fine actors who played in the New York and national companies.

A few months later we had an entry in the long-title derby: *A Funny Thing Happened on the Way to the Forum*. Style is a strange thing. The long titles currently in vogue are not in imitation of each other; they sprang up simultaneously, the way short skirts or narrow trousers do.

I entered this project late, and I found the authors almost swamped under half a dozen versions of this play. I took all the scripts up to the country and made such savage cuts that I feared my new associates would be horrified. Instead, I received heartwarming words of thanks. However, our problems were not over. The audience laughed at this show, but they didn't *like* it, and it was only after great travail—in fact, not until the last week of our tryouts in Washington—that we pulled it together and found a way to make the people out front laugh with us as well as at us. Of course my job was made immeasurably easier by the fact that Zero Mostel, Jack Gilford, David Burns and John Carradine are all great comics.

During the following summer John Wharton asked me to read a script called *Cradle and All*. It was underdeveloped, but it had good characters and a comic idea, and I thought I saw just what should be done to make it a hit. I was right; that's exactly what it became under the title, *Never Too Late*.

That June of 1962 a large party was given in honor of my 75th birthday, with suitable songs and skits of a satirical and sometimes eulogistic nature. It was heart-warming to have so many friends there to wish me well, but it also contained a faint unspoken valedictorian tone which I didn't like—as if my past was being celebrated, I was a dean, an honorary member. I preferred to feel as though I were still on the team. And so I got a particular pleasure out of the hits which were recorded that fall, for my score was as good as I could have desired, or as good as it had ever been. Once again I was represented by three plays running concurrently on Broadway. It was indeed like old times. And just as a bonus two musicals of my past had successful revivals off Broadway that same season. I hadn't been put out to pasture just yet.

Exit Music

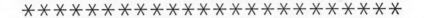

WHEN THE CURTAIN finally comes down and all the threads of the plot have been neatly tied together—an artifice quite at variance with life and as arbitrary as the masks which the ancient Greeks wore or the costumes which the Japanese wear in their current theatre—the orchestra plays while the audience walks up the aisles. Few of them listen to this music, but the sounds form a background for thoughts as they leave the theatre to resume their contact with the real world. And a few of them will hum the tune.

I am not sure what tune to play as my audience leaves. If I claim that I have had a very happy life and I lay down the rules for you to go and do likewise, that would be a bit smug. Perhaps if I only mention matters that affected me, without any assumption that they have any general application, it will sound less self-righteous.

Unfortunately one is seldom content to merely abide by the rules he has laid down for himself; he wants to proselyte; he wants to share; he wants to make others partake of his experiences.

Some deep instinct—the same instinct which makes boring people give you blow-by-blow accounts of conversations they have
had, or of golf shots they have made—makes the great scientist
wish to publish his discoveries for the good of the world. And
after all, a beautiful song is hardly a song unless there is someone
to hear it. I have, I confess, developed through the years a Pyg-
malion complex: I have wanted to mold the young. Teachers and
preachers have the same disease. Luckily for me, I had a captive
audience for my advice or theories. Not only on the stage but also
in my personal life. My business associates were usually young,
and so were the bulk of my friends.

I suppose that this tendency started years ago when I began
to champion actors whom I thought were deserving. My own
years of being unappreciated made me particularly empathic to
others following in the same path. Sometimes I would offer practical advice: I would tell the actor to take the road job, the aspiring director to take the out-of-town flop for the experience, or the
actress to take voice lessons, or not to have her nose bobbed or to
stand up straighter. This delightful egotistical feeling of interfer-
ing in other people's lives soon spilled over in other directions.
If I took a girl to the theatre or out dancing, she could have my
opinion on all existing problems as a bonus.

Was I a good influence? I thought so. But would the anxious
parents sitting at home in Akron, Ohio, think so? As we know,
only the most enlightened parents can release their grip on their
children. Also, parents tend to be conservative. They have entered a phase of life in which institutions are to be respected
and authority to be admired.

Now I don't believe that I'm conceited, and yet I feel I know
the answers to many of the enigmas of life. It seems to me that I
can think clearly about matters which seem to confuse a great
many people. Let me hastily add that I do not think that I pos-
sess superior intelligence; I am perfectly confident that if I took
an IQ test I would be no better than average. And yet I persist in
thinking that I am wise. The answer to this inconsistency is simply that thinking is done not with the intellect alone, but also with
the emotions.

Maurois once wrote that all the best thinking is done intui-
tively. When I read this, I thought it a ridiculous statement, but

upon further consideration, I began to agree. Our smartest thinking is done by instinct, as it were, not by ratiocination. Each of us has a peculiar, intuitive talent for his own business. Bernard Shaw said that making money wasn't done by brains, but was a gift just like having an ear for music. Haven't we all seen stupid, crass, insensitive men who could beat the daylights out of us in a business deal? Don't we all know how dumb some of our most successful financiers seem? A great general has convictions about his campaign which he does not need to analyze. Similarly, in my own unimportant career, I am aware of the fact that I can cut lines or change action on the stage without a conscious reason, but just because it is so obvious that it should be done.

Though the subconscious mind has stored up experience, our emotional reactions can work for us or against us. No man is free from prejudice or is able to separate his thinking completely from his emotions. For this reason the contrast between the intellectual theories of people and their actions is tremendous. The old adage, "Don't do as I do, do as I say," is a true one.

How many individuals can give dispassionate judgment when the argument involves certain ideas or even words which they have been conditioned to hate or to love? Think of the words that throw otherwise lucid people into a black fury: abortion, nigger, atheist, Pope, Nazis, Communist; or the words which blind them equally in the other direction: mother, church, country, home, baby, and so forth.

Throughout history, "atheist" has been one of the most rabble-rousing words in our vocabularies. Even today, when the world is less religious, it is a potent word which will cause men to react blindly. In the Golden Age of Greece, Pericles, an agnostic, had trouble at the height of his power to keep his friend Anaxagoras from being exiled or worse; and his dearest friend Asphasia also had to conform in religion in order to satisfy her critics. In Elizabethan days, heresy was the pretext used to cut off Sir Walter Raleigh's head. In America all our Presidents with the exception of Lincoln and Jefferson have been churchgoers, but I find it hard to believe that all of them were religious. I have attended a great many church services, but my mind has always wandered and I have found it an ordeal. It is not that I am not interested in ethical matters; I am a devoted reader of Emerson, for instance, and I have read and enjoyed Dr. Fosdick's sermons. It is what I consider the phony part of the service that gets me, the feeling that it is all done by rote. I also react against the formality; it seems to me ridiculous that the simple teachings of Jesus have been turned into a complicated ritual. The pattern obtains in other religions as well: Confucius and Buddha preached good will toward man, and man then molded their tenets into a formality.

We can look at the religions of a remote time dispassionately because our emotions are not involved. We can be amused at their naïveté, and yet it is perfectly clear that the men of ancient Greece who went to consult the Oracle at Delphi were as smart as our statesmen are today. They simply had an emotional blind spot; in their youth, certain lessons had been drummed into them. They knew well enough that the Oracle was a man-made contraption, but they revered it anyhow—even feared it. Likewise, in the Middle Ages, the ecclesiasts who gathered to debate the number of angels who could stand on the head of a pin were not simpleminded; they were brilliant men, masters of many languages and many skills.

Many great minds have made a botch of matters because their emotions fettered their thinking. Thomas Jefferson, who wrote so eloquently and thought so clearly about the problems which faced his country and his time, died with so many debts that his children were sold into slavery. Hetty Green, with a brain so keen that she could outwit Wall Street and become one of the richest people in the world, didn't have sense enough to buy a warm coat or have a comfortable place to live. And the stereotype of the inventor, poet, or absent-minded professor who is brainy but impractical is not just a cliché.

It seems to me that the quality of being adult, and therefore a quality of clear thinking, is attained only when the prejudices induced by the emotions are not allowed to interfere with rational judgment. And that is why I think that I may be smarter when it comes to assessing life than some other fellow who can beat the hell out of me at chess or a crossword puzzle.

My manners are certainly not perfect, but I do have very definite feelings on the subject. I detest the phony, and the conventional is often empty. The form is unimportant; the intent is everything. In other words, empty politeness is worthless.

As to the other trivia of life, I would say that I was a fairly faithful parrot of Polonius.

I incline toward the happy medium in dress and decorum. I believe that, business transactions excepted, people who borrow money rarely pay it back. It is foolish to lend with the expectation of return, and to borrow is to start a process that can last a lifetime. I would never give to a panhandler or a professional beggar. If I wish to give, I seek out the ones too proud and worthwhile to beg.

I detest the idea of keeping up with the Joneses.

I abhor lip service to ideas in which we don't believe. No intelligent man would contend seriously that thirteen was unlucky, and yet when some unborn archeologist digs up New York City, he is going to think that we were a nation of half-wits because most of our buildings have no thirteenth floor. But though I am not tolerant of superstitious people, I have felt ghosts walking behind me in the woods at twilight, and even now I think twice before I throw my hat on the bed—an actor's superstition.

The ambitious young are interested not only in what fork to use but also in ethical attitudes and in philosophy. My philosophy, if I may call it that, is a sort of optimistic skepticism. I am optimistic about life and our ability to enjoy it, but I am skeptical of many of our morals and mores. I am optimistic for the individual. There are so many things in life to make it exciting and joyous: the joy of work and the joy of dalliance, the joy which comes to our five senses from music, sunsets, sex, good things to eat and a host of others which are worth fighting for and achieving. But I am skeptical of conventional morals and laws. I do not believe that laws should attempt to control our personal lives. If a man wants to gamble or drink or commit suicide, it is his business. How cruel it is, for instance, to keep alive some old man or woman who lies in agony only wishing for surcease from this world. I do not believe that the law should control morality; I do not think a policeman should interfere in the moral realm unless it is to protect the individual.

I also confess to being highly skeptical of all schemes to do away with war and produce a better world through some organization. Until man conquers his greedy and unstable nature, governments will participate in war. Our instinct to fight and hunt and protect our own property is strong; for hundreds of thousands of years, the man animal has been trained in these matters and he will not easily change his nature. When I am driving a car and someone cuts in ahead of me I resent it; I have been encroached upon, somebody has infringed upon my turf. My immediate reaction is to fight for my place in line. In my reckless sixties, in the days before I became more philosophical, I would speed up my car and enter into a duel with my opponent. Now I am more logical; I realize that I am in no great hurry and I suffer the intrusion—but it still irks me.

When you see a man with a gun on his arm going out to hunt a deer, you see a man who has in him the instinct to hunt another man. The deer is considered "sport" because it can't shoot back.

There is not an ounce of thinking in one's patriotism or religion. Conviction in these matters depends entirely upon where you were born. If Senator McCarthy had been born in Russia, he would have been an unrelenting Communist; if Khrushchev had been born in Illinois, he would be in the Senate. And if you, dear reader, had been born in the Middle East, you would be prostrating yourself toward Mecca at prescribed hours every day. Of course, there would be compensation, you could look forward to a Jim Dandy type of heaven.

The people who believed in many gods were a little more logical than we are. If the Trojans prayed for victory and the Greeks won, the devout could rationalize the result as a private war between Juno and Aphrodite. We who have only one God cannot logically believe in the efficacy of prayer if we lose. Logically, I said, but we are told that we should have faith, not logic. At the time of the Spanish Armada, it was passionately believed by both sides that this was to be a test to prove whether God was on the side of the Protestants or the Catholics. God turned out to be on the side of the Protestants because he aided them with a great storm. Did anyone change sides?

My friends ask me why there is religion. How did it come about? It is universal; everybody believes in something; every-

body believes he has a soul. It seems to be natural that as the man
animal began to develop his brain, he had to inquire into the
source of his world and to seek a logic for its perversities. When
he was a child, his mother could solve all problems; he had someone to call to in time of trouble. As he grew to be a man, he
needed something to take the place of his parents. He was mature in body, but he was still a child in many ways, still insecure.
He needed someone to turn to in trouble, someone to help him
solve his problems and to punish him when he did wrong. The
gods appeared because he needed them and invented them. Perhaps those early peoples who worshipped the sun weren't so
wrong.

The riddle of our existence, a much debated subject, is a matter about which I feel no confusion. There are no big words involved, no sublime complexities; it is all simple and I suppose
naïve.

Life does not begin and end; it is a cycle. Birth, maturity,
death and rebirth, the seasons, the paths of the stars—all these
things change, but nothing is added and nothing is taken away.
There is no creation; whatever is, always was. In constant muta-
tion, going through millions of permutations and combinations, in
perpetual transformation, and yet not adding or subtracting one
atom: everything is subject to the same law. If God created the
world, who created Him? And on this subject I am wont to quote
a little Bible to back me up. "In the beginning was the Word,
and the Word was with God . . . in Him was life, and the life
was the light of men." In the beginning was God's law—the law of
nature, if you will. It always existed, and it is what controls life
and us.

Do I change anyone's thinking? Very little. As I was conditioned by a mother who rebelled against an upbringing so strict
and inflexible that it considered cards, dancing and laughter on
Sunday to be wicked, so have my friends each been conditioned
by the mores of their youth. But every one of us partakes of a
sort of immortality through the influences which he effects. The
geese fly south on a route prescribed by their ancestors. I despise
cant and pretensions because of my mother; I love trees because
of Neysa; and I carry with me the influences of dozens of others.
Perhaps some of the better parts of me may rub off; I may pass on

some worth-while trait through others. In the meantime, the fact that as an individual I have an unclouded outlook on life and that I am not distressed by the enigma of existence makes me a happier man and one freed from useless fears.

The other day a friend of mine said that he was sad that he had just visited Southampton because it reminded him that all the friends that he had known there were dead. I said that there must be some satisfaction in the fact that he was alive. "Oh," said my friend, "I'm not so sure I enjoy living." I realized that he was not joking, and I was shocked because I enjoy life very much.

And so as the orchestra plays this optimistic theme on a muted trumpet with a little support from the rhythm section, the customers file out of the theatre. Then the musicians pack their instruments in frantic haste and turn their thoughts to wives and children, gambling, food, girl friends, money troubles, or any of the other things which a good, red-blooded union man thinks about. Backstage, the actors wipe off their make-up, leave their glamour hanging in the dressing room, and take their mundane selves to the outer world. The ushers shoo out the last straggling couple and the porter locks the front door. Finally the stage-door man pulls a switch and the theatre is dark except for the little pilot light on center stage.

Tomorrow is another day.

George Abbott's Theatre

✳✳✳✳✳✳✳✳✳✳✳✳✳✳✳✳✳✳✳✳✳✳✳✳✳

KEY: (Act.) Actor; (A.) Author; (Co-a.) Co-author; (D.) Director; (Doc.) "Play-doctoring." Took over direction and rewriting on road after play was produced; (P.) Producer; (Co-p.) Co-producer.

YEAR	PLAY
1913	*The Misleading Lady* (Act.)
1916	*The Queen's Enemies* (Act.)
1918	*Lightnin'* (Act.)
	Daddies (Act.)
1920	*The Broken Wing* (Act.)
1921	*Dulcy* (on tour) (Act.)
1923	*Zander the Great* (Act.)
	White Desert (Act.)
1924	*Hell-bent fer Heaven* (Act.)
	Lazy Bones (Act.)
1925	*Processional* (Act.)
	The Fall Guy (Co-a.)
	A Holy Terror (Act.)
1926	*Love 'Em and Leave 'Em* (D., Co-a.)
	Cowboy Crazy (D.)
	Broadway (D., Co-a.)
	Chicago (D.)
1927	*Spread Eagle* (D.)
	Four Walls (D., Co-a.)
	Coquette (D., Co-a.)
	Bless You, Sister (Doc.)
1928	*Gentlemen of the Press* (D.)
	Ringside (D., Co-a.)
	Jarnegan (Doc.)
	Poppa (Doc.)

1930 *Those We Love* (Act., D., Co-a.)
1931 *Louder, Please* (D.)
1932 *Lilly Turner* (D., Co-a., Co-p.)
     The Great Magoo (D.)
     Twentieth Century (D., Co-p.)
1933 *Heat Lightning* (D., Co-p.)
     The Drums Begin (D., Co-p.)
1934 *John Brown* (Act., D., P.)
     Kill That Story (D., Co-p.)
     Small Miracle (D.)
     Ladies' Money (D., A.)
     Page Miss Glory (Doc.)
1935 *Three Men on a Horse* (D., Co-a.)
     Jumbo (D.)
     Boy Meets Girl (D., P.)
1936 *On Your Toes* (D., Co-a.)
     Sweet River (D., A., P.)
     Brother Rat (D., P.)
1937 *Room Service* (D., P.)
     Angel Island (D., P.)
     Brown Sugar (D., P.)
1938 *All That Glitters* (D., P.)
     What a Life (D., P.)
     The Boys from Syracuse (D., A., P.)
1939 *The Primrose Path* (D., P.)
     Mrs. O'Brien Entertains (D., P.)
     See My Lawyer (P.)
     Too Many Girls (D., P.)
     Ring Two (D., P.)
     The White-Haired Boy (D., P.)
1940 *The Unconquered* (D., P.)
     Goodbye in the Night (D., P.)
     Pal Joey (D., P.)
1941 *Best Foot Forward* (D., P.)
1942 *Jason* (P.)
     Beat the Band (D., P.)
     Sweet Charity (D.)
1943 *Kiss & Tell* (D., P.)
     Get Away, Old Man (D., P.)
1944 *A Highland Fling* (D., P.)
     Snafu (D., P.)
     On the Town (D.)

1945 *Mr. Cooper's Left Hand* (D., P.)
      Twilight Bar (P.)
      One Shoe Off (D., P.)
      Billion Dollar Baby (D.)
1946 *The Dancer* (P.)
      Beggar's Holiday (Doc.)
1947 *It Takes Two* (D.)
      Barefoot Boy with Cheek (D., P.)
      High Button Shoes (D.)
      You Never Know (Doc.)
1948 *Look Ma, I'm Dancin'* (D., P.)
      Where's Charley? (D., A.)
1949 *Mrs. Gibbons' Boys* (D., P.)
      Touch and Go (P.)
1950 *Tickets, Please* (Doc.)
      Call Me Madam (D.)
      Out of This World (Doc.)
1951 *A Tree Grows in Brooklyn* (D., Co-a., P.)
      The Number (D.)
1952 *In Any Language* (D., Co-p.)
1953 *Wonderful Town* (D.)
      Me and Juliet (D.)
1954 *Pajama Game* (D., Co-a.)
      On Your Toes (revival) (D., P.)
1955 *Damn Yankees* (D., Co-a.)
      Skin of Our Teeth (Act.)
1957 *New Girl in Town* (D., A.)
1958 *Drink To Me Only* (D.)
1959 *Once Upon a Mattress* (D.)
      Fiorello (D., Co-a.)
1960 *Tenderloin* (D., Co-a.)
1961 *A Call on Kuprin* (D.)
      Take Her, She's Mine (D.)
1962 *A Funny Thing Happened
        on the Way to the Forum* (D.)
      Never Too Late (D.)

About the Author

GEORGE ABBOTT's boyhood was spent in upstate New York and in Wyoming. Later he attended the University of Rochester, where he played on the football team and had enough success in theatricals to make him think he could be a playwright. After graduation he went to Harvard to take Professor Baker's famous course, and there was further encouraged by winning a play contest.

In 1913 Mr. Abbott went to New York to try to earn a living as an actor "until some smart producer snatched up one of my great plays." But it was a long wait, and in the meantime he became successful on the stage playing leads in such plays as *Processional* and the Pulitzer Prize play, *Hell-bent fer Heaven*. Finally in 1926 he had his first hit as a playwright, *Broadway*, written with Philip Dunning. *Coquette* and *Three Men on a Horse*, also collaborations, followed, and since that time he has usually been co-author, director or producer of one or two Broadway shows each season.

Mr. Abbott writes: "I have a daughter and three grandchildren. I like exercise: swimming, tennis, dancing and, of late, golf. I prefer to have lunch with men and dinner with women. In the spring and fall I live in New York, in the summer in the Catskills, and in the winter in Florida. My office, which I share with Harold Prince, is an exciting place. I love planning shows, writing, casting and rehearsing, but I dread opening nights."